$\mathcal{A}$dventure Guide to the
Cayman Islands

2nd Edition

Paris Permenter & John Bigley

HUNTER

HUNTER PUBLISHING, INC.
130 Campus Drive
Edison, NJ 08818-7816
☎ 732-225-1900 / 800-255-0343 / fax 732-417-1744
www.hunterpublishing.com
E-mail hunterp@bellsouth.net

IN CANADA:
Ulysses Travel Publications
4176 Saint-Denis, Montréal, Québec
Canada H2W 2M5
☎ 514-843-9882 ext. 2232 / fax 514-843-9448

IN THE UNITED KINGDOM:
Windsor Books International
The Boundary, Wheatley Road, Garsington
Oxford, OX44 9EJ England
☎ 01865-361122 / fax 01865-361133

ISBN 1-55650-915-4
© 2001 Paris Permenter & John Bigley

This and other Hunter travel guides are also available as e-books in a variety of digital formats through our online partners, including Amazon.com, BarnesandNoble.com, and eBooks.com.

Cover: *Diver with Tube Sponge, Cayman Brac,*
Shirley Vanderbilt / © Index Stock Imagery

Back cover: *Rum Point,* © Permenter & Bigley

Interior black-and-white photos © Cayman Islands Department of Tourism

Interior color photos © Permenter & Bigley, unless otherwise indicated

Maps by Kim André and Toni Wheeler Carbone, © 2001 Hunter Publishing

Indexing by Holly Day

4   3   2   1

ABOUT THE AUTHORS

John Bigley and Paris Permenter, a husband-and-wife team, fell in love with the Caribbean over a dozen years ago and have turned their extensive knowledge of the region into an occupation. As professional travel writers and photographers, the pair contributes travel articles and photographs on the US and the Caribbean to many national consumer and trade publications.

They are the authors of numerous other Hunter guides: *Adventure Guide to Jamaica, 4th Edition*; *Adventure Guide to Anguilla, Antigua, St. Barts, St. Kitts & St. Martin, 2nd Edition*; *Cayman Islands Alive!*; *Jamaica: A Taste of the Island*; *Jamaica Alive!*; *Nassau and the Best of the Bahamas Alive!*; *Antigua, Barbuda, St. Kitts and Nevis Alive!*; and *Bahamas: A Taste of the Islands*.

Paris and John are also frequent television and radio talk show guests on the subject of travel. Both are members of the prestigious Society of American Travel Writers (SATW).

Readers can follow the couple's travels on their Web sites: Travels with Paris and John (www.parisandjohn.com) and Lovetripper Romantic Travel Magazine (www.lovetripper.com).

ACKNOWLEDGMENTS

Writing a guide to the Cayman Islands is more a joy than a job, but like any project, it is one that is accomplished with more than a little help along the way.

This book has also had the support of many friends in the tourism business. We've received excellent assistance from the Cayman Islands Department of Tourism, whose expert advice has helped lead us to some of Cayman's most special spots. We'd like to thank Nicoela McCoy and Meloney Simms from the DOT public relations office on Grand Cayman. From the Cayman public relations office at Spring-O'Brien, we'd especially like to thank Alicia Selzer and Meredith Pillon for their expert assistance.

We'd also like to thank the friendly residents of the Cayman Islands. We have enjoyed meeting numerous islanders on our many trips, and their insight into island life has helped take us beyond the tourist track.

At home, we'd like to thank our daughter, Lauren Bigley. Her research and fact-checking skills helped us complete an accurate and up-to-date guide. As always, we'd like to thank Paris's parents, Richard and Carlene Permenter, for tending to the homefront while we were on the road.

CONTENTS

MAPS

Introduction

Once a few isolated islands populated by just a handful of residents, today the Cayman Islands garner the attention of both the travel and the business worlds. These islands are straight out of *Lifestyles of the Rich and Famous*, the kind of destination where business people might take care of banking chores in the morning and scuba dive in the afternoon. Have a good look around. See the sunglass-clad fellow on the next chaise lounge? He may well be in the islands to visit his bulging tax-free bank account. Two bikinis down may be a New York model taking a break from the workaday world or a businesswoman on-island to attend a board of directors meeting of an offshore insurance company.

A Diverse Destination

These islands are sought for their underwater attractions, boasting many of the best dive sites on the globe. Here, the waters have a clarity second to none, a diversity of sites to interest even the most well-traveled diver, and a variety of marine life that can't be beat. Vacations here center around those crystalline waters. Divers and snorkelers will find marine playgrounds around each of the islands. Fishermen wrestle with wily bonefish in the shallow flats or struggle with blue marlin, yellowfin tuna, or wahoo from deep-water charter boats. Those looking for a more leisurely pace enjoy sunset sails or long walks along powdery sand beaches.

Business travelers frequent the largest of the three Cayman Islands, **Grand Cayman**. Unlike many Caribbean islands, whose commerce is concentrated in inter-island trade, Grand Cayman is a major player in the world market. This tiny isle is the fifth-largest financial center in the world, with over 500 banks. More than 30,000 businesses are incorporated here, most of them nothing more than a plaque on a wall somewhere. The reason for the island's position as a business capital is its banking and trust laws and tax-free status. (Remember *The Firm*? Portions of that movie, based on the John Grisham book, were filmed right here and based on the island's banking secrecy laws.)

The affluence brought about by its position as a financial leader has both pros and cons for the vacationer. On one hand, you'll find the Cayman Islands are a safe destination, a place where you can walk on the beach, drive around in an open-air Jeep, and exercise no more than common-sense safety precautions. You will never be bothered by beach hasslers trying to hawk jewelry or braid your hair, something many vacationers resent on other Caribbean islands. And you won't feel a sense of guilt staying in a luxurious hotel while local residents live in poverty, a problem in neighboring Jamaica.

For the American traveler, perhaps no other Caribbean islands offer the creature comforts and the feeling of being at "a home away from home" found here. This is especially true of Grand Cayman. This island, together with its smaller "sister" islands, **Cayman Brac** and **Little Cayman**, enjoys the highest per capita income in the Caribbean. It is friendly, safe, and tailor-made for vacationers. Here you'll find all the comforts of the US, as well as an American standard of service in many restaurants, bars, and hotels. The islands' atmosphere is due largely to the many stateside expats who make their home here.

On the other hand, all this security and comfort comes at a price, and a steep one at that. When you step off the plane, 20% of your dollar is lost in the exchange rate. You'll be met by price tags that would be expensive if paid with a fully valued dollar; in paying with a dollar now worth only 80¢, you may find yourself gasping at some figures. There are ways to save money and do Cayman on just about any budget, though, and this book will help make your dollar go as far as possible.

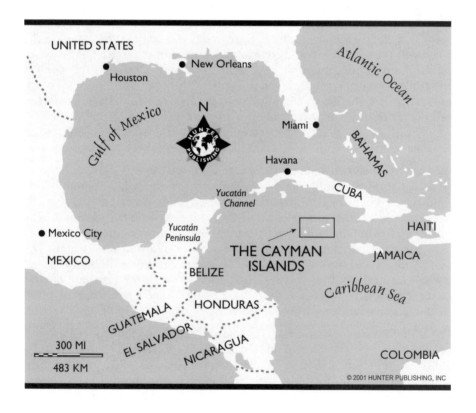

■ An Island For You

This guide will also help you select the island and the activities right for you. The three islands, although similar in terrain, flora, and fauna, are vastly different in atmosphere.

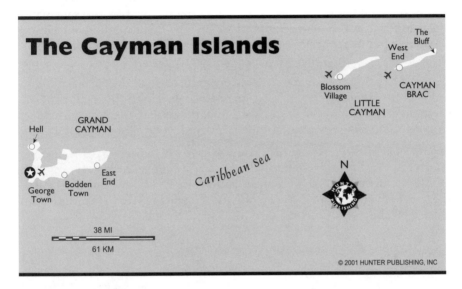

Grand Cayman

None of the Cayman Islands offers a rollicking experience of around-the-clock excitement, casino action, or frenetic shopping; travelers head to other islands for those experiences. But if you're looking for luxurious resorts, seaside golf, a little nightlife, and a playful atmosphere, Grand Cayman is the place for you. Here, a plethora of watersports operators offer every type of water adventure you could wish for, restaurants and bars line busy Seven Mile Beach, and vacationers from around the globe fill hotels, condominiums, time shares, motels, and accommodations to suit most budgets. The largest of the three islands, Grand Cayman offers several types of experiences, from fun-loving Seven Mile Beach to quiet, little-changed East End and historic George Town.

Grand Cayman visitors find that they can easily maneuver the entire landmass in one day. The island is shaped somewhat like a wrench, lying on its side with the jaws facing upwards, or north. The handle of the wrench is **East End**. One road circles the entire island, running east from **George Town** and following the shoreline as it snakes through small communities such as **Bodden Town** and **Spotts**. This road turns north at the end of the island and and continues its loop, but you can take a shortcut halfway down the island on **Frank Sound Road**, the route to the **Queen Elizabeth II Botanic Park**. When this road comes out on the north side, it travels west to **Rum Point**, a popular destination with vacationers who arrive by ferry from Seven Mile Beach and enjoy a day of fun in the sun.

South of Rum Point, **Cayman Kai** is a quiet residential area filled with beautiful, expensive homes, and some untouched land that's still good for birding.

Rum Point and Cayman Kai look west across a vast, shallow body of water called the North Sound. The sound lies between the wrench's open jaws. Where this body of water meets the sea is the home of **Stingray City**, a must-do for any Cayman visitor, diver or not. Read more about Grand Cayman's top attraction in the *East of George Town* section (pages 140-141).

Returning to the wrench, picture the top jaw of the tool. At the point where it meets the handle is is the location of **George Town**, the capital of the Cayman Islands and home of Owen Roberts Internationl Airport. Most visitors begin their vacation in this clean, orderly community.

From George Town, **Seven Mile Beach** sprawls to the north, tucked between the Caribbean Sea and the North Sound. This narrow strip of land may be small but it's not short on accommodations and restaurants; this is the heart of vacation land. Seven Mile Beach ends at **West Bay**, the clump of land on the westernmost side of the North Sound.

George Town Harbour, Grand Cayman.

And while Grand Cayman offers plenty of activities for even the most ac-tion-packed vacation, don't feel you're bound by this 76-square-mile is-land. It's a short hop from George Town to either of the sister islands for an overnight stay or just a day-trip. Also, inter-island flights connect Little Cayman and Cayman Brac, so you can, on any given day, do a little island-hopping for a totally different experience.

The Sister Islands

If you're looking for seclusion, a real getaway, head to the sister islands: **Little Cayman** and **Cayman Brac**. These are true hideaways. You'll find dive operators, fishing guides, and charter boats on these tiny isles, as well as adventure around every bend.

Whatever your choice, you're never limited to just one destination in the Cayman Islands. These isles are much smaller than their easterly neigh-bors, such as Cuba and Jamaica. You do not need to choose only one area or even one island for your vacation.

Who is the Adventure Traveler?

We've taken the broad view of adventure travel in this guide. Whether you've arranged a quiet stay in a Little Cayman or Cayman Brac villa or you're taking it easy at one of the Seven Mile Beach full-service resorts, you can still be an adventure traveler. In our view, an adventure traveler is one who wants to get out and see more of the Cayman Islands – to meet the people, explore what lies beneath the waves, see what is flitting about in the trees, learn more about these islands' his-tory, sample the island's cuisine, and discover its fascinating natural life, both above and below the water's surface. That might mean a wreck dive, a day of bonefishing, an afternoon of bird watching, or just an appreciation of the many walking trails on these islands.

What we've done in these pages is to help pave the way, to show you some of the options available. We want you to feel more comfortable, to schedule in some time for moving beyond the traditional stops.

■ Adventuring in the Cayman Islands

You'll find a full menu of activities throughout the Cayman Islands, whether you just have a few hours to explore off the beaten path or you're ready to head out on a week-long hike and camping adventure. For each region of Grand Cayman and for each of the sister islands, we've included a variety of adventures.

ON FOOT: This section covers walks, hikes, and beach strolls. If you'll be venturing off the beaten path alone, inform someone at your hotel of your planned route and ask for last-minute information on possible problems or warnings. It's always a good idea to leave your hiking plan with someone if you're striking out on your own. We've also included the names and numbers of many operators who specialize in hikes and walks. Most can add a lot to the experience, pointing out unique flora and fauna as well as the area's history along the way.

ON WHEELS: Along with scenic drives, this section includes cycling tours on each island. Again, remember that in Cayman driving is on the left. Cyclists will find busy traffic conditions along Seven Mile Beach, but miles of quiet drives on the east end of Grand Cayman and on the sister islands.

Note that Cayman follows the British tradition of driving on the left side of the road, so when crossing streets be sure to look right.

IN THE WATER: Scuba diving is an important feature of many vacations. In each chapter, we've covered the special aspects of that area's diving scene, including everything from wreck diving and wall dives, to reef dives. Top scuba sites for all abilities, from beginner to advanced, are offered, along with a list of scuba operators. We also cover snorkeling destinations.

ON THE WATER: Watersports abound, from sailing to windsurfing to kayaking. Unique opportunities are offered; some require skill and training, others can be learned in a simple lesson onshore. Fishing is another favorite pastime, and we cover that, too.

IN THE AIR: Hop in a prop plane and buzz over the islands for a unique way to tour. Parasailing along Seven Mile Beach is also a fun activity for the daredevil set.

ON HORSEBACK: For some travelers, a ride down the beach makes for a perfect afternoon activity.

ECO-TRAVEL: This section covers everything from birding to nature walks with do-it-yourself information as well as guided tours.

CULTURAL EXCURSIONS: Learn more about Cayman's unique culture, from its pirate history to its Welsh settlers to its days as a turtling capital. We'll explain more about the history and special features of the unique communities found along Cayman's roadsides.

RECREATION: Facilities for golf and tennis are covered on each island.

SIGHTSEEING: Museums, historic forts, historic homes, and more are covered in this section.

Using This Book

This book is divided into five main chapters. This chapter, the *Introduction*, looks at the geography, history, flora and fauna of the islands, as well as Customs and Immigration and some details that will help you get around, whether that means jumping in an open-air Jeep or an eight-seater island-hopping plane. The second chapter, *Where are the Adventures?*, is an overview of the types of adventures available in the Cayman Islands. The next three chapters give a more detailed view of each island in turn.

■ Adventures

Each of the chapters includes adventures to be had in its particular region. Throughout this book we offer a variety of sporting and eco-tourism options on both land and water. Whether your idea of adventure travel means wreck diving or birdwatching, you'll find it covered in these sections, but keep in mind that you should set your own boundaries here.

SAFE ADVENTURING

At this latitude, temperatures (and humidity levels) soar, draining away precious water and minerals from your body, making dehydration a real danger. At all times, it is important to maintain your **fluid levels**. Replenish them often, and be sure to carry water on all hikes and boating excursions.

The **sun**, while being one of the islands' biggest draws, is also a factor to be closely monitored. Wear a hat and a good sunscreen at all times (SPF 15 or higher).

Regardless of the type of activity you choose, know your limits. Scuba adventures in these islands range from beginners' dives in shallow, placid waters to deep wall and wreck dives. Hikes vary from strolls to sweaty workouts. On the water, the fun spans the spectrum as well, with some vacationers wrestling a fighting bonefish or marlin while others skip across the sea atop a Wave-Runner or breeze along in a catamaran.

■ Where to Stay

Each chapter also gives you nuts-and-bolts information on transportation, attractions, accommodations, and dining. Unless noted otherwise, pricing is given in US dollars, commonly used on all the islands.

We've sought to give a variety of price ranges in both accommodations and dining. Note, however, that rates change quickly, so use these as a gauge and not a figure set in stone. Accommodation rates are given in the listings for high season, but keep in mind that these vary greatly by season, soaring from mid-December through mid-April (and hitting a real peak the week between Christmas and New Year's), then dropping to a low during summer and fall months. Contact the hotels directly for the best prices and possible package deals that may save you money.

ACCOMMODATIONS PRICE SCALE
Prices listed are for a standard room for one night during high season (expect prices to be as much as 40% lower during the low season). The price scale refers to US $.
$ . . . . Under $100
$$ . . . . $100-$200
$$$. . . . . Over $200

■ Where to Eat

We've also covered an array of dining opportunities, from relatively inexpensive fast food to haute cuisine that will set you back the cost of a day's vacation. Prices do change, so use the scale below as a general guide.

DINING PRICE SCALE
The scale below indicates the approximate cost of a meal for one person, including drink and gratuity. The price scale refers to US $.
$ . . . . Under $15 per person
$$. . . . . $15-$30 per person
$$$ . . . . $31-$40 per person

History

■ The Beginning

 Cayman Brac and Little Cayman were spotted on May 10, 1503 by **Christopher Columbus** during his last journey to the New World. Actually on his way from Panama to Hispaniola (now home of the Dominican Republic and Haiti), Columbus was blown off course. This detour allowed him to sight the sister islands. He called these islands **Las Tortugas** after the many sea turtles he found there. In his notes, the explorer wrote "... we were in sight of two very small islands, full of tortoises, as was the sea about, inasmuch as they looked like little rocks."

Later maps referred to the islands as **Lagartos**, probably a reference to the large lizards (possibly iguanas) seen on the island. Later, the name became **Caymanas** from the Carib Indian word for caymans, the marine crocodile. On a 1585 voyage, Sir Francis Drake reported sighting "great serpents called Caymanas, large like lizards, which are edible." A few years later, a French map showed Cayman Brac with crocodiles in its waters, along with a manuscript that described the reptiles. No modern residents had ever seen the toothy lizards, but in 1993 an archeological dig on Grand Cayman (and three years later on Cayman Brac) proved the existence of the crocodiles. But it was the turtle that continued to bring sailors to this region. For years, the isles served only as a pit stop on these maritime runs.

In 1655 the islands came under **British** control when Jamaica was captured from the Spanish by Oliver Cromwell's army. Tucked near Jamaica and Spanish-ruled Cuba, the British thought that the Cayman Islands were strategically located. According to legend, some deserters from Cromwell's army fled Jamaica with escaped slaves and arrived in Cayman Brac and Little Cayman in 1658. Allegedly, their names were Watler and Bowden, and today some of those islands' oldest families, the Watlers and the Boddens, may be their descendants. The possession of the islands by the British Empire wouldn't be official until 1670, when they were ceded to Britain along with Jamaica by the **Treaty of Madrid**. The Brits tried to settle the formerly uninhabited island of Grand Cayman, but continuous problems with Spanish pirates sent the settlers back to Jamaica just a year later.

■ A Permanent Settlement

Slowly, the population increased and the first royal land grant in Grand Cayman came in 1734, marking the first permanent settlement. Through 1800, the island continued to grow in population with the arrival of shipwrecked mariners and immigrants from Jamaica. Cayman Brac and Little Cayman remained primarily uninhabited (some records show the tiny islands were settled but residents were attacked by pirates), only visited by turtle hunters during season.

For years, the Cayman Islands served as a magnet for pirates, and buccaneers such as **Sir Henry Morgan** enjoyed their sunny shores for at least brief stopovers. During the American Revolution, American privateers challenged English shipping, aided by the war ships and merchant ships of France, Spain, and Holland. By 1782, peace came to the seas and buccaneering drew to a close.

THE WRECK OF THE TEN SAILS

According to the latest research, in 1794, a great maritime trag-
edy took place off the east end of Grand Cayman. The Wreck of the
Ten Sails is still legendary on Grand Cayman, recalling the trag-
edy of the *Cordelia*, part of a convoy of merchant ships headed to
Britain from Jamaica. *Cordelia* ran aground on the reef at the
east end and frantically sent a signal to the other ships in the convoy to warn them off the dangerous coral. Sadly, the signal was
misunderstood and, one by one, they all ran into the reef. East
End residents were credited with their quick actions that saved
many lives, an act that King George III later recognized. Various
stories explain that the King granted the islands freedom from
conscription and other versions say that the king gave the islands
freedom from taxation.

In 1832 the citizens of the Cayman Islands met at what is today the oldest
remaining structure on the island, **Pedro St. James National Historic
Site**. Remembered as the "Birthplace of Democracy" in Cayman, this site
witnessed the first vote to create a legislature of representatives. This historic building has been renovated and is now open to the public (see page
146). By 1835, slavery had been outlawed by Great Britain and the islands
led a quiet existence, many of the population working as fishermen or
building turtling boats. The sea provided a livelihood for most residents,
who then traded for agricultural items that couldn't be grown on the island. Palm thatch was transformed into marine rope and offered in barter
for daily staples. During this time, shipbuilding became a major industry
as well.

For the next century, the Cayman Islands remained relatively isolated.
Residents continued their old traditions, but hurricanes, tidal waves, and
a depletion of the green turtle supply forced some residents to sail to Cuba,
Honduras, and Nicaragua to earn a living. The merchant seamen navi-
gated the waters and this sustained the economy of the islands until tourism and finance rose to prominence in the 20th century. During this time,
the islands were not only cut off geographically, but they also lacked much
communication with the outside world. The first wireless station wasn't
built until 1935.

■ Modern Times

The jump into the 20th century was aided by commissioner **Sir Allen
Cardinall**, who served on the island from 1934 to 1940. Linking the public
buildings of Grand Cayman with a network of roads, the commissioner
was also the first public figure to recognize the tourism potential, even not-
ing that one beach was "the most perfect bathing beach in the West
Indies."

In 1953, the first airfield in the Cayman Islands – the **Owen Roberts International Airport** on Grand Cayman – was completed. A year later, an airstrip opened on Cayman Brac. Within three years tourism began taking hold on Seven Mile Beach. By 1957, dive operator Bob Soto began the islands' first recreational diving business and introduced the world to these pristine waters.

The islands continued as a dependency of Jamaica, with both as protectorates of Great Britain, until 1962 when Jamaica became independent. The Caymanians had a far different view of the Union Jack than their Jamaican neighbors, however; in 1962 a vote overwhelmingly favored the islands' remaining a British dependency.

TIMELINE

- 1503 – Discovery by Christopher Columbus.
- 1586 – Sir Francis Drake's ships stop on Grand Cayman for two days.
- 1670 – Islands ceded to Britain (along with Jamaica) under the Treaty of Madrid.
- 1672 – First settlers arrived near Bodden Town.
- 1708 – Great Britain renamed islands Cayman Islands.
- 1790 – Fort George constructed.
- 1794 – Wreck of the Ten Sails.
- 1831 – Pedro St. James hosts Assembly, which decides to form democracy.
- 1835 – Emancipation of slaves.
- 1863 – Cayman becomes dependency of Jamaica.
- 1937 – First cruise ship visits.
- 1954 – First airfield.
- 1957 – First recreational diving business.
- 1962 – Cayman Islands vote to remain British Crown Colony.

Geography & Terrain

■ Location

 Set in the westernmost reaches of the Caribbean, Grand Cayman is about 180 miles west of Jamaica and 150 miles south of Cuba. It spans 76 square miles, approximately 22 miles long and eight miles at its widest point. The sister islands of Cayman Brac and Little Cayman are 80 miles east-northeast of Grand Cayman and are separated from each other by seven miles of ocean. Cayman Brac covers about 15 square miles and Little Cayman, 10 square miles.

■ Landforms

The three islands are similar, but not identical, in their landforms. Grand Cayman is irregularly shaped and includes the North Sound, a shallow bay of about 35 square miles. The elevation is low (about 60 feet above sea level at its highest point). These are not volcanic islands so you won't see mountains, just primarily low-level hills and bluffs.

The sister islands are each amoeba-shaped and small. Cayman Brac, about 12 miles long and a little over a mile wide, rises highest. The bluff, from which the island gets its name (Brac is Gaelic for bluff), soars to a nosebleed level – by Caymanian standards – of 140 feet above sea level. This cliff falls off into the sea and is one of the most picturesque features of the islands.

A few miles west, Little Cayman is the flattest of the three islands, reaching just 40 feet above sea level in its middle.

These three islands are the peaks of a submerged mountain range, **Cayman Ridge**, part of a chain running from Cuba to near Belize. The islands are actually limestone outcroppings with little soil, so vegetation is not as lush as that found on other Caribbean islands.

Two types of limestone form most of the surface: **bluff limestone,** formed about 30 million years ago, and **ironshore,** a substance created about 120,000 years ago, combining limestone with coral, mollusk shell, and marl. Ironshore accounts for the pocked surface that holds little pockets of soil (and makes walking barefoot just about impossible) on much of the islands.

The limestone is very porous and most rain is quickly absorbed, so the islands have no rivers or streams. Because there is so little runoff, there is greater clarity in the surrounding waters. Divers rave about the visibility, often as much as 100 to 150 feet. Each island is surrounded by coral reefs, producing some of the best snorkeling and scuba diving in the Caribbean. Divers have a chance at spotting a wide array of marine life, partly because of the deep water located nearby. The **Cayman Trough**, the deepest water in the Caribbean, lies between this nation and Jamaica, with depths that plunge over four miles into inky blackness.

Climate

Blessed with cooling trade winds, the Cayman Islands enjoy a temperate climate year-round. The hottest months are July and

August, when temperatures top out at 85 to 90°; the coolest month is February, when highs range from 72 to 86° and nighttime lows dip to the mid 60s or lower 70s. **Water temperatures** also drop during the winter months, ranging from 78 to 82°. During the summer, the waters warm to 82-86°, a balmy bath-like temperature that makes wetsuits strictly optional.

Rainfall varies with the season, reaching its peak during hurricane season. Average rainfall is 46 inches annually; May and October are traditionally the wettest months. The driest times are March and April. For a current weather report, call the **Cayman Islands National Meteorological Service** in George Town at ☎ 345-945-5773 or check the weather page on the islands' web site, **www.caymanislands.ky**.

■ Heat Dangers

In the Caribbean you'll find the mercury regularly rising to high levels and the humidity levels can make the temperature feel much higher. In these conditions, you'll need to take extra precautions to make sure you don't overdo your sun exposure.

The first concern is heat cramps – muscle cramps caused because water and salt are lost from the body. From there, it's not far to heat exhaustion, when the body tries to cool itself off and the victim feels, well, exhausted and even nauseous. Finally, heat stroke can set in, a life-threatening condition. It's easy to avoid these conditions.

HANDLING THE HEAT

- Drink water – lots of water. Don't wait until you're thirsty to reach for the water jug. Thirst is an early sign of heat stress, so start drinking before it reaches that point.

- Slow down. Curtail your activities whenever possible and do like the animals do in the high heat – move slowly.

- Take lots of breaks from exercise and activity.

- Stay out of the direct sunlight whenever possible.

- Make sure you are protected from the sun. Wear wide-brimmed hats and caps as well as sunglasses and sunblock.

- Avoid being outdoors between 10 am and 2 pm, when the sun's rays are the strongest. Enjoy an early morning hike, then kick back and take a swim break that afternoon.

Introduction

	CLIMATE		
Month	Avg. Temp. Morning (°F)	Avg. Temp. Afternoon (°F)	Rainfall (inches)
January	75	83	3.1
February	74	85	0.8
March	75	85	0.8
April	77	86	0.8
May	77	87	3.1
June	78	87	6.7
July	77	87	9.2
August	78	88	3.7
September	78	88	6.2
October	77	87	9.2
November	75	85	7.9
December	74	83	5.2

■ Hurricanes

Mention weather and the Caribbean in the same sentence and, quite predictably, the topic of hurricanes arises. These deadly storms are officially a threat from June through November, although the greatest danger is during late August through October (September is usually the worst).

Hurricanes are defined as revolving storms with wind speeds of 75 mph or greater. These counter-clockwise storms begin as waves off the west coast of Africa and work their way across the Atlantic, some gaining strength and eventually becoming tropical depressions (under 40 mph) or tropical storms (40-74 mph). Excellent warning systems keep islands posted on the possibility of oncoming storms. Radio Cayman (105.3 and 89.9) broadcasts current storm reports in the islands.

You'll find a list of hurricane shelters in the Cable and Wireless telephone directory. Keep in mind, however, that the Caribbean is a large region. We were on Grand Cayman when Hurricane Luis picked up strength on its way to batter St. Martin and Antigua in 1995, but we never saw surf above our ankles.

HURRICANE CATEGORIES

Atlantic hurricanes are ranked by the Saffir-Simpson hurricane intensity scale to give an estimate of the potential flooding and damage. Category three and above is considered intense.

Category	Winds (mph)	Damage
One	74-95	Minimal: Damage primarily to shrubbery, trees and foliage.
Two	96-110	Moderate: Considerable damage to shrubbery and foliage; some trees blown down. Some damage to roofing materials.
Three	111-130	Extensive: Foliage torn from trees; large trees blown down. Some structural damage to small buildings. Mobile homes destroyed. Flooding along the coastline.
Four	131-155	Extreme: Shrubs and trees blown down. Complete failure of roofs on small residences. Major beach erosion. Massive evacuation of homes within 500 yards of shore possibly required. Hurricane Andrew, which smashed into South Florida in 1992, is an example of a category four.
Five	155+	Catastrophic: Some complete building failures. Small buildings overturned or blown away. Low-lying escape routes inland cut by rising water three to five hours before the hurricane's center arrives. Hurricane Camille, a category five, struck Mississippi and Louisiana in 1969.

Flora & Fauna

■ Plant Life

The Cayman Islands are not as lush as neighboring Jamaica, but still boast a good variety of tropical flora and fauna. Since the islands were relatively isolated for centuries, residents became expert in the use of native flora for medicinal purposes. Some former uses of endemic plants include coconut water to relieve kidney problems; mulberry and almond leaves applied externally for the treatment of rheumatism; aloe to relieve burns and rashes; and periwinkle as a tea to treat coughs and diabetes.

Orchids

The **wild banana orchid** is the national flower, selected from among 27 indigenous orchid species. Blooming in April and May, this orchid is found on all three islands, but in different varieties. On Grand Cayman, look for *Schomburgkia thomsoniana*, with one-inch white blossoms and purple lips. On Cayman Brac and Little Cayman, the *Schomburgkia thomsoniana var. minor* is yellow in color with lighter purple lips. In all, 26 species of orchids are found on the islands, with five not found anywhere else (don't plan on viewing all the varieties, however; some are so small you'd need a magnifying glass to spot them!).

Trees

The national tree is the **silver thatch palm** (*Coccothrinax proctoril*). Named for botanist Dr. George Proctor, author of *Flora of the Cayman Islands* (see *Booklist*, page 243), the palm has a silvery underside with light green upper fronds. For all its beauty, this plant has far more than ornamental value, though. It has been used by islanders to form roofing, belts, baskets, rope, and more. Palm rope has long been a bartering tool, traded for staples.

Another often-seen species is the **bull thatch palm** (*Thrinax radiata*). A smallish tree that rarely grows taller than 20 feet, this palm looks much like the silver thatch but its leaves do not have the silvery underside of their cousins. You'll find bull thatch on both Grand Cayman and Little Cayman, usually in low areas.

Royal palms (*Roystonea regia*) are often seen in resort landscaping; their elegant, tall silhouette is easy to spot. Some of these trees soar to 80 feet high, with a sleek trunk and beautiful long, green fronds. Dead royal palms are often home to parrots.

Coconut palms (*Cocus nucifera*) are also a favorite landscaping tree. They are easy to identify by the large coconuts in the top of these tall trees.

Casuarina (*Casuarina Equisetifolia*) look much like willowy pine trees (so much so they're often called Australian pine) and are seen along the coastline.

Yellow mastic (*Sideroxylon foetidissimum*) is a native tree seen in the woodland areas. On Grand Cayman, it grows near Frank Sound Road; on Cayman Brac, it's seen in several areas on the bluff. When the tree flowers (not every year), the bloom is yellow and is followed by a small fruit.

Sea grape (*Coccoloba uvifera*) is seen along the coastlines; it's easy to spot with its clusters of grapes, which start as green and ripen to purple. The grapes are edible and are used for jelly; the plant itself is beneficial to the coast because its roots hold the sand during tropical storms.

Red birch (*Bursera simaruba*) has a smooth, red bark and yellow flowers. Called just "birch" by residents, cuttings from these trees are often used to make fenceposts. The posts then take root and form new trees, so be on the lookout for a fence line of trees that look like the barbed wired runs right through the tree – that's birch!

Fruit

The **mango** is the most plentiful fruit in the Cayman Islands, ripening in the month of June and continuing to produce fruit through September. The islands harvest about 65,000 pounds of this tropical treasure every season. There are 15 different varieties of the fruit; you'll find it at roadside stands and farmers' markets.

Guinep (*Meliococcus bijugatus*) grows on Grand Cayman and Cayman Brac. After a yellow flower blooms in the spring, the tree provides a harvest of guineps, a small fruit with a hard shell.

Wild guinep (*Exothea paniculata*) is found on Cayman Brac and is a favorite with the birdlife population for its fruits. The parrot population loves the black berries, which ripen in the spring.

■ Animal Life

A shy resident of these islands is the **agouti** (*Dasyprocta punctata*), a rabbit-sized rodent once hunted for meat. The agouti is a Central American native, introduced by the early settlers. Once kept as a pet and raised for food, today the rodent is rarely seen. The agouti has long, thin legs, hoof-like claws with three toes on its hind feet and five toes on its forefeet. A family of agoutis can be viewed at the Cayman Turtle Farm on Grand Cayman (see page 189).

The **hickatee** (*Trachemys decussata*), a freshwater turtle, is found in the freshwater and brackish ponds in the Cayman Islands and neighboring Cuba.

Although the Cayman Islands have no poisonous snakes, you might spot a harmless indigenous species, such as the grass snake (*Alsophis cantherigerus*).

A favorite sighting is the **blue iguana** (*Cyclura nubila lewisi*). This vegetarian species can grow to a length of five feet. It's often seen sunning itself (sometimes in the middle of the road). Little Cayman is home to over 2,000 rock iguanas (check out the "iguana crossing" signs around the island). On Grand Cayman, you can see a large male in the Queen Elizabeth II Botanic Park and a pair at Rum Point. Cayman Brac has a population of about 50 of these large lizards.

The Cayman parrot is the national bird of the Cayman Islands.

■ Bird Life

Bird life thrives. Parrots, ducks, cuckoos, herons, and others populate the wetlands. Birders are on the lookout for numerous species on all three islands.

Little Cayman in particular is a favorite with birders, who come to the tiny isle for the chance to spot red-footed boobies, magnificent frigate birds, West Indian whistling ducks, cattle egrets, black necked stilts, snowy egrets, tricolored herons, and others. Cayman Brac is favored for its parrot viewing, with a large reserve dedicated to these colorful birds. Grand Cayman is also home to several protected areas and ponds where both migrating and resident birds thrive.

Much of the credit for the proliferation and recognition of the Cayman Islands' bird life can be taken by former Governor Michael Gore. An avid birder, Gore worked diligently to secure the many sites and preserve them for future enjoyment.

One of the most exotic species is the Cayman national bird, the **Cayman parrot**. You might hear this bird even before you see its iridescent green feathers. Look for it in early morning and late afternoon when they return to roost in the stumps of palm trees. On Grand Cayman, look for the **Grand Cayman parrot** (*Amazona leucocephala caymensis*); Cayman

Brac boasts a subspecies, the **Cayman Brac parrot** (*Amazona leucocephala hesterna*), one of the world's rarest Amazon parrots. These parrots eat fruit, flowers and seeds in the dry woodlands and nest in hollow trees. Capturing of Cayman parrots is illegal. Formerly a popular house pet on the islands, both subspecies are now protected by law and cannot be taken from the wild.

AUTHORS' NOTE: *Don't scan the trees looking for parrots on Little Cayman. The island's parrots disappeared in 1932 with the Great Hurricane and never returned.*

Red-footed boobies (*sula sula*) are easily sighted on Little Cayman. Here you'll find over 7,000 boobies, about 30% of the Caribbean population. This beige bird, about 25 inches in size, nests high in the trees, constructing an easily-spotted rough nest of sticks. Its young are pure white.

Related to this bird is the **brown booby** (*Sula leucogaster*). This dark brown bird has a white lower breast. They're often seen along the bluff of Cayman Brac.

Each of the islands is home to many herons. **Least bitterns** (*Ixobrychus exilis*) are seen on Grand Cayman only; look for this small heron in swampy areas. The **great blue heron** (*Ardea herodias*) is far easier to see thanks to his four-foot height; he's also spotted in lagoons and ponds. The **great egret** (*Casmerodius albus*) is white and over three feet tall; look for him in ponds as well as mangrove swamps. **Snowy egrets** (*Egretta thula*) are also entirely white but smaller; while the great egret has a yellow bill, the snowy egret's is black. Don't mistake these white egrets for the smaller **cattle egret** (*Bubulcus ibis*); like its name suggests, they're often seen near livestock.

A common bird is the cooing **zenaida dove** (*Zenaida aurita*), which hunts for dried seeds. The colorful **bananaquit**, a yellow and black bird that's not shy about begging for crumbs (and its favorite treat, sugar) is another common sight. Although bananaquits are found throughout the Caribbean, the bananaquit (*Coereba flaveola sharpei*) found in the Cayman Islands is a unique subspecies.

Magnificent frigate birds are also sighted here. With a wingspan of over seven feet and wings sharply angled like boomerangs, the black frigate bird is fairly easy to spot. They soar high over the sea and are aggressive to other birds, often hitting the red-footed booby in flight in an attempt to make it disgorge its meal, an easy dinner for the frigate bird.

The only duck that breeds in the Cayman Islands is the long-legged **West Indian whistling duck** (*Dendrocygna arborea*), which resembles a goose. Look for this brownish duck in the swamps and lagoon areas. Other species of ducks you might spot are the **fulvous whistling duck** (*Den-*

drocygna bicolor), a brown duck who migrates through the area in the fall; the **mallard** (*Anas platyrnchos*), seen occasionally on Little Cayman; the **blue winged teal** (*Anas discors*), seen during the winter months on each of the islands; the **northern shoveler** (*Anas clypeata*), rarely seen in the fall months; the **American wigeon** (*Anas americana*), seen at Meagre Bay Pond and Colliers Pond on Grand Cayman in the winter months; and the **lesser scaup** (*Aythya affinis*), occasionally seen in the winter on lagoons and ponds on each of the islands.

■ Marine Life

The marine life here is some of the richest in the Caribbean. Gorgonians, barrel and tube sponges, and other colorful formations make the experience extraordinary for even the most seasoned divers.

Stingrays

There's no doubt that for many travelers the Cayman Islands are synonymous with stingrays, thanks to the popularity of Stingray City (see page 140). These fascinating creatures are most commonly seen in the area of the North Sound where the bay spills into the sea, but are sometimes sighted in other places as well. Many types of rays frequent this part of the Caribbean.

Southern Atlantic stingray (*Dasyatis americana*). This is the most common type of stingray and these are the fellows that will come up and nuzzle your hand at Stingray City and the Sandbar in the North Sound. They're found in shallow bays near the sandy bottoms where they feed on mollusks and crustaceans. Considered a choice meal by sharks, the rays have a barbed tail for protection. Like a scorpion's tail, the barb is brought up to defend the ray against attack from above. These rays are either a dark gray or brown with a white belly. They can reach up to six feet in width.

Eagle rays are spotted along the walls (most often along the North Wall of Grand Cayman) and are wary of people. Like the stingrays, eagle rays are also white-bellied but have patterned topsides, with spots and circles in a white or beige color against a dark gray or brown. These rays have angular pectoral fins and can measure up to eight feet across.

Manta rays. These are the largest of the ray family, growing over 20 feet across and sometimes weighing in at over 3,000 pounds. They have a unique fin structure around their mouths that forms a scoop to gulp plankton and small organisms. An immature manta was spotted for several years off Little Cayman but has not been sighted recently.

Sea Turtles

Other marine life often associated with the Cayman Islands are sea turtles. There's no missing the importance of this marine creature in the

Cayman Islands. Sir Turtle, the islands' peg-legged turtle "mascot," is seen on every brochure you'll find, and the most popular land attraction on this island is the Cayman Turtle Farm.

The **green sea turtle** (*Chelonia mydas*), which is such an integral part of Cayman culture, is found in the Atlantic Ocean, Gulf of Mexico, Mediterranean Sea, Pacific and Indian Oceans. These turtles have been observed to remain underwater for several days without surfacing for air. Even in its current protected state, the turtle does not lead an easy life; only one out of 10,000 eggs laid reaches maturity. The hazards are many: birds, animals, marine life, humans. Everything's a threat to these little guys. Nevertheless, the turtle thrives in Cayman waters.

Other Underwater Creatures

Sharks: The deeper waters around these islands are home to Caribbean reef sharks, bull sharks, and hammerhead sharks.

Barracuda: These long, silver fish are easily spotted by their toothy grin. A favorite with anglers, they can also often be seen by snorkelers.

Caribbean spiny lobster: These shy marine creatures have no claws like their northern relatives.

Common sea horse: These can be seen by divers hiding in soft corals.

Conch: You're probably familiar with this mollusk because of its shell: a beautiful pink curl nearly a foot long that, when blown by those in the know, can become an island bullhorn of a whistle. The shell covers a huge piece of white meat with a rubbery texture, as well as a "foot," the appendage used by the conch to drag itself along the ocean floor in search of food. Many Caribbean men swear conch is an aphrodisiac.

Four-eyed butterfly fish: This one is easy to spot: just look for a small yellow, gray, white and black fish who looks like he has four eyes! Two are actually fakes located near the tail, meant to throw off predators.

French angel fish: This gray fish has light moon-shaped markings. They're not very shy and, if you swim up slowly, you can get quite close to these lovely inhabitants.

Green moray eel: Often seen under rock crevices during the day, the moray looks frightening as it constantly opens and closes his mouth. Don't be afraid, though; the eel is just breathing and is generally harmless unless harassed.

Spiny puffer fish: Like his name suggests, the light beige puffer fish (also known as a balloon fish, and one look tells you why) looks like a little puffed-up ball scooting through the water with its micro-fins; it can inflate itself with water as a defense.

EARTH FRIENDLY

The Cayman Islands have taken strict measures to protect marine life. Today, the sea turtle is protected and no one may disturb, molest, or take turtles in Cayman waters without a license. Other marine conservation laws prohibit the taking of any marine life or damaging coral with anchors. Over 200 permanent boat moorings are in place around the islands.

■ Poisonous Species

Remember when your mom told you "look but don't touch"? Those words of wisdom come in handy on the islands. Although most plants and animals are harmless, you'll find a few creepy crawlies both in and out of the water, as well as some plants that are best avoided.

- **SCORPIONFISH:** A mottled pinkish fish that hangs out on coral and is so ugly it actually looks dangerous.
- **SEA URCHINS:** Painful if you step on their brittle spines.
- **JELLYFISH:** These cause painful stings with their tentacles.
- **STINGRAYS:** Dangerous if stepped on. Can be avoided by dragging your feet when wading, which kicks up the sand.
- **FIRE CORAL:** There are many varieties. All those edged in white will burn you if you brush against them.
- **MANCHINEEL:** Manchineel trees (*Hippomane mancinella*) present an unusual danger. These plants, members of the spurge plant family, have highly acidic leaves and fruit. During a rain, water dropping off the leaves can cause painful burns on your skin and the tree's tiny apples will also cause burns when stepped on. In most resorts, manchineel trees have been removed or are clearly marked, often with signs and with trunks painted red.
- **COWITCH** (*Mucuna pruriens* or *Helicteres jamaicensis*): Think of fiberglass on a vine. Think how much you'd itch if you brushed into this plant, covered with fine fibers, as you walked along in shorts. Think of avoiding this one.
- **COCKSPUR** (*Caesalpinia bonduc*): This shrub won't inflict any permanent damage, but it will rip at you with its hooked thorns as you walk past.
- **MAIDEN PLUM** (*Comocladia dentata*): Be prepared for a nasty rash if you come in contact with the sap of this weed. It is dark green with ovate-shaped leaves.
- **SAND FLEAS:** Tucked into that oh-so-wonderful sand lie tiny sand fleas, waiting to bite when the sand cools. You won't feel

their bites, but just wait a day or two: the welts will make themselves apparent and they'll itch for days. To avoid the no-see-ums, stay off the sand at sunset. The fleas are most active when the sand cools.

■ **SAND SPURS** (*Cenchrus genus*): Also called "wait-a-minute," this pesky thorn will penetrate unsuspecting bare feet that stumble across it in the sand. Best defense: follow mom's advice once again and wear your shoes.

■ **SNAKES:** The Cayman Islands do not have any poisonous snake species. You might come across a harmless grass snake (*Alsophis cantherigerus*), which feeds on frogs and lizards. The population of this reptile has been reduced by mongooses on the island.

Government & The Economy

 The Cayman Islands are a dependent territory, or a **Crown Colony**, of the United Kingdom. The islands are led by the **Governor**, an appointee of the Queen. The Governor heads the **Executive Council**, which includes three officials and four elected members. The **unicameral legislature** consists of 15 members. The government offices are found on Elgin Street in George Town, the capital of the Cayman Islands. Grand Cayman is divided into districts: Bodden Town, East End, George Town, North Side, Savannah, and West Bay.

Throughout the Cayman Islands, you'll see the official flag flying: a red banner with a small union jack in the upper left corner. The outside half of the flag includes a Caymanian coat of arms with a pineapple and turtle above a shield with three stars to symbolize the three islands. The pineapple symbolizes Cayman's association with Jamaica. Across the bottom reads the motto of the Cayman Islands: "He Hath Founded It Upon the Seas."

NATIONAL SYMBOLS

Unofficial national symbol – Sir Turtle, a peg-legged turtle

National bird – Cayman parrot

National tree – Silver thatch palm

National flower – Wild banana orchid

■ Tourism

The economy of the Cayman Islands is one of the strongest in the Caribbean and residents enjoy one of the highest standards of living in the world. Much of that affluence results from the successful tourism industry, with about 70% of the national product coming from that sector. Most visitors come from the United States. During the winter season, many vacationers arrive from the East and Midwest; in hot summer months a great number from Texas and the South make their way to these islands for their cooler temperatures.

■ Business

Offshore financial services play an integral role in the Cayman Islands' economy. Grand Cayman has nearly 600 licensed banks (including 47 branches representing the 50 largest banks worldwide). Banking secrecy laws passed in 1966 laid the groundwork for this profitable industry, which today puts the small island in the same league as financial giants such as Zurich and Tokyo. Just what is a Cayman banking account? Some are, as might be expected, multi-million dollar accounts, while others are on a much smaller scale. Both take advantage of the tax-free status and confidentiality laws, which protect all reputable transactions as a means for earning tax-free interest. You can open an account once the Caymanian bank receives a reference from your home banker, then you can deposit funds (in US dollars, if you like). There is no exchange control and money can be moved in and out of the country freely and privately. Banks normally don't accept huge amounts of cash.

Offshore insurance companies are also a growing business. Nearly 500 offshore insurance or captive insurance companies make their base here (captive insurance is a term used for insurance companies set up by a company or a trade association to serve its members or employees). Thanks to the Cayman Islands' generous tax-free status, many other companies choose to incorporate in the islands; currently almost 30,000 companies are registered there.

People & Culture

 The three Cayman Islands boast a total population just over 33,000. About 32,000 people reside on the largest island, followed by under 1,300 residents on Cayman Brac and fewer than 170 on Little Cayman.

It's a varied population, with cultures from around the globe. About a third of all residents are non-Caymanians; most non-natives are from the US, Canada, the UK and nearby Jamaica, although a total of 113 nationalities are represented.

■ Language

English is the primary language in the Cayman Islands, but you'll notice it is spoken with a unique lilt, one that's a little different from accents in other areas of the Caribbean. It's a reminder of the islands' earliest Welsh, Scottish, and English settlers. You'll often hear the Jamaican patois as well.

■ Cuisine

Caymanian cuisine reflects the riches of the sea. Traditional Caymanian food includes **turtle**, brought to the table in the form of soup, stew, or steak, and **conch** (pronounced konk), the mollusk that lives in the beautiful pink-and-white shell seen throughout the islands. Conch is a versatile dish and may be served as an appetizer in the form of fritters, a soup prepared as a chowder or thick with onions and spices as a stew, or even uncooked, marinated in lime juice as ceviche.

HOME COOKING

Interested in having a genuine Caymanian meal cooked for you in your villa or condo? Through Burton Ebanks (☎ 345-949-7222), you can make arrangements to have a private caterer prepare a homestyle meal right in your accommodation, a great way to learn more about the preparation of a Caymanian dinner.

The influences of nearby Jamaica are seen on island menus as well, especially in the **jerk seasoning** that ignites fish, chicken, and other meats. Jerk is meat or fish slathered with a fiery concoction of Scotch bonnet peppers, allspice, thyme, salt, garlic, scallions, and onions, then slow-cooked over a flame to produce a dish similar to a piquant barbecue. As in Jamaica, jerk is often served with rice and peas (often pigeon peas), a traditional Caribbean side dish.

Other Caribbean flavors and dishes found in the Cayman Islands include:

Allspice. The common term for pimento (see pimento).

Breadfruit. Breadfruit is kind of an all-purpose fruit: you can boil it, roast it, fry it, you name it. The giant green fruit came to the West Indies thanks to Captain Bligh (yep, of Mutiny on the Bounty fame). Breadfruit is a popular sidedish.

Cassava. The early Indians of the Caribbean, the Taino, first used this root, or yucca, to make flour. Also known as tapioca, cassava is poisonous until it is processed to remove the prussic acid. Today cassava is used to make "heavy cake."

Cayman style conch chowder. Unlike the white cream base of traditional conch chowder, Caymanian style conch chowder is tomato based with onions, peppers, and plenty of flavor.

Coconut. The coconut is a ubiquitous part of Caribbean diet, and every part is used, from its milk to its meat; even its brown shell has uses.

Fish tea. This spicy soup looks and tastes much better than it sounds. It's similar to bouillabaisse. Watch out for fish bones when you eat this popular favorite.

Heavy cake. This traditional Caymanian dessert is, well, heavy. Created from raw grated cassava, yam or breadfruit, some cooks add cornmeal to the mixture. This is combined with molasses or brown sugar to create a sweet, caramelized cake that recalls the days when flour was difficult to obtain on these islands.

Mango. The mango is always present on buffets. Long and oval, the mango is used in many desserts or, in its green stage, in chutneys and stews.

Guineps. These small green fruits look somewhat like a small lime. To eat one, pop the flesh out from the skin and suck on it (don't eat the seed).

Patties. The patty is to Jamaicans what the hamburger is to Americans although this dish has made its way to neighboring Cayman as well. The patty is actually a fried pie, dough filled with either spicy meat or occasionally vegetables.

Pimento. Pimento, called allspice in other parts of the world, is a star among spices. Without the pimento, Jamaica would not have jerk, that delightful side-of-the-road dish that has moved from fast-food status to a gourmet dish served in many Caymanian restaurants, even the finest.

Plantains. Don't get plantains mixed up with bananas. They may look similar, but the plantain is not an overgrown banana and tastes nothing like its sweet cousin. Plantains are used in recipes more like a potato and are often served sliced and fried.

Pumpkin soup. Caribbean pumpkins are not large and sweet like their American counterparts, but small and a favorite soup ingredient.

Rundown. This entrée is pickled fish cooked in a seasoned coconut milk until the fish just falls apart or literally "runs down."

Environmental Concerns

■ Marine Conservation

 The Cayman Islands have some of the strictest marine conservation laws in the Caribbean. They were first put into place in 1978

and were strengthened in 1993. The rules prohibit destructive acts such as damaging coral by anchor, chains or other means anywhere in Cayman waters; the taking of any marine life while scuba diving; the taking of any coral, sponges, sea fans or other marine specimens; the use of a spear gun or seine net; fishing with gill nets or poison; dumping anything into the water; exporting any form of marine life.

MARINE PROTECTION AREAS

The laws designate four special areas of protection: marine park zones, replenishment zones, environmental zones, and no-diving zones.

- In **marine park zones** it is illegal to take any marine life, alive or dead, except by line fishing from the shore or beyond the drop-off. Anchoring is permitted only at fixed moorings installed by the Department of Environment's Protection and Conservation unit.

- Lobster and conch are protected in the **replenishment zones**. Spear guns, pole spears, fish traps, and fish nets are prohibited in these regions; only line fishing is allowed. Anchoring is permitted.

- **Environmental zones** receive some of the strictest protection under the law. Here, no marine life may be taken or disturbed; anchoring is prohibited, as are all activities in the water. Part of the North Sound on Grand Cayman is covered by these stringent rules in order to protect breeding areas for fish and other marine life.

- **No-diving zones** were created to protect the cultural heritage as well as the environment of the Cayman Islands. This designation marks a region as off-limits for scuba diving to protect the waters for traditional Cayman fishing. These special zones have been set aside off the north coast of Grand Cayman.

Marine laws also limit the amount of catch. **Lobster** can be caught only during season (August 1 through January 30th). Even then, only adult spiny lobsters with a six-inch minimum tail size may be taken. Each person may take up to five, but no more than 15 per boat, per day. Up to 15 **conch** may be taken per person (or 20 per boat), per day. Only adult conchs, those with fully developed lips, may be harvested. **Grouper** are protected during the winter spawning season (January).

For more about the Marine Conservation Laws, ask for a copy of the brochure *Marine Park Rules and The Sea Code in the Cayman Islands*; or call the Cayman Islands Dept. of Environment's Protection and Conservation Unit on Grand Cayman at ☎ 345-949-8469 or fax 345-949-8912.

AUTHORS' NOTE: *The penalty for violation of any of these marine rules is strict. The maximum penalty is CI $5,000 (US $6,000) and one year in jail. The penalty for vessels convicted of illegally dumping waste is CI $500,000 (US $625,000).*

■ Environmental Groups

Several organizations welcome visitors to their regular meetings to learn more about the environment and culture of the island.

PRESERVATION INFORMATION SOURCES

- **National Trust for the Cayman Islands** – PO Box 31116 SMB, Grand Cayman, Cayman Islands, BWI, ☎ 345-949-0121, fax 345-949-7494, e-mail ntrust@candw.ky.

- **Cayman Islands National Archive** – Grand Cayman, Cayman Islands, BWI, ☎ 345-949-9345, fax 345-949-9727.

- **CAYFEST** – National Festival of the Arts, PO Box 30301 SMB, Grand Cayman, Cayman Islands, BWI, ☎ 345-949-5839.

- **Queen Elizabeth II Botanic Park** – Andrew Guthrie, Manager, PO Box 203 Northside, Grand Cayman, Cayman Islands, BWI, ☎ 345-947-9462, fax 345-947-7873, e-mail guthrie@candw.ky, www.botanic-park.ky.

- **Cayman Islands Bird Club** – c/o National Trust, PO Box 31116 SMB, Grand Cayman, Cayman Islands, BWI, ☎ 345-949-0121, fax 345-949-7494, e-mail ntrust@candw.ky. Meetings are held on the last Tuesday of every month, 7:15 pm, at the offices of the National Trust on Courts Road in George Town. Informal meetings are held most Saturday mornings; October is a very active month.

- **Garden Club of Grand Cayman** – PO Box 30447 SMB, Grand Cayman, Cayman Islands, BWI, ☎ 345-945-1709. Monthly meetings; annual flower show. Call for further information.

- **Grand Cayman Orchid Society** – PO Box 30083 SMB, Grand Cayman, Cayman Islands, BWI, ☎ 345-949-5564. Monthly meetings; call for scheduled meeting times.

Travel Information

■ When to Go

Regardless of when you visit, you're almost always assured of short-sleeve weather, balmy trade winds, and plenty of sun. Temperatures vary only about 10° from summer to winter. The hottest months are July and August when temperatures average 85 to 90°; the coolest month is February, when highs range from 72 to 86° and nighttime lows dip to the mid 60s to lower 70s.

The busiest months constitute "high season" – between December 15 and April 15. During this time, rates are at their peak (and really reach a peak during the week between Christmas and New Year's) and rooms can sometimes be difficult to come by at top resorts.

The "shoulder seasons," the months on each side of high season, are very pleasant weather-wise, yet you'll find prices much lower during this period. The lowest prices are offered during the summer months and the peak of hurricane season (August through October). Remember, hurricanes are forecast days in advance, so even during these peak months your chances of getting caught in a storm are small.

Water temperatures dip slightly during the winter months, when average temperatures varies from 78° to 82°. During the summer, the waters warm to 82° to 86 °, a bath-like temperature that allows divers to swim without wet suits, if they choose.

■ Costs

Cayman is costly, there's no denying it. The Cayman dollar is stronger than its US equivalent, and at this writing exchanged at a rate of about US $1.25 to CI $1. Prices in hotels, restaurants, stores, and attractions reflect that unfavorable exchange rate and the high standard of living enjoyed on the island. Just how expensive is it? Accommodation prices vary with the season. High season, spanning mid-December to mid-April, is the most costly time to visit. Rates are at their peak during this period and during the Christmas holidays they soar even higher. The least expensive time to visit is during the summer months when prices may be as much as 40% lower. To many visitors, the best combination of price and weather comes during the "shoulder seasons," the months before and after high season. Prices are lower, the seas are usually calm, and the livin' is easy.

MONEY-SAVING TIPS

- Consider bringing some food with you or making a stop at a supermarket in George Town.

- Pick up coupon booklets at the airport. These can include 10%-off coupons and other bargains at eateries on Grand Cayman or along Seven Mile Beach.

- Look for two-for-one specials (popular on Sunday nights).

- Buy rum on-island and make your own drinks.

- Double-check the gratuity. Some restaurants add a 15% gratuity to the bill, so make sure you don't inadvertently tip twice.

- Check for laundry facilities if you rent a condominium.

- Look for early-bird specials at some restaurants. Dining before six o'clock can save money.

Although room prices fluctuate with the season, food and transportation costs remain stable. Food prices, of course, vary with the type of restaurant, but expect to pay about 30% more than you'd pay at home for a comparable meal. Even fast-food establishments offer standard favorites with a price tag a little heftier than you are accustomed to seeing. To combat high prices, many repeat Cayman visitors prefer to prepare a meal or two a day "at home." Condominium units with full housekeeping facilities are exceedingly popular, especially on Grand Cayman. Some vacationers even go as far as bringing along ice chests packed with staples (although there are restrictions on bringing meat, fruit and vegetable products).

AUTHORS' NOTE: *Make sure you understand whether the menu prices you are reading are marked in US or CI dollars.*

■ Currency Conversion

Here are the basics for coverting currency to and from Cayman Islands dollars, using the exchange rate in effect at this writing.

- Multiply US $ by .8 (80%) to get approximate CI $
- Multiply CN $ by .53 (53%) to get approximate CI $
- Multiply British £ by 1.16 to get approximate CI $
- Multiply CI $ by 1.25 for US $; by 1.88 for Canadian $; and by .86 for British £ equivalents.

SAMPLE CONVERSIONS FROM CI $			
CI $	US	CN	British
$1.00	$1.25	$1.88	£0.86
$125.00	$156.25	$235.04	£107.56

SAMPLE CONVERSIONS TO CI $					
US to CI$		CN to CI$		£ to CI $	
$100	$80	$100	$53	£100	$116

SAMPLE PRICES in CI $

Coke . . . . 80¢

Bar of soap $1.00

Bag of chips $3.00

Gallon (imperial) of gas $2.57

Hamburger $2.29

Bottle of local beer $3.25

French fries $1.25

Mini-bottle of rum $2.10

You'll find that grocery prices are slightly higher on Little Cayman and Cayman Brac because all items must be brought in from the larger island.

■ Immigration & Customs

Entry Requirements

United States and Canadian citizens need to show proof of citizenship in the form of a passport or birth certificate. Visitors must also show a return airline ticket.

Travelers can remain in the islands for up to six months, provided they have sufficient funds and appropriate accommodations. Extensions must be obtained before a traveler leaves home, by writing to the Chief Immigration Officer, Department of Immigration, PO Box 1098, Grand Cayman. The Cayman Islands Department of Immigration grants each visa on its individual merit.

Visas are not required of citizens of member countries of the Commonwealth of Britain, or of Andorra, Austria, Belgium, Denmark, Finland, France, Germany, Greece, Iceland, Irish Republic, Italy, Japan, Liechtenstein, Luxembourg, Malta, Monaco, Netherlands, Norway, Portugal, San Merino, Spain, Sweden, or Switzerland.

 AUTHORS' NOTE: *Visitors can be refused entry if their appearance or behavior do not meet normal social standards.*

Visitors age 18 and over are allowed to bring in, duty-free, one liter of alcohol, four liters of wine or one case of beer, and 200 cigarettes, 25 cigars or 250 grams of tobacco.

For arrival into the Cayman Islands, you'll need to complete two forms: a Cayman Islands Customs Declaration and a Cayman Islands International Embarkation/Disembarkation card. One of each form is required per family name.

The customs declaration asks for your birthdate, address, citizenship, length of stay, airline and flight number. At the bottom, you'll find a chart for listing goods purchased and their value, and includes liquor and tobacco.

The embarkation card requests your name, birthdate, passport number, flight number, intended address in the Cayman Islands, occupation, and number of previous visits.

Obtaining a US Passport

To obtain a US passport, you may apply at any passport office (see chart on following pages) or at one of the several thousand federal or state courts or US post offices authorized to accept passport applications. For your first passport, you must apply in person.

 AUTHORS' NOTE: *Not every post office accepts passport applications; it's a service usually offered at the main branches in a city.*

We can't stress enough the importance of applying for a passport early. The heaviest demand period is January through August (because of summer travel), with September through December being the speediest period. Even during the latter, however, you should allow at least eight weeks for your passport application to be processed.

To obtain a passport, first get a passport application (DSP-11) from your local passport office or post office that handles passport applications. Do not sign the application. You'll also find passport applications and information online at http://travel.state.gov/passport_services.html.

You must provide proof of US citizenship. This can be an expired passport, a certified birth certificate (that means one with a raised, impressed, embossed, or multicolored seal). If you do not have a certified copy of your birth certificate, call the Bureau of Vital Statistics in the city where you were born. You also must provide identification, which could be an expired passport, a valid driver's license, a government ID card or certificate of naturalization or citizenship. Here's what won't work: Social Security card, learner's permit, temporary driver's license, credit card, expired ID card.

Next, provide two identical photographs of yourself no larger than 2x2 inches (the image of your head from the bottom of your chin to the top of your head must not be less than one inch or more than 1⅜ inch). Passport photos can be either color or black and white, but they may not be Polaroids or vending machine photos. The easiest way to get passport photos is to go to your local quick-copy or photo processing store and ask for passport shots.

Passports for adults 18 and over are $65 and are valid for 10 years. You may pay by check, bank draft, or money order. At passport agencies you may also pay in cash; some (but not all) post offices and clerks of court accept payment in cash.

When you receive your passport, sign it. The next step is to fill in the emergency contact page in pencil.

Need to talk with someone? The only public phone number for passport information is to the National Passport Information Center (NPIC). You can call there for information on passport emergencies, applying for a US passport, or to obtain the status of a passport application. Automated information is available 24 hours a day and live operators can be reached on workdays from 8 am to 8 pm, Eastern Standard Time. (Services are available in English, Spanish, and by TDD.) This is a toll call; the charge is 35¢ per minute for the automated system or $1.05 per minute for live operators. Call ☎ 900-225-5674 for either automated or live service, ☎ 900-225-7778 for TDD service. Calling from a number blocked from 900 service? Call ☎ 888-362-8668 (TDD ☎ 888-498-3648); you will be required to pay by credit card at a flat rate of $4.95 per call. You may also contact one of the individual passport offices.

- **Boston Passport Agency**, Thomas P. O'Neill Federal Building, 10 Causeway Street, Room 247, Boston MA 02222-1094, ☎ 617-878-0900. Region: Maine, Massachusetts, New Hampshire, Rhode Island, Upstate New York, and Vermont.

- **Chicago Passport Agency**, Kluczynski Federal Building, 230 S. Dearborn Street, Suite 380, Chicago IL 60604-1564, ☎ 312-341-6020. Region: Illinois, Indiana, Michigan, and Wisconsin.

- **Honolulu Passport Agency**, First Hawaiian Tower, 1132 Bishop Street, Suite 500, Honolulu HI 96813-2809, ☎ 808-522-

8283 or 522-8286. Region: American Samoa, Federated States of Micronesia, Guam, Hawaii, & Northern Mariana Islands.

- **Houston Passport Agency**, Mickey Leland Federal Building, 1919 Smith Street, Suite 1100, Houston TX 77002-8049, ☎ 713-751-0294. Region: Kansas, Oklahoma, New Mexico, and Texas.

- **Los Angeles Passport Agency**, Federal Building, 11000 Wilshire Boulevard, Suite 1000, Los Angeles CA 90024-3615, ☎ 310-575-5700. Region: California (all counties south of and including San Luis Obispo, Kern and San Bernardino), and Nevada (Clark County only).

- **Miami Passport Agency**, Claude Pepper Federal Office Building, 51 SW First Avenue, 3rd Floor, Miami FL 33130-1680, ☎ 305-539-3600. Region: Florida, Georgia, Puerto Rico, South Carolina, and US Virgin Islands.

- **New Orleans Passport Agency**, Postal Services Building, 701 Loyola Avenue, Suite T-12005, New Orleans LA 70113-1931, ☎ 504-412-2600. Region: Alabama, Arkansas, Iowa, Kentucky, Louisiana, Mississippi, Missouri, North Carolina, Ohio, Tennessee, and Virginia (except DC suburbs).

- **New York Passport Agency**, 376 Hudson Street, New York NY 10014, ☎ 212-206-3500. Region: New York City and Long Island. Note: New York Passport Agency only accepts emergency applications from those leaving within two weeks.

- **Philadelphia Passport Agency**, US Custom House, 200 Chestnut Street, Room 103, Philadelphia PA 19106-2970, ☎ 215-418-5937. Region: Delaware, New Jersey, Pennsylvania, & West Virginia.

- **San Francisco Passport Agency**, 95 Hawthorne Street, 5th Floor, San Francisco CA 94105-3901, ☎ 415-538-2700. Region: Arizona, California (all counties north of and including Monterey, Kings, Oulare, and Inyo), Nevada (except Clark County), and Utah.

- **Seattle Passport Agency**, Henry Jackson Federal Building, 915 Second Avenue, Suite 992, Seattle WA 98174-1091, ☎ 206-220-7788 or 808-5700. Region: Alaska, Colorado, Idaho, Minnesota, Montana, Nebraska, North Dakota, Oregon, South Dakota, Washington, and Wyoming.

- **Stamford Passport Agency**, One Landmark Square, Broad and Atlantic Streets, Stamford CT 06901-2667, ☎ 203-969-9000. Region: Connecticut and Westchester County (New York).

- **Washington Passport Agency**, 1111 19th Street, NW, Washington DC 20524, ☎ 202-647-0518. Region: Maryland, Northern Virginia (including Alexandria, Arlington County, and Fairfax County), and the District of Columbia.

■ Returning Home

Upon leaving the Cayman Islands, there is a departure tax of US $12.50 for every person 12 years or older. The fee, which includes a $2.50 environmental protection fee, is not payable by credit card. Some airlines include the cost of the departure tax in your ticket. There is no departure tax for inter-island travel within the Cayman Islands.

United States Customs

When you leave the US, then return home, you will pass through US Customs at your point of entry. You'll complete a Customs declaration form, one per household, identifying the total amount of your expenditures while out of the country. Each returning Cayman visitor has an exemption of $400. Families may pool their exemptions; a husband and wife can take an exemption of $800; a family of four, $1,600. Cayman crafts are exempt from this allowance, as are works of art, foreign language books, caviar, and truffles.

Each visitor can also return with one carton of cigarettes and two liters of alcohol (only visitors age 21 and over). Additional liquor purchases result in a duty approximately 15% above the duty-free cost.

Your duty-free allowance includes any items purchased in duty-free shops, gifts presented to you, gifts you bought in the islands for other people, and purchases you might be wearing, such as clothing or jewelry. The US Department of Agriculture also allows you to bring back up to one ounce of decorative beach sand.

To make your passage through Customs a little easier, you should keep your sales slips and pack so your purchases can be easily reached. Get a copy of the *Know Before You Go* brochure (Publication 512) from the US Customs Service at your airport or by writing the US Customs Service, PO Box 7407, Washington DC 20044, www.customs.ustreas.gov.

PROHIBITED ITEMS

- Books, cassettes or CDs made without authorized copyright ("pirated" copies)
- Any type of drug paraphernalia
- Firearms
- Fruits, vegetables and meats or meat by-products (such as pâtés)
- Plants, cuttings
- Tortoiseshell jewelry or any other tortoiseshell items
- Turtle products – shells, steaks, lotion, and shell jewelry – sold on the island cannot be brought back into the US or through the US in transit to other countries.

Canadian Customs

After an absence of 24 hours, Canadian citizens can claim up to CAN $200 worth of goods without paying duty or taxes. After an absence of seven days or longer, Canadians can claim up to CAN $750 worth of goods without paying duty or taxes.

British Customs

UK travelers have the following exemption: 200 cigarettes, 50 cigars or one liter of spirits for visitors age 17 or over and all other goods up to £36 value.

Japanese Customs

Japanese travelers have an exemption of up to Yen 200,000 and three bottles of liquor for travelers age 20 and over.

Festivals & Events

■ Major Festivals

 Throughout the calendar year, Cayman Islanders celebrate with special events. Activities are aimed at fishermen, preservationists, pilots, scuba divers, and those who just want to have a good time.

Million Dollar Month

June is Million Dollar Month, when fishermen from far and near come to try their luck. Residents as well as visitors from around the world enter this tournament. The grand prize is US $250,000, awarded to the first angler to break the existing Cayman Islands All-Tackle Record for Atlantic blue marlin. The current record of 584 pounds was set in 1984. Other prizes include US $250,000 to the boat landing the largest blue marlin over 300 pounds; US $50,000 each to the boats landing the heaviest dolphin, wahoo, and yellowfin tuna; and US $50,000 to the boat of a single angler landing the largest Grand Slam (heaviest combined weight of a dolphin, wahoo, and yellowfin tuna). The visiting angler who reels in the largest eligible fish is awarded US $5,000.

The tournament begins at The Links at SafeHaven. Registration is US $200 (plus boat charter expenses) and is open to amateur and professional anglers. Boat/group registration fees are US $1,000.

This tournament draws over 200 anglers. Conservation rules apply, and fishermen are encouraged to release any catches under 300 pounds. Only those fish caught in sanctioned Million Dollar Month boats are eligible for the cash boat prizes and registered anglers can fish only on the Queen's

Birthday (June 16), the day of the Mermaids Tournament, and weekends (Friday through Sunday). For more information, contact **MDM Headquarters**, PO Box 878 George Town, Grand Cayman, ☎ 345-949-5587, fax 345-949-5528.

Aviation Week

Another fun time is International Aviation Week in early June. Sponsored by the Cayman Islands Department of Tourism, Aviation Week features an air show over Seven Mile Beach, displays, safety seminars, and live air-sea rescue demonstrations. Private pilots from throughout the states (including many who might not be comfortable making the journey alone) travel in a caravan from Key West, Florida, across Cuba's Giron Corridor on the 330-nautical-mile route. In recent years, this "invasion" has included over 150 private planes. For information, contact the Department of Tourism, ☎ 800-346-3313 or 345-949-0623 or see www.caymanislands.ky.

Pirates Week

The biggest blowout of the year is Pirates Week, scheduled annually at the end of October. It's a shiver-me-timbers time when the islands celebrate their buccaneering history with treasure hunts, parades, and plenty of excuses to dress as pirates and wenches. The celebration begins with fireworks and continues with parades, a 5K run, an underwater treasure hunt, a golf tournament, triathlon, sailboard race, children's fun fair, and much more.

Although swashbuckling may be the theme of Pirates Week, Caymanian heritage is also emphasized during this festival. Re-enactments of an old-time Caymanian wedding, thatch craft, and more have entertained and educated visitors at past festivals. Local foods, such as stewed conch, fish tea, and coconut rundown are served, and traditional quadrille dancing is highlighted. For more information, call ☎ 345-949-5078 or 5859, fax 949-5449, www.piratesweekfestival.com.

■ Cultural Events

If you're interested in learning more about the culture of the Cayman Islands, an excellent time to visit is during Cayfest. Scheduled for several weeks in July, Cayfest is a national festival of the arts of the Cayman Islands. It includes theater, dance, painting, pottery, architecture, photography, and more. Check out traditional Caymanian arts and dances, such as the quadrille. For more information, contact the **Cayman National Cultural Foundation** at ☎ 345-949-5839.

PUBLIC HOLIDAYS

During public holidays, expect all government offices and most retail establishments to close.

January 1 . . . . New Year's Day

February/March . . . . Ash Wednesday

March/April . . . . Good Friday

March/April . . . . Easter Monday

Mid-May . . . . Discovery Day

Mid-June . . . . Queen's Birthday

July (first Monday) . . . . Constitution Day

Early November . . . . Remembrance Day

December 25 . . . . Christmas Day

December 26 . . . . Boxing Day

■ Festival Calendar

You'll find plenty of rollicking festivals throughout the year. Here's a sampling of some that are planned annually. For more about any Cayman events, call the Cayman Islands Department of Tourism, ☎ 800-346-3313 or 345-949-0623 or see www.caymanislands.ky.

January

Annual Cancer Awareness Week, Grand Cayman – This annual event is sponsored by Cable and Wireless and includes a half-marathon walk, candlelight vigil, and more.

February

Mardi Gras Parade, Little Cayman – This annual event welcomes participants in the parade, which begins at Head 'O Bay and continues to the airport.

CIBC Valentine's Mile Run, Grand Cayman – This event, now in its 15th year, is a favorite with runners. Contact John Cummings, ☎ 345-949-8666.

Annual Orchid Show, Grand Cayman – Held at the Queen Elizabeth II Botanic Park, this annual show is sponsored by the Cayman Islands Orchid Society and the park. Along with orchid displays, the event includes lectures on these plants, orchids for sale, and demonstrations. For more information, ☎ 345-947-9462.

March

St. Patrick's Day Jog, Grand Cayman – Co-sponsored by Hyatt Regency and Bank of Butterfield, this 5K race starts and finishes at the Britannia golf course. Visitors are welcome to participate.

Naul Bodden Wahoo Tournament, Grand Cayman – Hosted by the Cayman Islands Angling Club, this tournament has US $10,000 in cash prizes. For information, call Donna Sjostrom, ☎ 345-949-7099.

Cayman Islands Annual Humane Society Dog Show, Grand Cayman – For a decade, this annual event has been a favorite with dog lovers on the island. Held at the Agricultural Pavilion in Savannah.

AUTHORS' NOTE: *Grand Cayman is home to the **Cayman Islands Humane Society,** a nonprofit organization that offers low-cost neutering and spaying programs and finds homes for stray pets. For more information, ☎ 345-949-1461, www.humane.ky. Donations can be sent to the Cayman Islands Humane Society, PO Box 1167, George Town, Grand Cayman, BWI. The Humane Society operates a used bookstore called **The Book Loft** and a thrift shop, **Claws-It,** on North Sound Road. Stop by the animal shelter for information on taking a Caymanian animal home to the US or Canada.*

April

Little Cayman Easter Auction, Little Cayman – Held at the Information Centre Trust House, this event includes a silent auction and Caymanian dinner. For information, call Gladys Howard, ☎ 345-948-1010.

Cayman Islands International Fishing Tournament, Grand Cayman – Sponsored by the Cayman Islands Angling Club, this event is tops with anglers. Contact ☎ 345-945-3000 or 949-7099, or e-mail fishing@candw.ky.

CNCF's Cayfest "Seaside Regatta," Grand Cayman – This event is held at the Public Beach along Seven Mile Beach and is held to recapture the spirit of an old-time regatta.

Cayfest, Grand Cayman – This national culture and arts festival showcases the culture of the Cayman Islands through dance, song, food, and more.

Bracfest, Cayman Brac – Like Cayfest, this festival is designed to showcase the local spirit of the islands, in this case both Cayman Brac and Little Cayman. Events ranging from puppet shows to music.

Revelers at Batabano, the annual Festival of the Sea.

Round the Island Regatta, Grand Cayman – Sponsored by the Cayman Islands Sailing Club, this event attracts everything from 22-foot vessels to 80-foot catamarans. Events include a dinghy regatta, race to the Banks, and a leisure sail around the island to the North Sound on the final day. For more information, ☎ 345-947-7913.

May

Annual Rotary Batabano Carnival, Grand Cayman – This annual event is filled with carnival music, including soca and calypso bands. Many Caymanian and Caribbean dishes tempt visitors, who are welcome to bring their own costumes and participate in the parade, although only costumes designed and made in Cayman are eligible for judging.

June

Paramount Computer's "Jet Around Cayman," Grand Cayman – This Jet Ski competition features both international and local riders.

C. I. International Aviation Week, Grand Cayman – This event includes an air/sea show, displays, safety seminars, and a fly-in to Cayman Brac. For more information, contact the Special Aviation Desk at the Cayman Islands Department of Tourism, ☎ 800-346-3313.

Queen's Birthday, Grand Cayman – The official observance of this holiday includes a parade and a garden party at Government House.

Annual Taste of Cayman, Grand Cayman – Sponsored by the Restaurant Association, this event includes a taste of local restaurants, a chili cookoff, conch chowder cookoff, and a golf tournament. For details, contact the Cayman Islands Restaurant Association, ☎ 345-949-8522, fax 345-949-0220.

August

Governor's Cup, Grand Cayman – Sponsored by the Cayman Islands Sailing Club, this event features Cayman's J22 teams, many of which race internationally. Spectators can watch from boats.

September

Cayman Madness, Grand Cayman – This diving promotion includes everything from underwater treasure hunts to barbecues. Sponsored by Bob Soto's Diving, the Cayman Islands Department of Tourism, and Cayman Airways. For more information, call ☎ 800-BOB-SOTO or see www.caymanmadness.ky.

SITA's Brac Wreck Bash, Cayman Brac – This event celebrates the anniversary of the purposeful sinking of the MV *Captain Keith Tibbetts*, now a favorite wreck dive site. The event lasts the entire month with special events that include live music, dances, contests, and special discounts.

Annual Rotary Fishing Tournament, Grand Cayman – This event attracts many top anglers; the tournament is now in its 28th year. For more information, contact Sonny Boy Bodden at ☎ 345-949-8222.

October

Pirates Week – Held annually at the end of November; see page 37 for details.

Atlantic Supply J22 Ladies Regatta, Grand Cayman – Showcasing the ladies of the Cayman Islands Sailing Club (which might possibly have the largest percentage of female racers of any such club on the globe), this event is not to be missed. For information, ☎ 345-947-7913.

December

Christmas House Lighting Competition

Arrival of Santa Claus, Owen Roberts International Airport

Rotary Christmas Tree Lighting and Carols, George Town

Getting Here

■ By Air

 You'll arrive in the Cayman Islands at Owen Roberts International Airport, a stylish facility that resembles a Polynesian structure. The principle carrier into this port of entry is **Cayman Airways** (☎ 800-G-CAYMAN; www.caymanairways.com), a national carrier with flights from Miami, Tampa, Orlando, and Houston. Flight time to Grand Cayman from Miami averages 70 minutes.

Service is also available with **American Airlines, Continental Airlines, Delta Air Lines, Northwest Airlines, USAirways International**, and **America Trans Air**. Additional carriers include **Air Jamai-**

ca, **Canadian**, **Sunworld**, **Taesa**, **Royal**, **Sun Country**, **Cubana**, and **British Airways**, which offers twice-weekly service from London.

AIRLINES

Air Jamaica. . . . . ☎ 800-523-5585, 345-949-2300
www.airjamaica.com

American Airlines . . . . ☎ 800-433-7300
www.aa.com

Cayman Airways. . . . . ☎ 800-422-9626 or 345-949-8200
www.caymanairways.com

Continental . . . . ☎ 800-231-0856 or 345-949-5252
www.continental.com

Delta Air Lines . . . . ☎ 800-325-1999
www.delta.com

Island Air. . . . . ☎ 345-949-5252
www.islandaircayman.com

Northwest . . . . ☎ 800-225-2525
www.nwa.com

USAirways . . . . ☎ 800-622-1015 or 345-949-7488
www.usair.com

United. . . . . ☎ 800-241-6522
www.ual.com

Direct flights to **Cayman Brac** are available on Cayman Airways from Miami, Tampa, Atlanta, and Houston or from Grand Cayman. Service to **Little Cayman** is available only with Island Air from Grand Cayman or Cayman Brac.

■ Package Tours

Several charter companies offer low-cost flight and accommodation packages. Some of these are available only through travel agents; others can be booked directly with the company. Check with **Adventure Tours USA**, www.atusa.com, ☎ 800-999-9046 for discount tickets and air/hotel packages. **Apple Vacations** and **GoGo Tours** can be booked only through your travel agent.

Travelers can often get a good deal if they purchase the flight and accommodations as part of a package. Contact these outfits to see what they have on offer, keeping in mind that the more flexible you can be, the better deal you might get.

PACKAGE TOUR OPERATORS

Airline Packages

AA Fly-Away Vacations . . . . ☎ 800-321-2121
Cayman Airtours . . . . ☎ 800-247-2966
Cayman Airways Holidays . . . . ☎ 800-G-CAYMAN
Delta's Dream Vacations . . . . ☎ 800-872-7786

General Tours

Caribbean Concepts . . . . ☎ 800-771-3230
129 Hillside Avenue, Williston Park, NY 11596

Horizon Tours . . . . ☎ 202-393-8390
1634 Eye Street NW, Suite 301, Washington DC 20006

LTC Travel . . . . ☎ 800-216-9776
101 2nd Street, West Chaska, MN 55318

Adventure & Environmental Tours

National Audubon Society . . . . ☎ 212-979-3000
700 Broadway, New York, NY 10003

Smithsonian . . . . ☎ 202-357-3030
1100 Jefferson Drive SW, Room 3077, Washington, DC 20560

Diving Tours

Scuba Voyages . . . . ☎ 800-544-7631
(Little Cayman & Cayman Brac only)
595 Fairbanks Street, Corona, CA 91719

Tropical Adventures . . . . ☎ 800-247-3483
111 Second Avenue N, Seattle, WA 98109

Family-Oriented Tours

Rascals in Paradise . . . . ☎ 800-872-7225 or 415-921-7000
2107 Van Ness Avenue, Suite 403, San Francisco, CA 94109,
www.rascalsinparadise.com, e-mail trips@rascalsinparadise.com

---

■ By Ship

Grand Cayman limits the number of cruise ships that can be in port at any time to three or four, with a maximum capacity of 6,000 passengers daily. This limit ensures that everyone has a good experience while on the island and nobody feels overcrowded in George Town.

Grand Cayman is served by numerous cruise lines, including **Carnival**, **Celebrity Cruise Lines**, **Costa**, **Crystal Cruises**, **Cunard**, **Fred Olsen**, **Holland America**, **Norwegian**, **P&O Cruises**, **Princess Cruises**,

Radisson Seven Seas, **Regal**, **Royal Caribbean**, **Seabourn**, and **Silversea Cruises**.

Cruise ship passengers arrive by tender in George Town at either the **North** or **South Terminal** (just steps apart). Both terminals are right in the heart of George Town, just a stroll from shopping and dining. The clean waterfront brims with shops featuring fine jewelry, black coral, artwork, leather goods, and more.

CRUISE LINE CONTACT INFORMATION

Carnival Cruises . . . . ☎ 888-CARNIVAL
www.carnival.com

Celebrity Cruises . . . . ☎ 888-313-8883
www.celebritycruises.com

Costa . . . . ☎ 800-33-COSTA
www.costacruises.com

Crystal Cruises . . . . ☎ 310-785-9300
www.crystalcruises.com

Cunard Lines . . . . ☎ 800-7-CUNARD
www.cunard.com

Fred Olsen . . . . ☎ 011-44-1473-292200
www.fredolsencruises.co.uk

Holland America . . . . ☎ 800-426-0327
www.hollandamerica.com

Norwegian Cruise Line . . . . ☎ 800-327-7030
www.ncl.com

P&O Cruises / Princess Tours . . . . ☎ 206-336-6000
www.pocruises.com

Princess Cruises . . . . ☎ 800-PRINCESS
www.princesscruises.com

Radisson Seven Seas . . . . ☎ 800-477-7500
www.rssc.com

Regal . . . . ☎ 800-270-7245
www.regalcruises.com

Royal Caribbean Cruises . . . . ☎ 888-313-8883
www.royalcaribbean.com

Seabourn Cruise Line . . . . ☎ 800-929-9391
www.seabourn.com

Visitors arriving for the day will find plenty of drivers offering trips to Seven Mile Beach as well as island tours just steps from the cruise terminals. You'll find a selection of organized tours (typically to the Turtle Farm, Hell, and Seven Mile Beach) for around $25, which gives you about a two-hour tour around the island (see *Guided Tours*, page 49). To experience the island without the crowds, consider hiring a driver by the hour. A taxi stand is located at the terminal and a knowledgeable driver will take up to four persons for US $37.50 per hour.

If you'd rather spend your time on the beach, take a taxi directly to Seven Mile Beach, about three miles from town. Taxi fare is approximately US $4 per person each way. The beaches are public, although chair facilities are for hotel guests only.

Generally, the busiest cruise ship days are Tuesday, Wednesday, and Thursday. If you're not on board a ship and want to visit George Town during a quiet day, plan to shop on Monday or Friday (not all shops are open on Saturdays, and many close on Sundays).

Getting Around

■ By Air

Island-hopping is part of life in the Cayman Islands; both Little Cayman and Cayman Brac are served by small aircraft rather than ferries.

The flight from Grand Cayman to Little Cayman takes 45 minutes; the aircraft continues on to Cayman Brac after a short stop. Passengers may check up to 55 pounds of baggage free of charge; excess baggage is charged US 50¢ per pound.

Fares from Grand Cayman to Little Cayman or Cayman Brac are US $154 round-trip or US $110 for a day-trip (there and back in one day). Flights between Cayman Brac and Little Cayman are US $40 round-trip. Special fares are available for children under 12. **Island Air** (☎ 345-949-5252, www.islandaircayman.com) provides daily service between the three islands. **Cayman Airways** (☎ 800-422-9626 or 345-949-8200, www.caymanairways.com) provides service to Cayman Brac five days a week with evening arrival.

■ By Car

Renting a vehicle, at least for part of your stay, is often the easiest and most economical way to get around, especially if you plan to explore. Car rentals begin at about US $40-50 per day during the winter months and $30 during the summer; expect to pay about $48-65 per day for a 4x4 vehicle. Vans average US $70-75.

A temporary Cayman Islands driver's license is required. You can obtain this from a car rental agency by presenting a valid driver's license and paying the US $7.50 fee. You must also show a major credit card. You must be 21 or over to rent a vehicle; some agencies require renters to be 25 years of age.

Remember that driving is on the *left* side of the road throughout the Cayman Islands. Some vehicles are right-hand drive. Most 4x4s have a left-hand stick shift. If you'd like a left-hand-drive vehicle, check with the company when making your reservation (we think a left-hand-drive vehicle is easier for US drivers; you can concentrate on driving on the left side of the road instead without fumbling with your signals and windshield wipers).

CAR RENTAL AGENCIES

Airport

Budget Rent A Car . . . . ☎ 345-949-5605
budget@candw.ky

Coconut Car Rentals . . . . ☎ 800-941-4562 or 345-949-7703

Hertz/Ace Rent-A-Car . . . . . . ☎ 800-654-3131 or 345-949-2280
acehertz@candw.ky

Marshall's Rent A Car . . . . ☎ 345-949-7821
mar_rac@candw.ky

Soto's 4x4 Ltd. . . . . ☎ 800-625-6174 or 345-945-1232
www.sotos4x4.ky

Thrifty . . . . ☎ 800-THRIFTY or 345-949-6640
thrifty@candw.ky

George Town

Andy's Rent A Car, Airport Road. . . . . ☎ 345-949-8111
www.andys.ky

Budget Rent A Car, Walkers Road . . . . ☎ 345-949-5605
budget@candw.ky

Cayman Rentals, N. Church Street . . . . ☎ 345-949-6408
cayauto@candw.ky

Coconut Car Rentals, Crewe Road . . . . ☎ 800-941-4562
or 345-949-4377, www.coconutcarrentals.com

E. Scott Rent A Car, Airport Centre . . . . ☎ 345-949-8867

Economy, Airport Centre . . . . ☎ 345-949-9550
www.economycarrental.com.ky

Seven Mile Beach

Andy's Rent A Car (opposite Marriott). . . . . . . ☎ 345-949-8111
www.andys.ky

Avis Cico Rent A Car
Hyatt Regency. . . . . ☎ 345-949-8468
Westin Casuarina . . . . ☎ 345-947-5585

Coconut Car Rentals, Coconut Place . . . . ☎ 800-941-4562
or 345-949-4377, www.coconutcarrentals.com

Hertz Rent-A-Car, Marriott Hotel . . . . ☎ 345-949-8147

Just Jeeps, N. Church Street . . . . ☎ 345-945-2424
www.sotos4x4.ky, e-mail sotos4x4@candw.ky

Marshall's, 201 Owen Roberts Drive. . . . . ☎ 800-625-6174
or 345-949-7263

Soto's 4x4 Ltd. (two blocks north of Marriott) . . ☎ 345-945-2424
www.sotos4x4.ky

Cayman Brac

T & D Avis, Airport. . . . . ☎ 800-228-0668
or 345-948-2847

Brac-Hertz Rent-a-Car . . . . ☎ 345-948-1515
www.bracrentals.com

Four D's Car Rental . . . . ☎ 345-948-1599

B&S Motor Ventures . . . . ☎ 345-948-1599, 345-948-1646
www.bandsmv.ky

Little Cayman

McLaughlin Car Rentals. . . . . ☎ 345-948-1000
littlecay@candw.ky

■ By Taxi

Taxi rates are based on a maximum of three riders. The minimum fee is
CI $4 for the first mile, CI $1.75 for each additional mile. Waiting time is
charged at CI 75¢ per minute. There are taxi stands at the airport and the
cruise ship docks; taxis are also available at all resorts.

SAMPLE TAXI FARES ON GRAND CAYMAN

(All fares in CI $)

Airport to Hyatt Regency $11.20

East End to Westin Casuarina. $32.25

George Town to Treasure Isle Resort. $5.50

George Town to Villas of the Galleon $8.00

Sleep Inn to Westin Casuarina $6.50

Sleep Inn to Turtle Farm $14.50

Westin to Turtle Farm $11.00

Treasure Isle Resort to Hell $12.75

■ By Bus

Grand Cayman now has public bus service; fares range from CI $1.50 to $2. The bus terminal is located in George Town on Edward Street (next to the public library), but you'll find numerous stops along these routes:

- ■ **ROUTE 1:** George Town to West Bay. Travels to Shedden Road, Seven Mile Beach, Turtle Farm, Boatswains Bay, Hell.
- ■ **ROUTE 2:** George Town to West Bay. Travels Seven Mile Beach, Boatswains Bay, Hell, Mount Pleasant.
- ■ **ROUTE 3:** George Town to Bodden Town. Travels through Red Bay, Spotts, Savannah.
- ■ **ROUTE 4:** George Town to East End. Travels through Red Bay, Spotts, Savannah, Bodden Town, Breakers, High Rock, Gun Bay.
- ■ **ROUTE 5:** George Town to North Side. Travels via Red Bay, Spotts, Savannah, Bodden Town, East End, Gun Bay, Old Man Bay and returns on Frank Sound Road.
- ■ **ROUTE 6:** George Town to South Sound. Travels out via North Church Street, Eastern Avenue, Godfrey Mixion Way, North Sound Road, Dorcy Drive, Crewe Road, Heron Harbour; returns via Crewe Road, Walkers Road, South Church Street, Cardinal Avenue.
- ■ **ROUTE 7:** George Town to South Sound. Travels out via South Church Street, Walkers Road, Smith Road, Crewe Road, Grand Harbour; returns via Crewe Road, Dorcy Drive, North Sound Road, Godfrey Nixion Way, Eastern Avenue, North Church Street, Fort Street.
- ■ **ROUTE 8:** George Town to Hutland. Travels via Red Bay, Spotts, Savannah, Bodden Town, Frank Sound Road, Old Man Bay, and North Side.

■ On Foot

With the low crime rate in the Cayman Islands, travel on foot is fun and safe. Walking is the easiest way to get around George Town, especially along the waterfront area. Many travelers also walk along Seven Mile Beach, strolling to dinner and back to their hotel. If you are staying in East End or West Bay, however, consider another transportation option.

AUTHORS' NOTE: *Driving is on the left side on the Cayman Islands, so pedestrians should always look to the **right** before crossing the street.*

■ By Scooter

Scooters are available for rent at several locations on Grand Cayman. **Cayman Cycle Rentals** (☎ 345-945-4021) has a shop at Treasure Island Resort, the Hyatt Regency Grand Cayman, and Coconut Place; scooters average about $25 per day. A temporary Cayman islands license, available from the rental agency, is required to drive a scooter and riding experience is necessary; see pages 45-46 for details.

■ By Bicycle

With their relatively flat grade, the Cayman Islands are wonderful for bicyclists. On Grand Cayman, along West Bay Road, be prepared for extremely heavy traffic during morning and evening rush hours. On Little Cayman, bicycling is one of the best means of travel and complimentary bicycle use is available from most accommodations.

■ Guided Tours

Guided tours are a good way for first-time visitors to get a good overview of the nation. They are available from most taxi drivers for about US $37.50 per hour for four persons; you can also check with your hotel tour desk for possibilities. Island tours typically include the Cayman Turtle Farm, Hell, Seven Mile Beach, and other attractions. Prices start at US $25 for a two-hour tour and run up to about $66 for a full-day trip.

Tour Operators

- **Burton's Tours**, ☎ 345-949-7222, fax 345-947-6222. Burton Ebanks is a local resident with an extensive knowledge of the entire region. He does both group and private tours and we can highly recommend him for his comprehensive knowledge of Grand Cayman.
- **Majestic Tours**, ☎ 345-949-7773, fax 345-949-8647, e-mail majtours@candw.ky. Airport transfers and sightseeing tours.

- **McCurley's Tours**, ☎ 345-947-9626. Sightseeing tours as well as transfers available.

- **Reids Premier Tours**, ☎ 345-949-6531, fax 345-949-4770. Sightseeing tours, shopping tours, fishing trips, snorkel trips, and more offered.

- **Rudy's Travellers Transport**, West Bay, ☎ 345-949-3208, fax 345-949-1155. Rudy Powery, president of the Bird Club, leads guided birding tours as well as sightseeing trips.

- **Silver Thatch Excursions**, ☎ 345-945-6588, fax 345-949-3342. Both the history and natural history of the area can be learned on a trip with Silver Thatch Excursions. Six different tours are available, including the **Eastern Experience** (historic sites from Old Prospect to the Ten Sails Monument in East End); **Walk the Mastic Trail**; **Botanic Park Adventures** (choice of Historic Route or Environmental Route); **A Walk Back In History** (historic walking tour of West Bay); **Central George Town**; and a **Visit to Old Prospect** (Watler's Cemetery, Old Savannah Schoolhouse). They also offer Birdwatching Excursions to one or more natural wildlife habitats, including the Governor Michael Gore Bird Sanctuary, Meagre Bay Pond, Botanic Park and Malportas Farm. Hotel pickup/return, drink, and snack (sandwich and traditional Caymanian pastries) are included.

- **Tropicana Tours Ltd.**, ☎ 345-949-0944, fax 345-949-4507, e-mail tropicana@candw.ky. Sightseeing and watersports are handled by this agency.

- **Vernon's Sightseeing Tours**, ☎ 345-949-1509, fax 345-949-0213. Sightseeing tours, dinner transfers, shopping tours, fishing trips and more offered.

Concierge Services

Many hotels, such as the Hyatt Regency Grand Cayman and Westin Casuarina, have a concierge on staff to assist with making tours, booking rental cars, making dinner reservations, etc.

A company called **Cayman Concierge Service** (☎ 345-946-0142) offers a similar service for guests across Grand Cayman, regardless of your accommodation. The service makes restaurant reservations, arranges car rentals, and more; no booking fee is charged. Call the central office or visit one of the three locations for assistance and to pick up brochures and maps. All locations are on Seven Mile Beach: The Strand, Galleria Plaza, and West Shore Centre.

Another free service is the **Tourist Information and Activity Service** (☎ 345-949-6598). This is a one-stop reservation hotline to book restaurants, private cooks for your villa, sightseeing tours, fishing charters, babysitters, maids, car rentals, bike rentals, submarine dives, water-sports and more. Information is also available by e-mail at aatours@candw.ky.

Accommodations

You'll find a wide variety of accommodations in the Cayman Islands, especially on Grand Cayman. Luxury resorts, full-service hotels, lavish condominiums, budget hotels, guest houses, and bed-and-breakfasts are available.

Room prices vary greatly with type of accommodation, location, and time of year. High season (mid-December through mid-April) brings prices about 40% higher than in summer months. A Government tax of 10% is charged on all accommodations.

SAMPLE PRICES

(Prices quoted are in US $, based on high-season rates)

Seven Mile Beach resorts . . . . $160-$570

Small hotels, inns . . . . $175-$200

Condominiums . . . . $250-$650

Guest houses . . . . $60-$80

Villas . . . . $300-$1000

Cayman Brac properties . . . . $90-$250

Little Cayman properties . . . . $150-$400

■ Resorts & Hotels

The Cayman Islands are home to several resort and hotel properties, although they're outnumbered by condominiums and villas. Resort accommodations range from intimate to enormous. They generally offer a full menu of resources for guests, from concierge service to rental car desks to wedding coordinators.

Resorts offer many different packages. Not every package is available at every resort but check with yours when booking to select the best package for your needs and your budget.

ACCOMMODATION PLANS

- **EP** (European Plan): This is a room-only plan. You've paid for a place to sleep but all meals, drinks, and recreation are extra.

- **MAP** (Modified American Plan): Breakfast and dinner are included. This is a good option for those who plan to be out exploring the island during the day.

- **AP** (American Plan): All meals are included. Drinks may or may not be included, and tips and recreation are usually not part of the package.

- **AI** (All-inclusive): As the name suggests, all-inclusive means that all activities, meals, drinks, transfers, and tips are included in the price. This all-inclusive policy means that you're free to try anything you like without getting out the credit cards. You've already paid for it in the package price.

ACCOMMODATIONS PRICE SCALE
Prices listed are for a standard room for one night during high season (expect prices to be as much as 40% lower during the low season). The price scale refers to US $.
$ . . . . Under $100
$$ . . . . $100-$200
$$$. . . . . Over $200

■ Condominiums

Condominium properties are especially popular on Grand Cayman. They can be a good choice for the traveler who wants to get away from the resort scene and "live" on island for a few days or weeks. With a full kitchen in most condo units, guests can shop at local markets, prepare some meals in house, and travel more independently.

With their "almost-like-home" atmosphere, condos aren't for all visitors, but they do work well for some. In selecting a condo, like a villa, be sure to ask plenty of questions. If your condo is in a rental pool and the owner suddenly decides to vacation on the island the same week as your visit, what will happen? Will you be upgraded to another property in the rental pool? Be sure to get all contingencies in writing.

RENTAL AGENCIES

To book condominiums and villas, call the property directly or one of these booking agencies that handles reservations.

International Travel & Resorts . . . . ☎ 800-223-9815

Reef Fanta-Seas . . . . ☎ 800-327-3835

Cayman Kai Development Co.. . . . . ☎ 800-336-6008

Cayman Villas. . . . . ☎ 800-235-5888

Tradewinds Property Mgmt.. . . . . ☎ 345-947-3029

Tropical Property Mgmt.. . . . . ☎ 345-945-4787

Blossom Villas/McLaughlin Ent.. . . . . ☎ 345-948-1000
(Little Cayman)

■ Villas

If you want some elbow room, a villa just might fit the bill. There's now a large inventory of villas available, ranging from spacious condominium units to timeshares to private houses.

A recent trend in the market has been the increasing number of "... units put on the market as timeshares, such as the expansion at Morritt's Grand Resort and the recent opening of the new Grand Caymanian Resort," explains Doug Sears, board member of the Cayman Tourism Alliance. For complete information on these resorts, see pages 165-173.

The increasing number of luxury villas is also noted by Penny Cumber, managing director for **Cayman Villas** (☎ 800-235-5888, 345-945-4144, fax 345-949-7471, www.caymanvillas.com). "There is a growing demand for property; the price of beachfront space is growing. The properties that are being built are becoming more sophisticated." Cayman Villas's offerings include **The Great House** on Seven Mile Beach. This third-floor apartment was used by *The Firm* filmmakers.

Cumber's company represents over 50 private homes as well as many condominiums. She says that more and more private houses and exclusive, very deluxe condos are being built. Many have their own pools and staff and are well equipped with central air, cable TV/ VCR, and all amenities such as washer/dryer, dishwasher, and microwave.

■ Rentals

Along with luxury villas, Cumber points out that there are a substantial number of properties for travelers with a closer eye on the budget. "We have a tremendous range, from $100 to $2,000 per night, including studios and seven-bedroom properties. Most private houses are at Cayman Kai, but there are many other quiet beaches around Grand Cayman, Cayman Brac and Little Cayman on which we also have villas. Guests can be on their own private beach and in the midst of all the action."

Travelers can book Cayman Villas up to 13 months in advance. If the property you have booked is sold or becomes unavailable for any reason, you will be upgraded to a better property at no extra charge. See pages 165-173, for details about these properties.

Special Concerns

■ Banking

Here a bank, there a bank, everywhere a bank! With almost 600 branches on the island, you're never far from financial services. Most are found in George Town and offer all the services you'd expect at home, including ATMs.

■ Clinics & Hospitals

- **Chrissie Tomlinson Memorial Hospital**, Walkers Road, George Town, Grand Cayman, ☎ 345-949-6066. This new CI $30 million facility includes maternity, emergency and surgical units as well as 24-hour ambulance service (dial 911 or 555 in Grand Cayman).
- **Faith Hospital,** Stake Bay, Cayman Brac, ☎ 345-948-2356
- **Cayman Medical and Surgical Centre,** Rankin's Plaza, Eastern Avenue, George Town, ☎ 345-949-8150
- **Professional Medical Centre,** Walkers Road, George Town, Grand Cayman, ☎ 345-949-6066
- **West Bay Road Medical Clinic,** West Bay Road (next to Treasure Island Resort), Grand Cayman, ☎ 345-949-2080

■ Credit Cards

Major credit cards are widely accepted throughout the Cayman Islands.

■ Crime

One of the Cayman Island's greatest assets is its low crime rate. Vacationers and locals both enjoy walking on public beaches or strolling along busy West Bay Street after an evening meal.

Crime rates are especially low on Little Cayman. When you pick up your rental vehicle at the one agency in town, they'll tell you just to leave the keys in the ignition when you park. However, no destination is completely crime-free. Use the same common-sense precautions you would at home.

SAFETY TIPS

- Do not leave valuables on the beach while swimming. Invest in a waterproof pouch for keys and necessities and lock other items in your car or hotel room.
- Don't leave valuables in your unlocked rental car. Many of the Cayman Islands' rental vehicles are open-air Jeeps; leave possessions in your hotel room.
- Use hotel safes and safety deposit boxes.
- Don't walk in isolated areas alone at night.

■ Currency

The official currency of the Cayman Islands is the Cayman Islands dollar, which is exchanged at a rate fixed to the US dollar. The Cayman Islands dollar is issued in units of $100, $50, $25, $10, $5 and $1, with coins of 25¢, 10¢, 5¢ and one cent. For a currency exchange chart, see pages 30-31.

AUTHOR TIP

US dollars are readily accepted on the Cayman Islands. You may receive change back in Caymanian currency, but there's no need to exchange your money upon arrival.

■ Dress

These are casual islands, and many restaurants welcome casual dress (shorts, T-shirts) at dinner. Call for recommendations if you have doubts. Swimsuits are de rigueur on the beach, but wear a cover-up away from the sand and swimming pool. Nude and topless sunbathing are prohibited throughout the Cayman Islands.

■ Dentists

Grand Cayman

- **Cayman Dental Services**, Mirco Commerce Centre, North Sound Road, George Town, ☎ 345-945-4447
- **Merren Dental Centre**, 37 Hospital Road, George Town, ☎ 345-949-2554

- **Dr. Robert Parr**, Cayman Medical Centre, Eastern Avenue, George Town, ☎ 345-949-7645

Cayman Brac

- **Dr. David Wolfe**, Snug Harbour, West Bay Road, ☎ 345-945-4388

■ Drugs

Be warned that the Cayman Islands exercise strict anti-drug laws. Marijuana is an illegal substance and possession of it can result not only in large fines, but also in a prison term.

■ Electricity

Electricity is 120 volts at 60 cycles. US appliances will not need adapters.

■ Emergency Numbers

Police . . . . ☎ 911

Fire. . . . . ☎ 911 or 555

Hyperbaric chamber . . . . ☎ 911 or 555

Air ambulance. . . . . ☎ 345-949-0241 or 6027

■ Gratuities

A 15% gratuity is standard. Some establishments add the gratuity to the bill automatically, so be sure to check first.

TIPPING GUIDELINES

Restaurants: 15% of bill, but check first to see if a service charge has already been included.

Bars: US $1 per drink.

Taxis: 10-15% for longer rides, but not expected for short ones.

Hotel bell desk: US $1 per bag or to call a cab.

Hotel housekeeping: US $1 per person, per day (except at all-inclusive resorts).

Hotel room service: 15% of bill (except at all-inclusives).

Haircare and other personal services: 15% of bill.

■ Groceries

There are numerous grocery stores on Grand Cayman, most found on Seven Mile Beach and in George Town. Generally, they are open Monday through Saturday only; you'll need to visit a pharmacy (see below) or gas station for small items on Sunday.

Grand Cayman

- **Fosters Food Fair**, The Strand, West Bay Road, Seven Mile Beach, ☎ 345-945-4748
- **Fosters Food Fair**, Airport Road, George Town, ☎ 345-949-5155
- **Kirk Supermarket**, Eastern Avenue, George Town, ☎ 345-949-7022

Little Cayman

- **Village Square and Village Inn**, Blossom Village, ☎ 345-948-1069

Cayman Brac

- **Billy's Supermarket**, Cotton Tree Bay, ☎ 345-948-1321

■ Hyperbaric Chamber

A two-person, double-lock recompression chamber is available for emergency treatment on Grand Cayman at the George Town Hospital. It is staffed 24 hours a day by trained operators and supervised by a physician specializing in hyperbaric medicine. In the event of an emergency, call ☎ 911 or 555.

■ Internet Service

Good Internet service is available, whether you bring your laptop or not. Connections can be made by dialing locally, ☎ 345-976-4638; the cost is CI 12¢ per minute. No computer? You'll find two Internet cafés along Seven Mile Beach: **P.D.'s Pub**, Galleria Plaza, West Bay Road, ☎ 345-949-7144; and **Dickens Internet Café**, Galleria Square, ☎ 345-945-9195. Both cafés offer Internet services on several computers; at press time, the rate was CI 12¢ per minute.

■ Liquor

Liquor can't be sold in stores on Sundays, although you can buy drinks in hotels and restaurants on that day. The legal drinking age in the Cayman Islands is 18.

■ Marriage

Getting married in the Cayman Islands is a simple process. Non-residents need to arrange in advance for a Marriage Officer and must apply for a special marriage license (US $200) at the Chief Secretary's office, Fourth Floor, Room 406, Government Administration Building, George Town, ☎ 345-949-7900. You can get a free copy of the brochure, *Getting Married in the Cayman Islands*, by writing to Government Information Services, Broadcasting House, Grand Cayman, ☎ 345-949-8092, fax 345-949-5936.

Procedures

You must contact the Chief Secretary's office at the address listed above before your visit to obtain an application and the name of a Marriage Officer (who will need to be named on your application). You'll then complete the form with your names, occupations, permanent addresses, and your temporary address while staying in the Cayman Islands (no residency period is required). You will also need to present the following:

- Valid passports or birth certificates verifying that you are at least 18 years of age (the minimum age for marriage without parental consent).
- The original (or a certified copy) divorce decree or death certificate, if applicable.
- A letter from the authorized Marriage Officer who will officiate at your ceremony.
- A Cayman Islands International Immigration Department pink slip showing proof of entry. Or, for cruise passengers, a boarding pass. If you are arriving on a cruise ship, have the purser call ahead to the ship's agent for assistance.
- Two witnesses.

Catholic Ceremonies

The Marriott can also arrange Catholic wedding ceremonies in a Catholic church. The couple must first go to their own priest for pre-nuptial requirements and fax the required paperwork from the church to the priest in Grand Cayman. (Original copies of the paperwork must be given to the priest upon arrival.) Certificates of baptism are also required along with a letter from the home priest, which grants permission to the Grand Cayman priest to perform the ceremony.

The **Westin Casuarina Resort** (☎ 345-945-3800, fax 345-945-3804) works with local companies to handle the wedding arrangements and help couples plan receptions and honeymoons at the resort. Their honeymoon package includes a bottle of chilled champagne on arrival, room service breakfast the first morning, one-day Jeep rental, round-trip passage for two on the Rum Pointer Ferry, full massage for two, sunset cruise for two, and a 10% discount on clothing at all Red Sail Sport shops.

Another option for nuptially minded travelers are bridal consultants based in the islands. **Cayman Weddings** (☎ 345-949-8677, fax 345-949-8237, www.cayman.com.ky/com/weddings) and **A Wedding For You** (☎ 345-947-6942, fax 345-947-7659) offer a variety of wedding services.

Wedding Planners

The job of getting married can be made even easier with the help of a wedding consultant at one of the larger resorts on Grand Cayman or an independent wedding planner. **Hyatt Regency Grand Cayman** (☎ 345-949-1234, fax 345-949-8528) has an on-site consultant to handle the paperwork. For US $800 per couple (including taxes and gratuities), you can purchase a package that includes a marriage officer, license/documentation, bridal bouquet and groom's boutonniere, wedding cake and a champagne toast. The package is available to resort guests, cruise ship passengers and other visitors.

The Honeymoon

Honeymoon packages are also available at the Hyatt Regency Grand Cayman. Packages include a honeymoon breakfast for two, a couples' massage, a sunset cruise, a round of golf, a Jeep rental for a day (the driver must by 25 years or older) and a bottle of champagne upon arrival.

Grand Cayman Marriott Beach Resort (☎ 345-949-0088, fax 345-949-8088) offers four wedding packages to guests and non-guests. The **Seabreeze** package, priced at CI $320 or US $400, includes the services of a minister, a Cayman marriage license, a recorded certified copy of the license, witnesses and a decorative marriage certificate. For CI $535 or US $665, the **Island Dream** package adds a basic tropical wedding bouquet and boutonniere, a wedding cake, a bottle of champagne and recorded wedding music. The services of a photographer who shoots two rolls of film (given to the couple for developing and reprinting as desired) are included in the **Paradise Found** package, priced at CI $725 or US $895. The **Ultimate Splendor** package, which runs CI $935 or US $1,165, includes both the photographer and the services of a videographer. Weddings can be held on the beach, in the garden courtyard, the ballroom, poolside or other site.

Introduction

■ Pharmacies

Because grocery stores are closed on Sundays, pharmacies are particularly important for last-minute shopping, and many sell some basic food items.

- **Strand Pharmacy**, The Strand Shopping Centre on West Bay Road, Seven Mile Beach, ☎ 345-945-7759
- **Cayman Drug**, Kirk Freeport Center, George Town, ☎ 345-949-2597
- **Island Pharmacy**, West Shore Centre, West Bay Road, Seven Mile beach, ☎ 345-949-8987
- **Foster Food Fair Pharmacy**, The Strand, Seven Mile Beach, ☎ 345-945-7759
- **Grand Harbour Pharmacy**, Grand Harbour Centre, Red Bay, ☎ 345-947-3784
- **Kirk Pharmacy**, Eastern Avenue, George Town, ☎ 345-949-7180

■ Religious Services

Anglican

St. George Anglican Church, George Town Cts., off Eastern Avenue, George Town, ☎ 345-949-5583

Bahai

Boggy Sand Road, West Bay, ☎ 345-949-3435

Baptist

First Baptist Church, Smith Road, George Town, ☎ 345-949-0692

Catholic

St. Ignatius, Walker's Road, George Town, ☎ 345-949-6797

Christ the Redeemer Mission, West Bay

Church of England

South Sound Community Centre, ☎ 345-949-2757

Church of God

Walker's Road, George Town, ☎ 345-949-9395

Methodist

Wesleyan Holiness Church, Turtle Farm Road, West Bay, ☎ 345-949-3394

Mormon

Church of Jesus Christ of Latter Day Saints, Smith Road, George Town, ☎ 345-949-4499

Presbyterian

Elmslie United Church, Harbour Drive, George Town, ☎ 345-949-7923

Seventh Day Adventist

Creme Road, George Town, ☎ 345-947-5279

■ Room Tax

A 10% government tax is charged on all accommodations. Most hotels add gratuities ranging from 6-10% to this amount.

■ Sunburn

Nothing will slow down your vacation faster than a sunburn, your biggest danger in the Caribbean. You'll be surprised, even if you don't burn easily or if you already have a good base tan, how easily the sun sneaks up on you. At this southern latitude, good sunscreen, applied liberally and often, is a must. This ailment ranks as the number one travelers' concern throughout the Caribbean. You are especially vulnerable while on the water; sea breezes may cool the skin but they don't prevent burns. Many snorkelers wear T-shirts to protect exposed backs from these strong rays.

AUTHOR TIP

Sunscreen lotion is sold on all the islands, but prices are steep; plan ahead and bring your favorite brand from home.

■ Telephone

Area Code

The area code for the Cayman Islands is 345.

Toll-free calls

Most 800 numbers will not work from the Cayman Islands. To access toll-free numbers, substitute 400 for 800. Callers are charged for these calls.

Long-distance Calls

AT&T, MCI Direct and US Sprint services are available for dialing from the islands to home. Access numbers are: **US Sprint**, ☎ 888-366-4663; **MCI Direct**, ☎ 800-888-8000; **AT&T USA Direct**, ☎ 800-872-2881.

Local Calls

The cost for local calls within Grand Cayman is 9¢ for the first three minutes, 3¢ for each additional minute. Calls within either Little Cayman or Cayman Brac are charged a flat fee of 9¢ per minute. Calls between Grand Cayman and the sister islands are 3¢ per minute. Calls between Little Cayman and Cayman Brac are 9¢ per minute.

Public Telephones

Throughout the islands, you'll find many public phones. Some accept coins only; others accept phone cards only; some accept both. You can purchase phone cards in denominations of $10, $15 and $25 from Cable and Wireless, which has offices in Anderson Square on Shedden Road in George Town and on Cayman Brac, as well as from most service stations.

■ Time

The Cayman Islands do not observe daylight saving time; eastern standard time is observed throughout the year. Dial ☎ 844 for the current local time.

■ Video Rentals

Because of all the condominium properties with VCRs, you'll find a good selection of rental businesses on Grand Cayman. **Blockbuster** has locations at the Eden Centre in George Town (☎ 345-949-9500) and on West Bay Road in the Westshore Centre (☎ 345-949-4500).

■ Water

Water throughout the Cayman Islands is drinkable, although many resorts use desalinated water produced by reverse osmosis; the result is safe, potable water. Still, some visitors prefer the taste of bottled water, which is available at restaurants and grocery stores throughout the islands.

Information Sources

■ Tourism Offices

i When on Grand Cayman, visit the **Cayman Islands Department of Tourism** office at Elgin Avenue, Cricket Square, in George Town, ☎ 345-949-0623, fax 345-949-4053. You'll also find information booths with maps and brochures at the Owen Roberts International Airport and the North Terminal cruise ship dock.

Excellent information is also found online at the Department of Tourism web site, www.caymanislands.ky, and at www.divecayman.ky, the official Cayman Islands dive information web site. For general information and reservations from the US, call the Department of Tourism at ☎ 800-346-3313; from Canada, ☎ 800-263-5805.

Before your trip, contact the Cayman Islands Department of Tourism office nearest you for brochures and information.

DEPARTMENT OF TOURISM LOCATIONS

Miami: 6100 Blue Lagoon Drive, Suite 150, Miami, FL 33126-2085, ☎ 305-266-2300, fax 305-267-2932.

New York: 420 Lexington Avenue, Suite 2733, New York, NY 10170, ☎ 212-682-5582, fax 212-986-5123.

Houston: Two Memorial City Plaza, 820 Gessner, Suite 170, Houston, TX 77024, ☎ 713-461-1317, fax 713-461-7409.

Los Angeles: 3440 Wilshire Boulevard, Suite 1202, Los Angeles, CA 90010, ☎ 213-738-1968, 213-738-1829.

Chicago: 9525 W. Bryn Mawr Avenue, Suite 160, Rosemont, IL 60018, ☎ 847-678-6446, fax 847-678-6675.

Canada: 234 Eglinton Avenue East, Suite 306, Toronto, Ontario, Canada M4P 1K5, ☎ 416-485-1550 or 800-263-5805, fax 416-485-7478.

United Kingdom: 6 Arlington Street, London, SW1A 1RE, England, United Kingdom, ☎ 011-44-207-491-7771, fax 011-44-207-409-7773.

■ Tourist Publications

While on-island, pick up a copy of the free *Key to Cayman* or *Destination Cayman* magazines for information on shopping, dining, and nightly entertainment. *What to Do Cayman* and *What's Hot! in Cayman* look at places of interest to visitors. Another good source of information is the Cayman Airways in-flight magazine, **Horizons**. These publications are distributed at the Owen Roberts International Airport as well as at most hotels.

■ Newspapers

The local newspaper is the tabloid-sized **Caymanian Compass**, published Monday through Friday. The Friday edition is especially useful for travelers because of it's **Wha' Happening?** list of the week's shows, club events, and special events.

You'll also find US newspapers for sale, although at a higher price than you would pay in the States. Some hotels offer the **New York Times** via fax, with a small selection of top stories and news items.

■ Television & Radio

Three local television stations serve the Cayman Islands. **CITN** (channel 27), **CTS** (channel 24) and **CCT,** Cayman Christian Television (channel 21), provide local broadcasting. Most residents and practically all resorts and hotels receive satellite television broadcasts from the States.

Several local radio stations broadcast in the islands. **Radio Cayman** (89.9 FM and 105.3 FM; 93.9 and 91.9 FM on Little Cayman and Cayman Brac), owned by the government, is broadcast on all the islands. **Z-99** (99.9 FM) and **ICCI-FM** (101 FM) at the International College of the Cayman Islands and **Heaven 97** (97.9 FM), a religious music station.

■ Web Sites

Web sites are provided throughout the book; the section titled *Useful Web Sites*, pages 240-243, has additional listings.

Where Are The Adventures?

The Cayman Islands present a variety of adventure opportunities, no matter what your fitness or activity level. Most adventures in the Cayman Islands revolve around the water, whether that means scuba diving or snorkeling, sailing or deep-sea fishing, or just plain beachwalking and sunworshipping, although activities on land are available as well.

On Foot

■ Walking & Hiking

 Because of the Cayman Islands' flat grade, walking is a popular activity on all three islands. There's plenty to see and, except along West Bay Road (parallel to Seven Mile Beach) and in George Town, there's very little traffic to contend with. Walking is a good way to meet local residents; it's traditional to greet others with "Good morning," or "Good afternoon," and a smile.

Hikers will also find marked trails. The **Mastic Trail** on the east end of Grand Cayman features several eco-areas and guided walks. Another excellent hike, this one self-guided, is found at the **Queen Elizabeth II Botanic Park**; for more information about these trails and hikes, see the *Grand Cayman* chapter, pages 130-132. Cayman Brac also has many marked trails of special interest to birders. More about these are found in the *Cayman Brac* chapter, pages 201-202.

AUTHOR TIP *Midday heat can be intense, especially once you enter the interior of the island away from the cooling trade winds. Always carry water with you and be aware of the symptoms of heat exhaustion and sunstroke.*

■ Caving

If you have an interest in caving, set aside time on **Cayman Brac**, at least for a day-trip. The caves here don't require any special gear other than a flashlight, and most can be reached easily using ladders or steps at the site. Some caves are home to bats, and most are composed of only a few rooms; see pages 202-203 in the *Cayman Brac* chapter for details.

■ Golf

There are several courses on Grand Cayman. In the Seven Mile Beach area, golfers can choose either the par 71 course at **The Links at SafeHaven** or the **Britannia** course at the Hyatt Regency. Under development is a nine-hole course at the new **Ritz-Carlton Grand Cayman**. Also on Grand Cayman is the **Sunrise Family Golf Centre** in East End. See pages 134 and 156-158 for details.

■ Running

Hash House Harriers (running club), Box 525 GT, Grand Cayman, Roger Davies, ☎ 345-949-2001. The club meets every Monday at 5:30, at a variety of locations.

■ Tennis

On **Grand Cayman**, most of the larger resorts have tennis facilities. You'll find courts at Caribbean Club Villas, Grand Caymanian, Grand Cayman Marriott Beach Resort, Hyatt Regency Grand Cayman, Royal Reef Resort, Treasure Island Resort and Westin Casuarina.

Among condominium properties, courts are found at The Anchorage, Aqua Bay Club, The Avalon, Britannia Villas, Casa Caribe, Christopher Columbus, Coralstone Club, Plantation Village Beach Resort, Sea Island, Seven mile Beach Resort and Club, Silver Sands Condominiums, Tamarind Bay Condominiums, Treasure Island Condominiums, Turtle Beach Villas, and Victoria House.

Villa properties with tennis courts are found at Barefoot Kai, The Bridge House, Kai Ku, Rum Run Villa, Thatch Hill, Villa Zara, Finger Tip, Gardens of the Kai, Island Houses, Kaiboose, Pools of the Kai, Tara Flora, Tara Sand, and We'll Sea.

On **Cayman Brac**, tennis courts are found at Brac Reef Beach Resort. On **Little Cayman**, tennis facilities are available at Little Cayman Beach Resort and the Southern Cross Club.

See the *Where to Stay* section in each chapter for a full description of the facilities. For information on special events, call the **Tennis Club**, Box 1813 GT, Grand Cayman, Scott Smith, ☎ 345-949-9464.

In the Water

■ Scuba

 The Cayman Islands are universally recognized as a top dive destination. Since 1957, with the founding of the Caribbean's first dive operation on Grand Cayman, these islands have caught the attention of the diving world. Bob Soto established that first operation and today over 40 such establishments provide service on the three islands.

The **Cayman Islands Watersports Operators Association (CIWOA)** estimates that about a third of all overnight visitors are scuba divers and about 80% enjoy some form of watersports during their stay (plus, about a fourth of the cruise ship passengers enjoy watersports). The popularity of these activities continues to grow but, because of the large number of dive sites in these islands, visitors can still enjoy a feeling of discovery. Strict marine laws protect the beautiful reefs and ensure pristine dive sites.

DIVING THE CAYMAN ISLANDS

- Dive sites start close to shore in shallow water (25 to 60 feet).
- A variety of dive experiences is available, for beginners as well as advanced divers.
- Quality dive operations are found throughout the islands.
- Instruction is readily available through any of the certification agencies (PADI, NAUI, SSI, NASDS, and YMCA).
- Green sea turtles are often sighted on dives.
- Scuba instruction is available in many languages.
- Much of the marine life is approachable, such as the rays at Stingray City.
- Visibility is excellent year-round.
- Calm water is assured on the leeward side of each island (dive operations are so confident of this that many guarantee diving 365 days a year).
- Strict conservation laws protect the reefs.
- The Caribbean's oldest underwater photography school, Cathy Church's, is located here.
- A hyperbaric recompression chamber is available 24 hours a day.

EARTH FRIENDLY

ECO ALERT: *Every year, members of CIWOA organize and participate in reef and ocean floor clean-up projects. The organization also works to encourage young Caymanians to consider a career in the dive industry by offering free PADI certification courses and snorkeling lessons for local schoolchildren and scout groups during special programs. Call the CIWOA at ☎ 345-949-8522 for more information.*

Over 200 sites lure divers of all abilities, from beginners looking for shore excursions and shallow reef dives to advanced divers seeking wreck and cave explorations. You'll find professional assistance from dive operators on each of the three islands. These include resort courses, where you can sample diving after a one-day course; full certification courses, which will award you a "C" card; and advanced courses to teach you the use of scuba computers, the skills of drift diving, and even underwater photography.

Incredible visibility, measured at 100 to 150 feet, helps make these islands such spectacular dive destinations. With year-round water temperatures of 77° to 83°, visitors can dive comfortably and enjoy an underwater playground that's filled with marine life.

The Cayman Islands is one of the best dive destinations in the world.

Grand Cayman offers approximately 130 dive spots, many less than half a mile from shore. The island is surrounded by approximately 60 miles of drop-offs. One of the most popular shallow dive sites is **Stingray City** on the North Sound. This 12-foot dive is memorable for presence of many southern Atlantic stingrays that divers and snorkelers can feed by hand.

Cayman Brac also offers drop-offs as well as coral gardens and caves. **Little Cayman** is especially noted for **Bloody Bay Wall**, a drop-off that begins at just 18 feet below the surface and plunges to over 1,000 feet. Visibility here often ranges to 200 feet.

The appeal of these dive sites has been maintained even in the face of rising tourism and an increasing number of divers. Strict marine conservation laws ensure the safety of the reefs and the marine life (see *Marine Conservation*, pages 26-27). Dive sites are protected with permanent moorings (over 200 in the islands) so boats can moor rather than anchor and risk damage to the fragile reefs.

To protect both the safety of the reefs and the divers who come to this island, Cayman Islands watersports operators adhere to strict regulations. The CIWOA was founded in 1981 to ensure the safety of the divers and the reefs. Members emphasize good neutral buoyancy techniques to prevent damage to the reefs resulting from improper positioning in the water. Also, CIWOA dive boats visit only those sites with moorings installed by the Department of the Environment's Protection and Conservation unit.

Divers who want to advance their skills will also find technical instruction on Grand Cayman. **Divetech Ltd.** offers technical diving instruction, including certification in the use of Nitrox/EANx.

ENRICHED AIR DIVING

Nitrox is a combination of nitrogen and oxygen that has long been used by military and technical divers and has now been approved for use by the CIWOA. Typical air has 79% nitrogen and 21% oxygen. Combinations with a greater percentage of oxygen are called Enriched Air Nitrox (EANx). The EANx mixture has 36% oxygen and is often used for cave and wreck diving.

This mixture increases the safety factor, making the nitrogen accumulation on a deep dive the same as for a dive in waters 10 to 20 feet shallower. It reduces the possibility of both decompression sickness and fatigue following a dive. Also, divers can enjoy more bottom time with no decompression or a shorter decompression time beyond those limits. These factors make it desirable for divers not in peak physical condition and for older divers.

To use EANx, you must be a certified advanced open-water diver with a minimum of 10 open-water dives logged. The course for EANx use runs about US $200-225, including four hours of classroom instruction and two EANx dives.

Adventures

Several companies, including **Ocean Frontiers**, **Sunset Divers**, and **Reef Divers**, offer rebreather certification. Rebreathers offer divers a silent dive with no bubbles or noise and are available for rent to divers certified in their use.

To share the company of other divers, contact the **British Sub Aqua Club** (Cayman Islands Divers, branch #360 BSAC, PO Box 1515 GT, Grand Cayman, ☎ 345-949-0685). Visiting divers are welcome to join activities.

> *The "Diver Down" red and white flag is required throughout the Cayman Islands for both divers and snorkelers in the water outside an identified swimming area.*

Diving in the Cayman Islands is taken seriously as a business and the operators here are excellent, upholding the highest safety standards. Two local organizations, Cayman Islands Watersports Operators Association and Cayman National Watersports Association, help maintain the excellent professional level.

Dive Operators

In this section we've listed the many dive operators on **Grand Cayman**. Because of the island's small size, many operators offer complimentary shuttles to pick divers up at their hotels and bring them to their departure sites. **Cayman Brac** and **Little Cayman** dive operators are listed in the *Adventures - In the Water* sections of those chapters. For more on scuba diving and dive operators, don't miss the tourism board's official dive web site at www.divecayman.ky.

UNDERWATER ADVENTURE COSTS

(These represent average prices in US $)

Snorkel trip . . . . $30-$63

Stingray City snorkel trip . . . . $30-$45

Snorkel equipment rental . . . . $5-$10

Stingray City dive. . . . . $45-$50

One-tank dive. . . . . $40-$61

Two-tank dive. . . . . $65-$85

Three-tank dive . . . . $100-$125

Scuba tanks (per tank). . . . . $5-$9

BCD . . . . $12-$15

Wet suit rental . . . . $10-$16

Night dive	$39-$55
Resort course	$75-$100
Scuba certification course	$325-$450
Nitrox certification course	$150-$200

Abanks' Diving, 96 South Church Street, George Town, ☎ 345-945-1444, www.abanks.com.ky. This NAUI- and PADI-affiliated operator offers two dives daily. Along with certification courses, they also offer snorkel rentals.

Ambassador Divers, George Town, ☎ 345-949-8839, www.ambassadordivers.com. This PADI-affiliated operation specializes in computer diving. They offer two daily dives on a 12-person boat.

Aqua Adventures, Seven Mile Beach, ☎ 345-949-1616. This company takes up to a maximum of eight divers, with five dives daily.

Aquanauts Ltd., Seven Mile Beach, ☎ 888-SUN-NUTS or 345-945-1990, www.aquanautsdiving.com. With PADI, NAUI, and SSI affiliations, this operator offers four daily dives on a 16-person boat. Instruction and customized dive packages available.

Bob Soto's Diving, Seven Mile Beach, ☎ 800-BOB-SOTO or 345-949-2871, www.bobsotosdiving.com.ky. The Cayman Islands' first dive operator, in business since 1957, this company has five Seven Mile Beach locations. Grand Cayman's only PADI 5-Star Development Center. Also affiliated with NAUI, SSI, NASDS, and YMCA. Four daily dives offered.

Cayman Diving Lodge, East End, ☎ 800-TLC-DIVE or 345-947-7555, www.divelodge.com. For over 25 years, this small diving lodge has offered diving, including one- and two-tank dives, night dives, and instruction. PADI affiliated.

Cayman Diving School, George Town, ☎ 345-949-4729, www.caymandivingschool.com. Specializing in instruction, this school caters to all skill levels, from resort to dive master. The PADI- , SSI- , and YMCA-affiliated operation has been in business for 13 years and offers instruction in several languages.

MULTILINGUAL DIVE INSTRUCTION

Cayman Diving School offers dive instruction in English, German, French, Italian, and Spanish. International visitors will also find multiple languages on their web site, www.caymandivingschool.com.

Divetech/Turtle Reef Divers, Seven Mile Beach, ☎ 345-949-1700, www.divetech.com. Specialty and technical training (including Nitrox) are available at this operation, now in its fifth year in business. Certification, resort course, and night dives offered. PADI and NAUI affiliated.

Divers Down, Coconut Place, Seven Mile Beach, ☎ 345-916-3751, www.diversdown.net. This operation now in its fourth year is PADI affiliated and runs three dives daily.

Divers Supply, Seven Mile Beach, ☎ 345-949-7621, e-mail diversup@candw.ky. This PADI operation has certification and resort courses, as well as Stingray City and night dives. In operation for 12 years.

Don Foster's Dive Cayman Ltd., George Town, ☎ 800-83-DIVER or 345-945-5132, www.donfoster.com. This operator is PADI, NAUI and SSI affiliated and offers three dives daily. Their boat has space for 20 divers.

Eden Rock Diving Center Ltd., George Town, ☎ 345-949-7243, www.edenrockdive.com. With its proximity to the cruise ship terminal, this is a popular operation that's been in business 15 years. Unlimited shore diving available to some of George Town's best sites. PADI, NAUI, and SSI affiliated. In operation 17 years.

Fisheye of Cayman, Seven Mile Beach, ☎ 800-887-8569 or 345-945-4209, www.fisheye.com. This operator has three custom-built boats and operates a complete underwater photography operation with rentals, processing, and repairs. PADI, NAUI, and YMCA affiliated.

Ocean Frontiers, East End, ☎ 800-544-6576 or 345-947-7500, www.oceanfrontiers.com. This company offers free shuttle service to its East End location. Four or five dives daily. PADI affiliated. In operation five years.

Ollen Miller's Sun Divers, Seven Mile Beach, ☎ 345-947-6606, e-mail sundiver@candw.ky. Groups of up to eight divers are accommodated by this PADI-affiliated shop that offers three dives daily.

Peter Milburn's Dive Cayman, Seven Mile Beach, ☎ 345-945-5770, www.petermilburndivecayman.com. For 20 years, this operator has run dives for many skill levels. Three dives daily. PADI, NAUI and SSI affiliated.

Red Sail Sports, Seven Mile Beach, ☎ 800-255-6425 or 345-945-5965, www.redsail.com. With a main location adjacent to the Hyatt Regency Grand Cayman and other locations at Westin Casuarina Resort and Marriott Grand Cayman, this operator has three dives daily with a boat capacity of 24. Complete dive packages available. PADI, NAUI, SSI, and NASDS affiliated.

Seasports, West Bay, ☎ 345-949-3965, e-mail seasport@candw.ky. For 28 years, Seasports has catered to small groups, taking only two to eight divers per boat. Pickup by boat from hotels and condos along Seven Mile Beach. PADI and NAUI affiliated.

Sunset Divers, George Town, ☎ 800-854-4767 or 345-949-7111, www.sunsethouse.com. At Sunset House. This 29-year operation has at least five daily dives as well as offshore diving at Sunset Reef. PADI, NAUI, SSI, YMCA, and NASDS affiliated.

Tortuga Divers Ltd., East End, ☎ 345-947-2097, e-mail tortugad@ candw.ky. Located at Morritt's Tortuga Club, this operator has taken out divers for four years. PADI affiliated.

Treasure Island Divers, George Town, ☎ 800-872-7552 or 345-949-4456. Behind Treasure Island Resort, this 14-year-old facility has four dives daily. PADI, NAUI and SSI affiliated.

ADVENTURE TALKS: SUNSET DIVERS

Ken Thompson of Sunset House and Sunset Divers talked with us about the world of Cayman diving. He can be reached at ☎ 800-854-4767.

■ *How would you classify the diving in the Cayman Islands?*

Diving in the Cayman Islands would not necessarily be classified as typically "adventurous," although it would probably be argued by some that it is. When I think of adventurous diving, isolated dive sites that are difficult to get to, or dangerous to attempt, come to mind. Neither of those qualities applies to diving in Grand Cayman.

We do have some of the best diving in the Caribbean, and there is growing interest in the niche area of technical diving. But rather than divers attempting to go deep, or seeking caves to explore, these divers are looking for the next logical step up from recreational diving, which will introduce them to new areas of interest. I'm referring to the use of nitrox and to rebreathers.

Both of these areas are readily available to the average diver and do not require incredible stamina, huge investments of time to learn, or a massive number of dives to master. Sunset Divers has invested in the qualified instructors and the necessary equipment in order to offer these programs. We stay ahead of most of the dive operations on the island.

■ *What can you offer the average diver?*

We have not abandoned the regular diver who comes down for his or her week of great diving in a safe, controlled environment. Rather, these are programs that can make a holiday more exciting and challenging. We still have some of the best wall diving in the world, the water is warm year-round, and the conditions make most other destinations envious.

■ *What can you tell us about your dives?*

Our dive boat, *Manta*, offers all-day, three-tank dive trips to the more distant dive sites on the northeast and east end of Grand Cayman. These sites are not regularly dived by operations on the west side of the island as the distance is too far. But the *Manta*, the largest day boat on the island, regularly travels to these spots to do extended computer diving. For those who do not want to be out all day, we still offer computer diving on our regular dive boats so guests can maximize their bottom time, without spending additional money.

■ *What sets your operation apart from others on the island?*

One feature that sets us apart from almost every other hotel on the island is that our boats leave from the hotel dock, and exciting shore diving is available right in front of the hotel. So when people read in our literature that shore diving is included in their dive package, they know they can step out of their hotel room and be in the water in minutes. It's so convenient.

What else do we offer? Towels on all our boats, drinking water, fresh fruit between dives to freshen the palate, and some of the most experienced dive instructors on the island. Sunset Divers' staff are qualified to teach open-water certifications, advanced or specialty ratings, as well as those divers wanting their instructor rating. We can teach recreational instructors to become technical instructors.

We understand what divers want, and give it to them. We have 48 secure lockers so guests can store tanks and gear near the dive area, and not have to carry it back and forth to their rooms. Our outdoor bar and patio are set up to allow divers to dress in casual attire (read bathing suits), to have lunch without having to worry about dressing up or drying off; and they don't get cold as they would in an air-conditioned restaurant. But if they want more formal dining, we have the full-service Sea Harvest Restaurant on the property.

Live-aboards

For those divers who want to eat, sleep, and drink diving, the live-aboard is a good choice. You'll be with others who share your interest, and you won't waste time reaching dive sites; what seems like your personal yacht just whisks you there.

Cayman Aggressor, ☎ 800-348-2628 or 345-949-5551, www.agressor.com. This George Town-based live-aboard has five professional staff members and a maximum of 18 guests. In operation for 15 years, it is PADI, NAUI and SSI affiliated and offers still- and video camera rentals. Divers enjoy sites off all three islands. The cost is approximately $2,000 per person, per week.

Little Cayman Diver II, ☎ 800-458-BRAC or 345-948-1429, www.little-caymandiver.com. Based off Little Cayman, this live-aboard accommodates 10 passengers in five cabins, each with a private bath. PADI, NAUI,

SSI, NASDS, and YMCA affiliated, this operator has been in business for 10 years. Video camera rentals available. The cost of a one-week all-inclusive stay is $1,395-$1,595.

E-BUDDY NEWSLETTER

The Cayman Islands Department of Tourism's dive web site, **www.divecayman.ky**, offers a free scuba diving newsletter via e-mail. The monthly newsletter includes dive packages and news of interest to divers. To sign up, visit their web site.

Resort Courses

Want to give scuba diving a try without the expense and time of a certification course? Try a resort course. This quick class gives basic instruction, practice in a swimming pool, and a shallow open-water dive with plenty of help from your divemaster. Your course is only good for that day's dive, but it is a good way to get a feel for the sport. Resort courses start about US $60.

■ Tethered Scuba

For those curious about the undersea world but not ready to take the plunge for a full certification course, a tethered scuba experience (also called SASY) to depths of 20 feet is offered even to children (see pages 95 and 108 for more information).

■ Snorkeling

If scuba diving is not for you, consider snorkeling. Many of Cayman's scenic reefs can be enjoyed in water just a few feet deep with equipment as limited as a mask and a snorkel. Snorkeling is an excellent introduction to the underwater beauty and rich marine life found in the Cayman waters. Just yards from shore, you can enjoy a look at colorful corals, graceful fans, and fish that include friendly sergeant majors, butterfly fish, and shy damselfish.

And don't feel that wreck diving is just for scuba divers. In Grand Cayman snorkelers can also view a wreck just a short swim from George Town's shores. The wreck of the *Cali* sits in shallow water and is an easy snorkel trip (see page 108). Most resorts offer snorkel equipment at little or no charge.

AUTHOR TIP

To prevent your mask from fogging, rub saliva on the inside of the lens. Dishwashing liquid and special alcohol-based non-fogging formulas may also be used.

Snorkel trips are offered by most dive operators, the most popular being the excursion to Stingray City (see page 140). Typically, these trips include drinks and often lunch following the snorkeling adventure. Complimentary shuttle services are sometimes offered.

The following are additional operators on Grand Cayman who offer guided half- and/or full-day snorkel excursions. Snorkeling operators on Cayman Brac and Little Cayman are listed in the *Adventures* sections of those chapters.

Cayman Delight Cruises, West Bay, ☎ 345-949-8111, www.cayman.org/caymandelightcruises

Tourist Information & Activity Services, Seven Mile Beach, ☎ 345-949-6598

■ Submarines

For underwater fun, *Atlantis* **Submarines**, *Nautilus*, and **Seaworld** *Explorer* provide a peek at the marine world (see the *George Town* section, pages 110-112). *Atlantis* plunges to a depth of 100 feet below the surface; Seaworld *Explorer* and *Nautilus* are semi-submersibles similar to a glass-bottom boat.

A unique operation called **SEAMobile** offers two-person submarine rides; you can even pilot the vessel; call ☎ 877-252-6262 or 345-916-DIVE or see www.seamagine.com for information.

NAUTILUS SUBMARINE

Grand Cayman has long been the home of the *Atlantis* submarine, and it is now home base for the *Nautilus* as well. This 80-foot semi-submersible vessel takes groups on a one-hour tour to view the rich marine life of the bay. The sub goes out about three-fourths of a mile offshore, offering visitors a chance to view two shipwrecks and to watch a diver feed a variety of tropical fish. Good for families with children. Tours are offered at 10:30 am and 2:30 pm daily, with additional tours scheduled on Tuesday, Wednesday and Thursday mornings as needed. The tours are priced at $35 per person and $19 for children.

The *Nautilus* also offers a unique tour on Thursday evenings. The Murder Mystery Theater is scheduled from 6:30 to 8 pm and includes a professional actor who interacts with the audience in trying to solve a "murder" on board. Unlimited hors d'oeuvres as well as beer, wine, and rum punch are available throughout the evening. These tours are priced at $43.75; call ☎ 345-945-1355.

■ Underwater Photography

As home of the Caribbean's oldest underwater photography school (Cathy Church's), Grand Cayman draws beginning and advanced underwater photographers. Stop in at any of these shops to rent underwater camera equipment, take lessons, or to have your shots developed. Many dive shops also offer camera rentals.

Grand Cayman

Cathy Church's Underwater Photo Centre, Sunset House Hotel, South Church Street and Coconut Place on West Bay Road, ☎ 345-949-7415, fax 345-949-9770, www.cathychurch.com. One of the Caribbean's best known underwater photographers, Cathy Church, operates Cathy Church's Underwater Photo Centre at Sunset House Resort in George Town. Classes, rentals, and processing services are available.

Divers Supply, West Shore Centre on West Bay Road, ☎ 345-949-4373, fax 345-949-0294.

Don Foster's Ocean Photo, Seven Mile Beach, ☎ 345-945-5132; www.donfosters.com.

Fisheye Photographic Services, Cayman Falls on West Bay Road, ☎ 345-945-4209, fax 345-945-4208, www.fisheye.com.

Cayman Brac

Brac Aquatics Dive and Photo Centre, Brac Caribbean Beach Village, West End, ☎ 800-544-2722 or 345-948-1429.

Reef Photo Video Center, Brac Reef Beach Resort, ☎ 345-948-1340.

Photo Tiara, Divi Tiara Beach Resort, ☎ 345-948-1553.

Little Cayman

Reef Photo & Video Centre, Little Cayman Beach Resort, ☎ 345-948-1033, fax 345-948-1040.

AUTHOR TIP *If you're not ready to gear up with the full underwater photography outfit, at least buy a disposable underwater camera. These generally work to a depth of 15 feet and are perfect for capturing memories of snorkel trips, Stingray City, and the underwater beauty of the Cayman Islands.*

■ Video Camera Rentals

Along with the photo centers listed above, many dive shops (see pages 71-73) offer video camera rental. Check with your dive shop of choice for availability.

On the Water

■ Swimming

 If swimming's your thing, call the **Stingray Swim Club of Cayman** (☎ 345-949-8105). The club hosts several competitions and visitors are welcome to participate in local events.

Swimming along **Seven Mile Beach** is usually easy, with little current. However, keep an eye out for watersports activity – it's a popular spot for windsurfers, Jet Skis, and kayaks, too.

AUTHOR TIP

 All beaches in the Cayman Islands are public. This doesn't mean that you can enter any beach, however; land access to some beaches is private.

■ Fishing

Fishing is more than just a popular activity, it's a national obsession. Tournaments draw locals and visitors alike for a chance at prize dollars and the opportunity to show off trophy fish (see *Festivals & Events*, page 36, and *Tournaments*, page 82, for more information). Catch-and-release is encouraged by local captains and applies to all catch that will not be eaten and all billfish that aren't record contenders. Fly-fishing continues to grow in popularity.

Regardless of your experience level, you can go on a fishing jaunt. There are half- and full-day excursions; most include services of a captain and crew as well as tackle and bait. Most of the fishing trips average four to six passengers.

Be sure to book your charter at least 24 hours in advance and plan to put down a hefty deposit (about 50%). In making arrangements and paying your deposit, make sure you are working directly with the captain or crew members themselves. Also, see what items you'll be expected to provide, such as food and drinks. Charter operators on **Grand Cayman** are listed below; those on **Cayman Brac** and **Little Cayman** are listed in the *Adventures* sections of those chapters.

AUTHOR TIP

If you take a charter, it's traditional to tip the captain and crew. Tips average 10-15% of the charter fee.

FISHING CHARTER COSTS

Taking out a charter boat is not an inexpensive proposition, but for many visitors it's the highlight of their trip. The cost of a half-day charter begins at about US $400 and may run as high as $1,000-$1,500 for a full-day excursion with state-of-the art equipment and tackle. Prices vary with the operator, and some charge an additional fee for more than four anglers, but here's an idea of what this outdoor adventure will run.

Deep-sea charters, full day	$600-$1,500
Deep-sea charters, half-day	$450-$700
Bone/tarpon/reef fishing, full day	$325-$900
Bone/tarpon/reef fishing	$250-$500

Charters seek gamefish, including blue marlin, yellowfin tuna, wahoo, dolphin (dorado) and barracuda, all caught year-round (the blue marlin is the most prized catch). Strikes occur as close as a quarter-mile from land at the point where the turquoise waters drop into inky darkness and deep water begins.

BLUE MARLIN: This top gamefish is often caught on light tackle while trolling the deep water around the islands. It is a fighter, a favorite with deep-sea fishermen, and can be caught both on artificial lures and with whole bait fish. Blue marlin here don't reach the proportions of those found off some islands (they average 200 pounds or less in the Cayman Islands), but they are caught year-round.

EARTH FRIENDLY

The government of the Cayman Islands encourages the catch and release of the blue marlin to help maintain numbers in these waters. It also offers free citations to anglers who release their marlin; a request form can be obtained from the boat's captain or the charter boat booking office. Also, captains can point anglers to local taxidermists that make trophy mounts for released fish based on their estimated size.

DOLPHIN: Not the mammal. This gamefish is noted for its heavy "forehead" and high speed. At 10 to 15 pounds each, the bright blue-and-yellow dolphin are found near floating debris or patches of seaweed. Drawn to feathers and spoons, the fish also like bait such as flying fish (its favorite diet), squid, and mullet. Summer is the best time for landing dolphin.

YELLOWFIN TUNA: Summer months especially bring this fighting fish to Cayman anglers. Averaging 30 to 40 pounds, the yellowfin is a powerful swimmer. It is usually caught on heavy line (its size can run much larger than average). The yellowfin is highly sought after and is commonly voted the best tuna for eating. Yellowfin tuna usually are caught during the spring.

BLACKFIN TUNA: This tuna is often caught by drift fishermen and is an excellent fighter. Weighing six to eight pounds, the blackfin is a good eating fish.

SKIPJACK TUNA: This tuna is sometimes caught by fishermen trolling for larger tuna. It averages 12 to 15 pounds.

WAHOO: Considered one of the best gamefish because of its fighting ability, the wahoo can obtain a speed of up to 50 mph. This deepwater fish is good for eating, and is a member of the mackerel family. Fish for wahoo from November through March. The following booking agencies and independent Caymanian captains can arrange charter excursions and fishing off the Cayman coasts.

AUTHOR TIP

Fly-fishermen should bring all their equipment, as guides and charters do not supply saltwater fly rods.

Charter Operators

Bayside Watersports, Seven Mile Beach, ☎ 345-949-1750. This operator has 10 boats ranging from a 20-foot Seacraft to a 53-foot sport-fisherman (max. of eight persons). Deep-sea, bone, tarpon, and reef fishing available.

Black Princess Charters, Seven Mile Beach, ☎ 345-949-0400/3821, www.fishgrandcayman.com. These 17- to 54-foot boats offer deep-sea fishing (full- or half-day) or a half-day of bone, tarpon and reef fishing.

Burton's Tourist Information and Activity Services, Seven Mile Beach, ☎ 345-949-6598, aatours@candw.ky. This company can arrange any type of fishing charter.

Captain Asley's Watersports, George Town, ☎ 345-949-3054, cayfish@candw.ky. Both deep-sea and reef fishing are offered by this company, which has three boats ranging from 25 to 41 feet for 10-35 persons.

Captain Ronald Ebanks, Seven Mile Beach, ☎ 345-947-3146, www.flyfishgrandcayman.com. If you're interested in fly fishing, call this operator who has a 17-foot and a 24-foot boat.

Island Girl Charters, George Town, ☎ 345-947-3029, e-mail islgirl@candw.ky. Island Girl specializes in deep-sea fishing and live-bait, drift fishing for yellowfin tuna and marlin. Also offers night fishing for snapper and shark. Charters for up to four participants are offered on a 28-foot boat.

Just Fish'n, Hyatt Canal, Seven Mile Beach, ☎ 345-916-0113.

Peacemaker Charters, Seven Mile Beach, ☎ 345-947-8548, e-mail peace@candw.ky. Up to eight persons may be accommodated on this 48-foot boat for deep-sea and reef fishing.

Sea Star Charters, Seven Mile Beach, ☎ 345-949-1016. This operator has three vessels and offers bonefishing as well as deep-sea fishing for up to five or six anglers.

Shore Fishing

BONEFISH: These three- to eight-pound fish are found in shallow flats and afford any angler a good fight. On Grand Cayman, good bonefishing can be found in the North Sound, South Sound, and Frank Sound areas as well as the coastal flats of South Hole Sound Lagoon. Another hot spot is off Little Cayman and on the southwest coast of Cayman Brac in the shallows. These fish can often be seen mudding in the shallow areas.

Bonefish can be caught at any time of day, although your success rate depends on many factors, such as weather and tides. Bonefish are caught on the catch-and-release system.

TARPON: Tarpon up to eight pounds (and up to 15 pounds on Little Cayman), are found on Grand Cayman's North Sound and in Tarpon Pond, a landlocked, mangrove-shaded 15-acre pond on Little Cayman. Tarpon are also caught above the mosquito-control dikes on Grand Cayman. These fish average three to four pounds. To locate the canals, ask a local resident (and bring along insect repellent – they don't call these mosquito-control dikes for nothing!). Light tackle and saltwater fly rods are preferred for catching these fighting fish. Tarpon are caught on a catch-and-release system.

PERMIT: Weighing up to 35 pounds, permit are caught on light tackle in shallow waters. A good fighter, the permit is a cousin of the common pompano. The permit has a jack-shaped body and is found over sandy bottoms.

COMMON POMPANO: Much smaller than the permit, the common pompano averages about eight pounds and is found in schools along Seven Mile Beach as well as on the North Sound side of Barkers. They are caught with bait or artificial lures.

BARRACUDA: This toothy species strikes spoons and can also be caught by fly-fishermen. A good fighter with a strong runs and frequent jumps, the fish is usually found just below the surface.

Barracuda should not be eaten, due to the risk of contracting ciguatera, or tropical fish poisoning. Barracuda consume fish that have dined on algae containing microorganisms that produce toxic substances. The toxin remains in the barracuda and can be deadly.

Reef Fishing

The many miles of reefs that surround these islands provide a playground for fishermen in search of light tackle action. After chumming to attract the fish, a variety of species can be sought, usually with live bait, such as squid and conch.

GROUPER: The grouper is the largest family of saltwater fish and makes an excellent meal. The Nassau grouper, with mottled coloring, is the most popular in these waters and is usually under three feet in size.

JACK CREVALLE: A tireless fighter, this jack averages five to eight pounds and is often found in large schools.

MUTTON SNAPPER: Another good dining choice, the mutton snapper is brightly colored and has a black spot on each side of its body. Running five to 10 pounds, this fish is often caught with bucktails and plugs.

YELLOWTAIL SNAPPER: This snapper is sought for its tireless fighting, as well as for its tasty flesh. Usually weighing one to 1½ pounds, the fish is often taken while drift fishing near the reef after chumming.

Fishing Tournaments

Fishing tournaments are major events in these islands. The largest is the **Million Dollar Month,** held in June. This event attracts anglers from around the world who come to test their skills. The tournament takes place at The Links at SafeHaven. Registration is $200 (in addition to boat charter expenses) and is open to amateur and professional anglers. Boat/group registration fees are US $1,000. See *Festivals & Events*, page 36, for details on prizes and contacts.

The **Cayman Islands Angling Club** and the **Rotary Club** also sponsor local fishing tournaments for both residents and visitors. The CI Angling Club holds tournaments in February, March, May, at the end of August and in November. If you'd like to meet other anglers, call about attending one of their meetings (☎ 345-949-7099, e-mail fishing@candw.ky); they welcome visitors. Another good way to "talk fish" is to stop in at the **Flying Bridge Bar** at the Indies Suites (☎ 345-945-5025). Tournament fishermen Ronnie and Bunnie Foster hear plenty of tall tales here. The Rotary Club hosts its tournament in September; for details, ☎ 345-949-8206.

■ Watersports

Sailing & Boating

Sailing excursions are another popular way to enjoy the islands. Charters, sunset cruises, booze cruises, rollicking "pirate" cruises, and more are offered to entertain vacationers, especially on Grand Cayman. Do-it-yourselfers will find plenty of smaller watercraft: ocean kayaks, Sunfish, Hobie Cats, WaveRunners, and more. Sailors can contact the Grand Cayman Sailing Club (Box 30513 SMB, Grand Cayman, BWI, ☎ 345-945-4383 or 947-7913) for information on sailing programs.

RENTALS

Rental prices vary, but expect to pay anywhere from $25 to $125 an hour, depending on the type of craft. These listings are on Grand Cayman.

Cayman Islands Sailing Club . . . . ☎ 345-947-7913

Cayman Windsurfing . . . . ☎ 345-947-7492

Red Sail Sports. . . . . ☎ 877-RED-SAIL
or 345-945-5965, www.redsail.com

Yachting

Unlike other Caribbean islands, such as St. Martin, Antigua, and the Virgin Islands, the Cayman Islands do not offer bareboat charters or crewed yachts. In fact, the islands have only limited yachting facilities. The **Cayman Islands Yacht Club** (PO Box 30985 SMB, Grand Cayman, BWI, ☎ 345-945-4322, fax 345-4432, e-mail ciyc@candw.ky) has 152 slips. It offers berthing facilities, fuel, electricity, and water hook-ups for craft up to 70 feet. No laundry, store, restaurant, or other amenities are available at this North Sound marina.

The **Harbour House Boatyard and Marina** (PO Box 10550 AP, Grand Cayman, BWI, ☎ 345-947-1307, fax 947-6093, e-mail hhmroger@candw.ky) provides dockage, a small boat slipway, small and large boat storage, and more. This is a working dockyard. The marina is located on Marina Drive at Prospect Park.

Sailors can contact the **Grand Cayman Sailing Club** (PO Box 30513 SMB, Grand Cayman, BWI, ☎ 345-945-4383 or 947-7913) for more information on sailing programs.

Adventures

WATERSPORTS ADVENTURE COSTS

(The following represent average prices in US $)

Windsurfing rentals, per hour $35

WaveRunner rentals, per half-hour. . . . . $50-$65

Ocean kayak rentals, per hour. $15-$22

Catamaran rentals, per hour $40

Banana boat rentals, per hour $35

Glass-bottom boat ride, per trip. . . . . $19-$35

Dinner cruises . . . . $45-$68

Day-sail. . . . . $40-$65

■ Water Toys

You'll find plenty of water fun in the islands as well, especially at the major resort centers. WaveRunners, aqua trikes, viewboards, Sunsearcher floats, banana boat rides, paddle cats, paddleboats, and toys for kids of all ages are available to rent. Look for this fun along Seven Mile Beach on Grand Cayman, and, to a much more limited extent, at Brac Reef Beach Resort on Cayman Brac, and Little Cayman Beach Resort on Little Cayman.

■ Windsurfing

Windsurfing operators are found on Seven Mile Beach and in East End, the top choice for serious windsurfing aficionados. There are two dedicated windsurfing operators in Grand Cayman. **Cayman Windsurf** (☎ 345-947-7492), on the east end at Morritt's Tortuga Club and on Seven Mile Beach at SafeHaven, is a BiC Center; beginners are welcome. The east end is a top windsurfing area because of its stronger winds. Trade winds of 15 to 25 knots blow during the winter months, dropping to 10 to 15 knots in the summer.

■ Sunset Cruises

Fortunately, you don't have to do all the work on your vacation. Let someone else man the helm and just relax for awhile aboard a sunset cruise. It's a great chance to watch for the "green flash," that peculiar meteorological phenomenon that occurs when the sun falls from a cloudless sky into a calm sea. Watch the horizon as soon as the sun begins to touch the sea and continue to watch for a momentary green flash, one that's often sought but rarely seen.

SUNSET & DINNER CRUISE OPERATORS

Bayside Watersports . . . . ☎ 345-949-1750

Black Princess Charters. . . . . ☎ 345-949-0400

Bob Soto's Diving Ltd. . . . . . . ☎ 800-262-7686 or 345-949-2022

Cayman Delight Cruises. . . . . ☎ 345-949-6738

Crosby Ebanks C & G Watersports . . . . ☎ 345-945-4049

Jolly Roger . . . . ☎ 345-945-SAIL

Kirk Sea Tours, Ltd.. ☎ 345-949-7278

Peacemaker Charters . . . . ☎ 345-916-2478

Red Sail Sports . . . . ☎ 800-255-6425 or 345-949-8745

In the Air

■ Aviation Clubs

Private pilots may contact the **Cayman Islands Flying Club**, Carl McCoy, President, PO Box 1725 GT, Grand Cayman, ☎ 345-949-2891, fax 345-949-6821.

If you are a pilot, don't miss **Aviation Week**, held each June. The event features a fly-in from the US across Cuba; up to 150 planes have taken part in recent years. The event also includes an air show over Seven Mile Beach, displays, safety seminars, and live air-sea rescue demonstrations. For information, contact the Department of Tourism, ☎ 800-346-3313 or 345-949-0623 or see www.caymanislands.ky.

■ Flying Tours

During high season (December through June), **Island Air** offers flight-seeing tours. These are conducted by **Seabourne Flightseeing Adventures** and cost about $60 for a 30-minute tour. For information, ☎ 345-949-6029, or see www.islandaircayman.com.

DAY-TRIPS

When you're ready to see a more secluded side of the Cayman Islands, consider a day-trip to Cayman Brac or Little Cayman. The sister islands are excellent destinations for serious fishermen and divers and a good way to sample the islands (and perhaps consider them for your next trip).

Flights depart Grand Cayman in the early morning, stopping first on Little Cayman and continuing to Cayman Brac. Once on the ground, you can rent a vehicle (a Jeep on Little Cayman) and enjoy a self-guided tour of the island, birdwatching, scuba diving, snorkeling, or fishing. Guided tours are available on Little Cayman; a special package including flight, tour, and lunch is offered through **Island Air** (Monday-Friday, 9 am to 5 pm; ☎ 345-949-5252, fax 345-949-7044). With daily service from Grand Cayman, flights depart on the 45-minute trip several times daily (times vary by season). The day-trip package costs US $110.

■ Parasailing

If you're ready to enjoy a bird's-eye view of Grand Cayman, sign up for a parasail ride over Seven Mile Beach. This is the only place in the Cayman Islands where parasailing is offered. Cost is about $60.

PARASAILING OPERATORS

Abank's Watersports & Tours, Ltd.	☎ 345-945-1444
Aqua Delights	☎ 345-945-4786
Bob Soto's Diving Ltd.	☎ 800-262-7686
Cayman Skyriders	☎ 345-949-8745
Kirk Sea Tours and Watersports	☎ 345-949-6986
Parasailing Professionals	☎ 345-916-2953
Red Sail Sports	☎ 345-949-8745

On Wheels

■ Bicycling

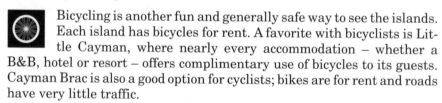

Bicycling is another fun and generally safe way to see the islands. Each island has bicycles for rent. A favorite with bicyclists is Little Cayman, where nearly every accommodation – whether a B&B, hotel or resort – offers complimentary use of bicycles to its guests. Cayman Brac is also a good option for cyclists; bikes are for rent and roads have very little traffic.

For more on cycling, contact the **Cayman Islands Cycling Association**, Box 456, George Town, Grand Cayman, BWI, ☎ 345-949-8666. The association has events scheduled throughout the year. Also, check *The Caymanian Compass* on Fridays for information.

■ Jeeping

Open-air Jeeps are so ubiquitous they could be considered symbols of the adventurous Cayman lifestyle. They're available from most of the car rental agencies (see list on page 46).

On Horseback

 Horseback riding provides an excellent opportunity to tour some of the island's quieter sections as well as its beaches. You'll find three operators on Grand Cayman.

Most horseback riding on the island is along the powdery beaches, an excellent place for practiced riders to romp and beginners to enjoy a slow walk on cushioned sand.

Honey Suckle Trail Rides (☎ 345-947-7976 or 916-3363) offers rides for both experienced and new riders with special attention to children. Both Western and English tack is available, as well as a variety of horses from thoroughbred to quarter horse. Guided trail rides and sunset rides are popular. Rides start at US $65.

ADVENTURE TALKS:
HONEY SUCKLE TRAIL RIDES

Penny Rivers of Honey Suckle Trail Rides spoke with us about her trail rides.

■ *What types of rides do you offer?*

Our rides are approximately an hour and 15 minutes on the beach, through the water, along a short trail and back down the beach. If we do a walk-ride, the cost is US $70 per person; a trot/canter/gallop and walk is US $80 per person. We also offer a two-hour guaranteed private ride, all captured on video, for US $100 per person.

■ *What should visitors wear?*

Jeans and sneakers are fine; people even wear shorts.

■ *What level of riders do you accommodate?*

We can accommodate experienced riders, novices and children.

■ *What types of horses do you have?*

We have quarter horses, paints, Appaloosas (including a former barrel racer) and a thoroughbred. When visitors book the ride we need to know their skill level so we put them on a horse to suit.

Again, we can accommodate all riders. We also provide pickup service within the Seven Mile beach area.

Experienced and new riders can enjoy beach rides with **Pampered Ponies** (☎ 345-945-2262 or 916-2540, fax 345-945-2262, www.ponies.ky). The operator offers early morning beach rides as well as romantic sunset rides. Full moon rides are especially popular, and private rides are also available. Rides start at US $75 for a one-hour beach ride; private rides are US $85 per person. Moonlight rides are US $100 per person for one hour.

ADVENTURE TALKS: PAMPERED PONIES

Danny Catt of Pampered Ponies spoke with us.

■ *What types of rides do you offer?*

We offer a 9 am and a 5:30 pm ride during the summer and we add a 10:30 am and 4 pm ride in the winter. We can accommodate large groups up to 12 riders. The one-hour daytime rides are US $75 per person. We also offer a moonlight ride, starting three days before the night of the full moon. It also lasts one hour; the cost is US $125 per person. We also offer private rides (just you or your group) for an additional US $10 per person. We accept Visa, MasterCard, travelers checks and cash. All of our rides are guided. We have one guide for small rides and two for larger groups. We will send two guides with two riders if requested and we pay close attention to children. We are the only horseback riding establishment in The Cayman Islands with insurance provided by Lloyds of London.

■ *What should visitors bring with them? Jeans? Swimsuits?*

Visitors should dress comfortably. We have everything they will need to enjoy the beach rides. We do suggest they bring a camera because they will want to remember this for a long time.

■ *What level of riders do you accommodate?*

We can accommodate any type of rider. We have gentle well-trained horses that seven-year-old children ride and we have some horses that allow the customers to do a little Caribbean beach jumping. We use washed up driftwood for jumps along the beach. We are also willing to split a group ride. If there are six riders and only three want to run, one trail guide will run with the first three and another guide will stay and walk with the other three riders. If the trail boss feels that the riders are good enough, then they will be allowed to run ahead of the pack by themselves (within eyesight of the guide) and then run back to the pack. We do have large, first class, big and beautiful horses. They are powerful but gentle. We have a professional trainer on site.

■ *Describe the itinerary for one of your rides.*

The rides all start the same. We expect at least one tourist to be somewhat afraid at first. After we are all loaded up we head down to the beach. We start out at a walk to warm up the horses and the riders. This also gives the guides a chance to sum up the riders' abilities. As the riders get comfortable we offer to pick up the pace and offer the chance for you to run. Some are ready at this point and some are not. All of our customers leave our ranch with a smile and most of them come back and ride on their next visit.

Nicki's Private Beach Rides (☎ 345-916-3530 or 945-5839) offers guided 90-minute rides along quiet trails; groups are no larger than four riders. No children under 12 are accepted. Prices for summer rides begin at CI $50 or US $63; winter rates are CI $56 or US $70, and transportation to the departure site is included.

Eco-Travel

■ Birding

One of the most popular eco-tourism activities in these islands is birding. Approximately 200 species of birds make their home on these small islands (50 species are known to breed here), from the magnificent frigate bird, with a seven-foot wingspan, to tiny humming-birds and Cayman parrots.

Silver Thatch Excursions offers specialized birding trips to birding sites such as the Governor Michael Gore Bird Sanctuary, a haven for waterfowl, as well as Meagre Bay Pond, Queen Elizabeth II Botanic Park, and the Willie Ebanks Farm to view endangered West Indian whistling ducks. Founders Geddes and Janet Hislop offer private tours at US $40 per hour or group tours for US $50 per person. ☎ 345-945-6588, fax 345-949-3342, e-mail silvert@hotmail.com.

ADVENTURE TALKS: SILVER THATCH EXCURSIONS

We spoke with Geddes Hislop, of Silver Thatch Excursions

■ *How do your tours differ from a traditional guided tour?*

Unlike most other tours, Silver Thatch offers a more intimate and participative look at Cayman's natural and historic heritage. These are not just sightseeing trips. Participants can expect some walking and "close encounters" with native plants, wildlife, etc., and come away with not only pictures, but an experience.

■ *What would you say to encourage travelers to get off the beach for a while and see more of the island's interior? What surprises await them?*

Let's face it: Cayman has beautiful beaches, but there is more to a vacation (and life) than sitting on a beach. Besides, you can't honestly say you've seen an island if you've only been "sitting on the edge;" You've got to get out beyond the beach and see what we're really about! Picturesque villages and gardens, beautiful roadside scenery and historic treasures are hidden along side roads waiting to be discovered.

■ *Can you tell us more about your Mastic Trail tour?*

This is one of my personal favorites. It's one of Cayman's oldest and best-preserved traditional footpaths. It runs through the Mastic Reserve, the second largest nature reserve on the island encompassing reputedly the oldest stand of native woodland left on the island. There is nowhere else in the Cayman Islands like it: historic sites, medicinal plants, Cayman parrots, woodpeckers, doves and other colorful bird life abound; magnificent trees – rare, large and some twisted into unusual shapes. At the right time of year, the trail is lush with wildflowers, including common and rare native orchids. Participants can expect a leisurely but interesting two-hour walk through this magnificent woodland where even many locals have not trod!

■ *Can you tell us more about your birdwatching tours?*

Again one of my favorites! I personally like birdwatching because my style is to find the birds instead of picking "one good spot" and staying there for an hour to see what shows up. With my background in wildlife management and research, my approach is to think of the birds as a function of their habitat. So, depending on the time of year, the weather, the interests of the participants (parrots are almost always on the list!), we get in the vehicle early in the morning and we're gone for about five hours. Imagine sipping coffee while sitting on the edge of a meadow waiting for the parrots to rouse and fly across just as the sun rises!

■ *What ecological and historical offerings of Grand Cayman would you especially like travelers to explore?*

Without hesitation I would recommend the Mastic Trail as our unique and ultimate eco-experience. For the history-minded, I offer walking tours of the West Bay and the capital, George Town's, historic districts. This brings you face to face with the historic architectural treasures hidden within Cayman's modern façade.

Serious birders should consider attending a meeting of the **Cayman Islands Bird Club**. The group meets monthly to discuss seasonal sightings. Call the National Trust at ☎ 345-949-0121 to check on meeting times.

Another good source of birding information is Rudy Powery of **Rudy's Travellers Tours** (☎ 345-949-3208, fax 345-949-1155). The president of the Bird Club, Powery organizes birding tours around the island.

Each of these islands includes protected sanctuaries and good birding sites. Little Cayman, home of the largest colony of red-footed boobies in the Caribbean, is a favorite with serious birders. Guided walks are available on Sundays. The island is also home to Patricia Bradley, author of *Birds of the Cayman Islands* (see *Booklist*, page 243), considered the best source of information on the islands' feathered residents.

■ Turtle Releases

Grand Cayman now offers an eco-tourism activity that is a favorite with both children and adults: turtle releases. Offered by the **Cayman Turtle Farm** in West Bay (see page 189), these annual events release tagged green sea turtles at the public beach; occasionally, groups sponsor special releases at other sites throughout the island.

■ National Trust Projects

Many of the conservation projects on the Cayman Islands have been brought about due to the efforts of the National Trust. Founded 1987, the trust is charged with conservation of lands, national features and submarine areas of beauty, historic or environmental importance, and the protection of flora and fauna. The National Trust has committees representing each of the eight districts on Grand Cayman and one for Little Cayman and Cayman Brac. To meet its goals, the work of the trust includes several ongoing programs.

The Land Reserves Program sets aside land for nature preserves throughout the islands. These important facilities include the Mastic Reserve, Salina Reserve, Queen Elizabeth II Botanic Park and the Governor Michael Gore Bird Sanctuary on Grand Cayman; the Brac Parrot Reserve on Cayman Brac; and the Booby Pond Nature Reserve on Little Cayman.

Children at the annual Cayman Islands turtle release.

The Biodiversity Program encourages scientists to visit the islands for their research and to assist in trust projects.

The Priority Species Program identifies local wildlife in need of special protection. These projects have included the Blue Iguana Conservation Program. Volunteers also take a census every three years of the parrot populations on Grand Cayman and Cayman Brac to monitor this bird. Research has also been conducted on the West Indian whistling duck. Other projects include a bat conservation program and an endangered plant program.

To learn more about these projects, check out the trust's web site at www.caymannationaltrust.org or write National Trust for the Cayman Islands, PO Box 31116 SMB, Grand Cayman, ☎ 345-949-0121, fax 345-949-7494; e-mail ntrust@candw.ky. While in George Town, stop by the offices on Courts Road off Eastern Avenue.

NATIONAL TRUST HERITAGE PASSPORT

Recently the National Trust began a new program called **Heritage One**, an attraction "passport." The passport allows a 25% discount on admission to four popular attractions: the Cayman Islands National Museum, Cayman Turtle Farm, Pedro St. James National Historic Site, and Queen Elizabeth II Botanic Park.

Each time the passport is used, it is stamped. You'll also receive a special coin as a souvenir from each attraction with its logo on one side and the Heritage One logo on the other.

To purchase a Heritage One pass, visit one of the four attractions, or check with your hotel concierge, car rental office, post office, or the tourism board. The cost of the passport is CI $19.95 for adults and CI $10.95 for children. There is no expiration date on the card.

One of the largest projects of the National Trust is the Salina Reserve, a 650-acre nature reserve on the north coast. Although not open to the public, the reserve is an important ecological project that combines wetlands and woodlands and offers nesting sites for parrots, caves with bat roosts, and several acres of habitat for the rare blue iguana.

Another major project is the conservation of the Central Mangrove Wetland, a long-term effort to preserve the wetland that flows into the North Sound. Fundamental to many natural processes, the wetland filters the ground waters and provides a flow of nutrients into the sound. Those nutrients are essential for the food chain upon which the marine life of the North Sound thrive. About 1,500 acres of this area is currently protected as an Environmental Zone under Marine Parks Law (see page 27 for a description of the current Marine Protection laws). The trust is now working to increase the wetland protection with land purchases. The entire wetland spans about 8,500 acres and is still largely undeveloped. The wetland also provides moisture that later falls in the form of rain over the central and western regions of the island (a rainfall that's 40% greater than seen on the eastern side of the island). This region is the home of many species, such as West Indian whistling ducks, Grand Cayman parrots, hickatees, agoutis, and marine life.

Cultural Excursions

■ Attractions

 Along with its eco-tourism activities, the National Trust is charged with preserving the natural, historic, and maritime history of Cayman through preservation of areas, sites, buildings, structures, and objects of historic or cultural significance. One of the first of such projects undertaken by the Trust was the conservation of the remains of an original wall of **Fort George** in downtown George Town (see page 118). Other projects have included the **Old Savannah Schoolhouse**, a typical 1940s one-room government schoolhouse; the **Guard House Park**, which recalls the history of Bodden Town, Cayman's first capital; and the **East End Lighthouse Park**.

The trust has gone on to create walking tour brochures for its most interesting historic districts: **West Bay**, **George Town**, and **Bodden Town**. These brochures (available for $1 from the Cayman Islands National Museum, the National Trust, and visitors information booth) introduce visitors to Caymanian architecture and are a wonderful way to learn more about the history that makes these islands special.

The National Trust has also played a major role in the preservation of **Pedro St. James Castle**, the oldest known stone structure in the Cayman Islands. For more on this project, check out the *East of George Town* section, page 146.

But it's not just the most important historic structures that have drawn the attention of this group; everyday homes and buildings also earn its respect. The National Trust has an ongoing Historic Buildings and Sites Inventory, a computerized reference list of places of historic and architectural interest built before 1950.

To encourage the public to recognize the value of these historic buildings, the trust has a historic plaque program. It also honors private citizens who have made a commitment to maintain, rehabilitate or restore historic buildings and sites with an annual "Award of Distinction for the Preservation of Historic Places."

■ Guided Tours

Grand Cayman

Both the history and natural history of the area can be learned on a trip with **Silver Thatch Excursions**. These tours are operated by Geddes Hislop, former Public Education Manager Officer for the National Trust, and his wife, Janet. Hislop worked on the interpretive development of two of the island's top environmental attractions: the Queen Elizabeth II Botanic Park and the Mastic Trail. Six different tours are available, including The Eastern Experience (historic sites from Old Prospect to the Ten Sails Monument in East End); Walk the Mastic Trail; Botanic Park Adventures (two options, including the Historic Route and the Environmental Route); A Walk Back In History (historic walking tour of West Bay, central George Town, visit to Old Prospect, Watler's Cemetery and Old Savannah Schoolhouse); and Birdwatching Excursions to one or more natural wildlife habitats, such as Governor Michael Gore Bird Sanctuary, Meagre Bay Pond, the Botanic Park and Malportas Farm.

Hotel pickup and return, drink, and a snack (sandwich and traditional Caymanian pastries) are included. For information, ☎ 345-945-6588, fax 345-949-3342. For more information about tours offered by Silver Thatch, see pages 50 and 89.

Cayman Brac

Visitors to Cayman Brac have an excellent source of free tours; local resident T.J. Sevik leads specialized nature and eco-tours, custom designed for your interests; for arrangements contact Kenny Ryan or Mrs. Wanda Tatum, ☎ 345-948-2651, fax 345-948-2506.

For other tour options, check with these operators:

D&M Taxi-N-Tours, Spot Bay, ☎ 345-948-2307. Customized tours of the island, including the bluff and the lighthouse, are available through this company.

Elo's Tours and Taxi Service, The Bight, ☎ 345-948-0220. This company offers guided tours around the island including the caves. Trips to the lighthouse cost extra.

Hill's Taxi, Spot Bay, ☎ 345-948-0540. These tours cover the caves, lighthouse, museum, and more.

Maple Edwards Taxi, Spot Bay, ☎ 345-948-0395. These tours include the museum, bluff, caves, and more.

Little Cayman

LCB Tours, Blossom Village, ☎ 800-327-3835 or 345-948-1033, e-mail lcbr@candw.ky. This tour company visits the bird sanctuary, museum, and more; snorkel trips are also available.

Family Adventures

 Bringing the kids along on vacation might seem like an adventure in itself, but in the Cayman Islands it's an easy task. The island has many family-friendly accommodations (there are twice as many condominiums as hotels on Grand Cayman) that make children welcome. Condominium units generally accommodate four to eight people and usually include televisions with VCRs as well as full kitchens – to cut back on dining costs and to satisfy picky eaters. The low crime rate in the Cayman Islands also makes this a top destination for families.

■ Attractions & Activities

CAYMAN TURTLE FARM, West Bay: Children of all ages delight in the tiny newborn turtles and the massive breeders. Kids enjoy picking up turtles in the special tanks (bring along the camera for this excursion) and school-age children find the trip an education.

SCUBA RESORT COURSES: Children can take a resort course from one of the many operators. The course begins in a swimming pool and is followed by a shallow-water dive.

SASY: Thanks to a new program operated by Red Sail Sports, children as young as four can now have a taste of scuba diving. SASY, or Supplied Air Snorkeling for Youths, is a scuba unit customized for young bodies. Developed in the Cayman Islands by Captain Wayne Hasson, a father of two young children, the unit combines a regulator so young divers can breath from a continuous air supply and a buoyancy compensator to keep them floating safely near the surface. Units are available for use at Red Sail Sports (www.redsail.com) locations at the Hyatt Regency Grand Cayman, Westin Casuarina Resort and Marriott Grand Cayman.

"Grand Cayman is the perfect place for kids to learn to use SASY," explains Red Sail Sports Operations Manager Rod McDowell. "The waters here are clear and calm, and there's a lot for them to see. Parents can now take their children along on a dive boat, and together the whole family can explore our underwater world."

GLASS-BOTTOM BOAT RIDE: Families with children of all ages enjoy the Seaworld *Explorer*, a semi-submersible that gives you a peek into the undersea world.

ATLANTIS SUBMARINE, George Town: Submerging up to a depth of 100 feet, this submarine is good for children but not recommended for those who might be prone to tantrums or fits in enclosed situations (there's no taking unruly kids out of this attraction).

PIRATE SHIP, George Town: Yo ho ho! The kids will love a two-hour cruise aboard the *Jolly Roger*, a replica of a 17th-century Spanish galleon.

PIRATE CAVE, Bodden Town: Take a look at indigenous Cayman animals – the agouti and a parrot – before heading down to the cave. Pretend you're a pirate in the damp, dark recesses or on the lookout for pirate treasure.

WATERSPORTS, Seven Mile Beach and Rum Point: The youngest kids enjoy just splashing in the gentle surf or digging in the sand; older children can ride the banana boat, try their luck on a windsurfer, or snorkel in the clear waters.

CHILDREN'S RESORT PROGRAMS: The Hyatt Regency Grand Cayman offers Camp Hyatt for kids three-12 years old. Westin Casuarina Resort has Camp Scallywag for children four-12.

CARDINAL D'S PARK, George Town: A small zoo that gives youngsters a look at the Cayman parrot, blue iguana, agouti, whistling ducks, and turtles. Their petting zoo is popular with young visitors.

O2B KIDZ, Merrens Shopping Complex, North Church Street, ☎ 345-946-5439. This expansive indoor playland is a great rainy day option for children under 12. Kids have a range of games and play equipment; there's a toddler area for the smallest travelers.

SMYLES, Islander Complex, Harquail Bypass, ☎ 345-946-5800. On the premises of World Gym, Smyles includes plenty of activities for young travelers.

MINIATURE GOLF, West Bay Road in front of the Hyatt Regency, Seven Mile Beach, ☎ 345-949-1474. An 18-hole mini course that is great for kids (and kids at heart), with a jungle theme including elephants and even a waterfall.

PLANET ARCADIA, Grand Harbour, Red Bay, ☎ 345-947-4263. This video game arcade has simulator games, pinball, air hockey, you name it.

RAINY DAY ACTIVITIES

Into every vacation a little rain may fall, so if clouds prevail during your vacation, don't despair. Here's a list of activities that don't depend on sunshine. And remember that most tropical rainstorms are short-lived.

- Cayman Turtle Farm (Grand Cayman's West Bay area). Although much of the farm is located outdoors, the tanks can be enjoyed in all but the worst weather.
- National Museum (George Town)
- Scuba diving
- Shopping in George Town
- Pirate Cave (Bodden Town, Grand Cayman)
- Pedro St. James (Savannah, Grand Cayman)

- *Nautilus* semi-submersible (George Town)
- Caves (Cayman Brac)
- Seaworld *Explorer* (George Town)
- *Atlantis* Submarines (George Town)

■ Spectator Sports

Cricket

Cricket Association, c/o Jimmy Powell, Box 1377, ☎ 345-949-8197, (weekdays), ☎ 345-949-3911 (home). The Association holds weekend matches from January through June at the Cricket Oval off Thomas Russell Way.

Dirt-Track Racing

Grand Cayman is now the home of dirt-track racing through the **Cayman Motorsports Association**. Races include front-wheel-drive cars, rear-wheel-drive cars, and motorbikes. Between races, children and teens race go-carts and dirtbikes.

Races take place the first Sunday of the month. At press time, work was underway on a new paved track with a drag racing strip on the east end. For information, call the Cayman Motorsports Association hotline, ☎ 345-945-1213.

Rugby

Rugby Club, c/o Campbell Law, ☎ 345-949-9876 (wk), or Bernard Knight, ☎ 345-949-2039, Box 893 GT. Matches are played at the South Sound Rugby Club pitch from September through March.

Soccer

Cayman Islands Football (Soccer) Association, c/o Jeff Webb, President, PO Box 178 GT, ☎ 345-949-4733/6164. The season runs from September though March with games played at different locations.

Adventures

Packing For Adventure

In addition to basic travel documents, there are items that are either difficult to find, or are available but may be more expensive to purchase in the Islands; bring what you'll need for the length of your stay.

WHAT TO BRING

General Travel

- Proof of citizenship; driver's license for car rental
- Airline tickets
- Swimsuit and snorkel sear
- Sunscreen, aloe vera gel
- First aid kit, prescriptions (in original bottles)
- Cameras, flash and film
- Cooler
- Mini address book

Divers

- "C" card
- Compass
- Dive tables
- Dive computer
- Weight belt
- Mesh bag
- Dive boots
- Dive skin or light wetsuit
- Dive light and Cyalume sticks
- Batteries
- Logbook
- Emergency medical information
- Proof of insurance/DAN membership card

Anglers

- Polarized sunglasses
- Camera to record your catch
- Wading shoes or non-skid boating shoes
- Fly-fishing tackle

Hikers

- Hiking shoes (broken-in)
- Extra socks
- Compass
- Insect repellent

Birders

- Binoculars
- Bird list
- Copy of *Birds of the Cayman Islands* (see *Booklist*, page 243) or your favorite guide

Adventures

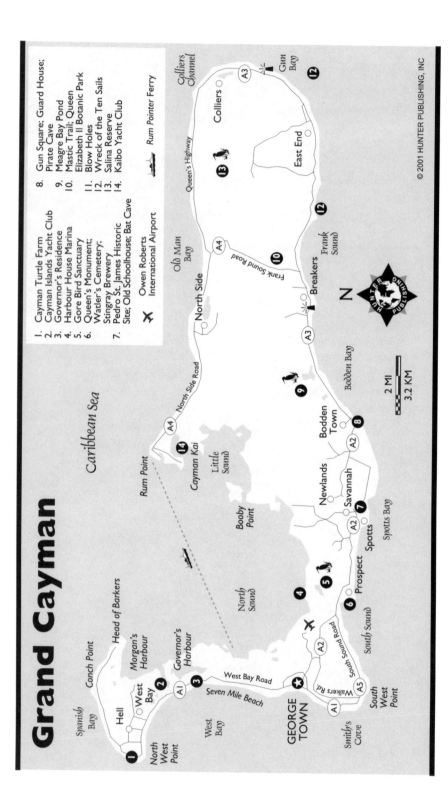

Grand Cayman

1. Cayman Turtle Farm
2. Cayman Islands Yacht Club
3. Governor's Residence
4. Harbour House Marina
5. Gore Bird Sanctuary
6. Queen's Monument;
   Watler's Cemetery;
7. Stingray Brewery
   Pedro St. James Historic
   Site; Old Schoolhouse; Bat Cave

8. Gun Square; Guard House;
   Pirate Cave
9. Meagre Bay Pond
10. Mastic Trail; Queen
    Elizabeth II Botanic Park
11. Blow Holes
12. Wreck of the Ten Sails
13. Salina Reserve
14. Kaibo Yacht Club

✈ Owen Roberts
   International Airport

⛴ Rum Pointer Ferry

Caribbean Sea

N HUNTER PUBLISHING

2 MI
3.2 KM

Grand Cayman

This chapter covers the island of Grand Cayman, the heart of Caymanian tourism and the destination for most travelers. For easy navigation, we have divided this chapter according to the island's four regions.

- *George Town* covers the capital city, the heart of the business and banking industry that has made these islands so affluent. The stop of all cruise ship passengers, George Town is also the best place for those looking to learn more about Caymanian history, to do some duty-free shopping, and to enjoy some of the island's best underwater fun.

- *East of George Town* takes a look at the land stretching east of the capital city of George Town, much of it unimproved swamp and buttonwood forest. A favorite of birders, hikers, and those seeking a look at the flora and fauna of the islands, the east end is little changed from its days before the boom in Cayman tourism. This is the quietest part of Grand Cayman and well worth a day-trip even for those staying on other areas of the island.

- The *Seven Mile Beach* section explores what for many travelers *is* the Cayman Islands, a stretch of powdery beach lined not just with palms and casuarina trees, but also with resorts, condominiums, and innumerable watersports operators. The heart of the Caymanian tourism business, this is one of the most popular beaches in the Caribbean.

- *West Bay* takes a look at the region to the north of Seven Mile Beach, a quiet residential section that's also home to some of the island's top tourism attractions: the Cayman Turtle Farm and Hell.

Getting Around

Upon arrival at the **Owen Roberts International Airport**, continue through the airport past the baggage claim and outside to the pick-up area. Here, vans and mini-buses offer passenger service to local hotels for a fixed fee. Hotels in the Cayman Islands are not allowed to send a courtesy van for airport pickup, so be prepared to pay for a ride or rent a car.

Transportation around George Town and throughout Grand Cayman is easy. Take your pick from taxis and group vans as well as rental cars, Jeeps, bicycles, and scooters.

■ By Car

Renting a vehicle for at least part of your stay is often the easiest and most economical way to get around, especially if you plan to explore. Car rentals begin at about US $30 per day during the summer months and near US $50 per day during winter months.

Several rental companies offer pickup at the airport (offices are directly across from the airport); larger accommodations also have car rental desks.

A temporary Cayman Islands driver's license is required; you can obtain this from the rental agency by presenting your valid driver's license and paying the US $7.50 fee. You must be 21 or over to rent a vehicle from local operators, 25 at larger agencies. Insurance policies of some rental agencies do not cover drivers under 25.

Remember that driving is to the *left* throughout the Cayman Islands. Most vehicles are right-hand drive; most 4x4s have a left-hand stick shift.

A car is not necessary to enjoy Seven Mile Beach, but it is handy if you'd like to tour the entire stretch of beach and venture to other areas of Grand Cayman. Rentals are available at several nearby agencies; most offer free pickup and dropoff at Seven Mile Beach. Rentals begin at about US $50 per day in the winter to US $30 per day in the summer.

If you are staying in West Bay or East End, you'll want a car. Taxi service is available, but rates to other parts of the island are not cheap. For example, a taxi from Spanish Bay Reef Resort on the far north side of West Bay to the airport area of George Town runs US $27, one-way.

For a complete listing of rental car companies throughout the islands, see page 46.

■ By Scooter

A popular way to buzz around the island is on a scooter. You must have riding experience to rent one; expect to pay about $25 per day. You will also need a temporary Cayman Islands drivers license, as you do for driving a car; see above. You should know that traffic along Seven Mile Beach's West Bay Road can be brutal.

Scooters are available for rent at several locations on Seven Mile Beach. **Cayman Cycle Rentals** (☎ 345-945-4021) has rentals at Treasure Island Resort, the Hyatt Regency Grand Cayman, and Coconut Place.

■ By Bicycle

Prices vary but average about US $12 per day for a 10-speed bike and $14 for a mountain bike. Note that traffic can be extremely heavy along West Bay Road during morning and evening rush hours. A good option for a quiet ride is the Harquail Bypass. This road, which links Seven Mile Beach with the airport area, usually has light traffic and is lined with tropical vegetation.

 AUTHORS' NOTE: *Two-wheel enthusiasts will find that the East End is probably the best area in Grand Cayman for leisurely bicycle trips. The grade is flat and traffic is light.*

Call **Cayman Cycle Rentals** (☎ 345-945-4021) or stop by the offices at Coconut Place on West Bay Road, the Hyatt Regency Grand Cayman, or Treasure Island Resort, all on Seven Mile Beach. Ten-speed mountain bicycles are also available here. **Soto's 4x4** also rents bikes at their Seven Mile Beach location (☎ 345-945-2424). Take your pick on Seven Mile Beach: taxi or rental car, pedal or foot power. They're all good options.

Bicycling, as well as walking, is also a good option in West Bay. With quiet neighborhood streets throughout much of this area of the island, you'll find good opportunities for foot and pedal power.

■ On Foot

With the low crime rate in the Cayman Islands, travel on foot is fun and safe. Walking is the easiest way to get around George Town, especially along the waterfront area. Remember, however, to look *right* when crossing streets.

■ Guided Tours

Guided tours are an excellent way for first-time visitors to get a good overview. They are available from most taxi drivers for about US $37.50 per hour for four persons; you can also check with your hotel tour desk for possibilities. Here are several tour operators that offer varying packages:

A.A. Chauffeur and Transportation Services, ☎ 345-949-7222, e-mail aatours@candw.ky. This company offers sightseeing tours as well as airport pickup and chauffeuring.

Burton's Tours, ☎ 345-949-7222, fax 345-947-6222. Burton Ebanks is a local resident with extensive knowledge of the entire region. He does both group and private tours and we can highly recommend him for his complete knowledge of Grand Cayman.

Majestic Tours, ☎ 345-949-7773, fax 345-949-8647. Tours and airport transfers.

McCurley's Tours, ☎ 345-947-9626. Sightseeing tours as well as transfers available.

Reids Premier Tours, ☎ 345-949-6531, fax 949-949-4770. Sightseeing tours, shopping tours, fishing trips, snorkel trips, and more.

Rudy's Travellers Transport, West Bay, ☎ 345-949-3208, fax 345-949-1155. Rudy Powery, president of the Bird Club, leads guided birding tours as well as sightseeing trips.

Silver Thatch Excursions, ☎ 345-945-6588, fax 345-949-3342. This company specializes in the cultural and natural history of the area. George Town tours include A Walk Back In History, a walking tour to the region's most historic sites. Birding and nature tours also available. Hotel pickup and return, drink, and a snack (sandwich and traditional Caymanian pastries) are included.

Tropicana Tours Ltd., ☎ 345-949-0944, fax 345-949-4507. Sightseeing and watersports.

Vernon's Sightseeing Tours, ☎ 345-949-1509, fax 345-949-0213. Sightseeing tours, dinner transfers, shopping tours, fishing trips and more offered.

George Town

For most vacationers, a visit to George Town marks the beginning and end of their stay. This capital city is home of both the international airport and the cruise terminal, so a majority of the 1.3 million visitors spend at least some time here.

The capital is the social and economic hub of the islands, home to over half the 30,000 residents of Grand Cayman and the base for most of the business and government activity. Don't look for a bustling city, however; George Town is still very much an island community; you'll feel at home strolling the streets, eating at a seaside diner, and enjoying watersports just as you would in the resort areas of Seven Mile Beach.

Once, this community was known as **The Hogsties**. Today, it's a major financial center that ranks right up there with Zurich and Tokyo. Modern, clean, and efficient, this capital city hasn't forgotten its historic roots, however. Just off Hog Sty Bay, historic homes, churches, and other structures are now part of a self-guided walking tour designed by the National Trust.

Much of the activity in George Town takes place along **North** and **South Church Streets**, which run parallel to the shoreline. These roads face out to George Town Harbour and are lined with duty-free shops, restaurants, and tourist-oriented businesses. The intersection where South Church Street forks right onto Shedden Road or continues onto North Church Street (adjacent to the cruise ship terminal), is the heart of town.

East of the shoreline, government buildings and banking centers carry on the work of the Cayman Islands, helping the nation hold its spot as one of

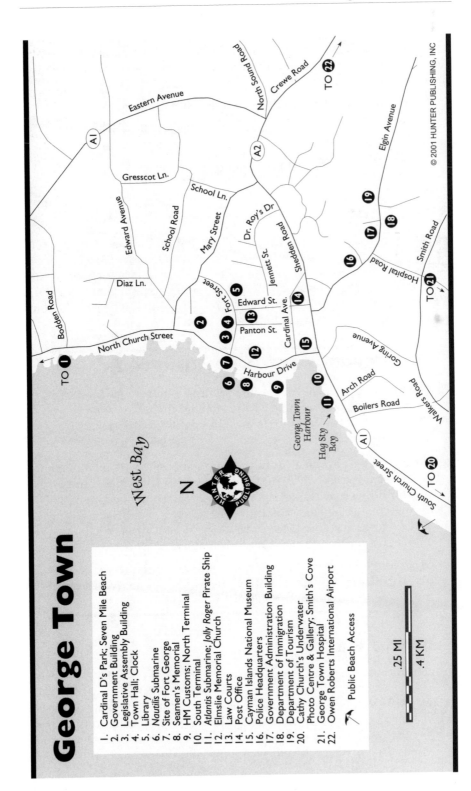

George Town

1. Cardinal D's Park; Seven Mile Beach
2. Government Building
3. Legislative Assembly Building
4. Town Hall; Clock
5. Library
6. *Nautilis* Submarine
7. Site of Fort George
8. Seamen's Memorial
9. HM Customs; North Terminal
10. South Terminal
11. *Atlantis* Submarine; *Jolly Roger* Pirate Ship
12. Elmslie Memorial Church
13. Law Courts
14. Post Office
15. Cayman Islands National Museum
16. Police Headquarters
17. Government Administration Building
18. Department of Immigration
19. Department of Tourism
20. Cathy Church's Underwater
    Photo Centre & Gallery; Smith's Cove
21. George Town Hospital
22. Owen Roberts International Airport

↗ Public Beach Access

.25 MI

.4 KM

Grand Cayman

© 2001 HUNTER PUBLISHING, INC

the monetary centers in the world. Farther east, the airport is located on the edge of North Sound, the shallow body of water that divides George Town, Seven Mile Beach, and the west end from the less developed east end of the island.

South of town, South Church Street winds it way through elegant residential districts, lined with beautiful seaside homes and a few quiet businesses.

Adventures

■ On Foot

Slip on a pair of comfortable shoes and take off on a walking tour of George Town. A brochure, titled *An Historical Walking Tour, Central George Town*, which is produced by the National Trust for the Cayman Islands, covers a self-guided walking tour of about two hours in length; copies are available from the National Trust office, at the tourism office, and at the National Museum, for $1.

GEORGE TOWN WALKING TOUR

The tour begins at the cruise ship landing and includes the site of **Fort George**, built around 1790 to defend the island from Spanish invasions. The fort site is located at the intersection of Harbour Drive and Fort Street.

Nearby, the **Seamen's Memorial** remembers 153 Caymanians lost at sea. Across the street, the **Elmslie Memorial Church** was built by shipwright Captain Rayal Bodden using shipbuilding techniques; inside, the ceiling resembles a schooner's hull. The adjacent cemetery has grave markers that resemble houses, a typical style seen in the island's cemeteries.

Other stops on the walking tour include the **Legislative Assembly Building**, the **post office**, and walk-bys of **traditional houses** with Caymanian raked sand gardens.

■ In the Water

Scuba

Although George Town may be the capital city, it is by no means just a business center: here it's just as appropriate to don a mask and tank as a three piece suit. The waters off George Town are protected as a marine park and boast numerous dive sites. For a complete

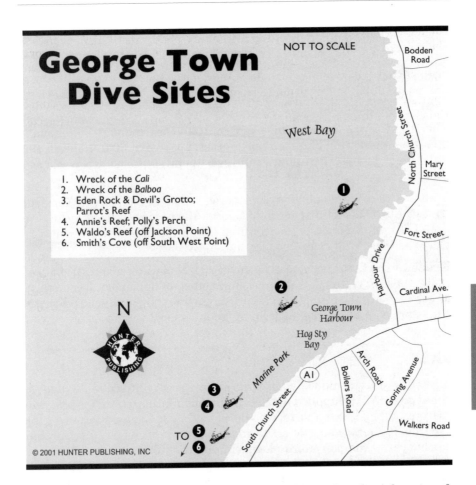

George Town Dive Sites

NOT TO SCALE

West Bay

1. Wreck of the *Cali*
2. Wreck of the *Balboa*
3. Eden Rock & Devil's Grotto; Parrot's Reef
4. Annie's Reef; Polly's Perch
5. Waldo's Reef (off Jackson Point)
6. Smith's Cove (off South West Point)

George Town Harbour

Hog Sty Bay

© 2001 HUNTER PUBLISHING, INC

list of dive operators on Grand Cayman, see *Where Are the Adventures?*, pages 71-73.

Eden Rock and Devil's Grotto: Eden Rock Dive Shop on South Church Road is the entry point for one of George Town's most popular dive sites. Eden Rock and the Devil's Grotto, located about 150 yards from the shore, are shallow dives but unique. Both are labyrinths of grottos running out from the shore. Eden Rock is popular not only with divers but also with snorkelers who enjoy the easy entrance and a view of the tunnels and often large tarpon. Eden Rock and Devil's Grotto have a depth of 30-50 feet.

Parrot's Reef: Parrot's Reef and, beyond that, Sunset Reef, are dive sites filled with marine life. They are just yards from shore. Parrot's Reef has a depth of 30-60 feet.

The Wreck of the *Balboa*: The hurricane of 1932 accounted for the wreck of this freighter, which today lies 25 to 40 feet below the surface. Some of the ship remains intact, but other parts were blown away to clear the traffic channel. This is a popular night dive because of the depth (and because this site sits right in the George Town Harbour waterway, which is busy during the day). Rich with marine life from corals to sponges to brilliant parrotfish, this is one of Grand Cayman's top dive sites.

Soto's Reef: This reef lies just offshore from the Lobster Pot (see *Where to Eat*, page 126). Ranging in depth from five to 35 feet, the reef is dotted with coral formations.

The Black Forest: Beautiful black coral and waving gorgonians make this site indeed seem like the Black Forest. Located at 60 to 100 feet, this wall dive is just off the island's southwest point, but isn't accessible as a shore dive.

Smiths Cove: Although often considered a snorkel site, Smiths Cove (off South Church Street just south of George Town) is an easy shore dive as well. The reef starts just a few feet from the surface and divers can also explore the West Wall from this location.

Wreck of the *Cali*: Located in just over 20 feet of water about 100 feet offshore, the *Cali* is a shallow dive recommended for beginners. Experienced divers can save the *Cali* for departure day, when they can't scuba dive; the site offers a great snorkel experience and is a good way to finish off your Cayman vacation.

SASY

If you'd like to introduce your children to the joys of scuba diving, you might give SASY (Supplied Air Snorkeling for Youths) a try. This program, operated by Red Sail Sports, was developed by a Cayman father for his children. It allows young divers to breath from a continuous air supply and has buoyancy compensator to keep children floating safely near the surface. For more about this program, see page 95. Units are available for use at **Red Sail Sports** (www.redsail.com) locations at the Hyatt Regency Grand Cayman (☎ 345-949-8745), Westin Casuarina Resort (☎ 345-949-8732), and Marriott Grand Cayman (☎ 345-949-6343).

INTERNATIONAL SCUBA DIVING HALL OF FAME

In March 2000, the Cayman Islands established the International Scuba Diving Hall of Fame with 19 inductees who have made a significant contribution to the world of recreational scuba diving. The Hall of Fame is temporarily located in the Port Complex in George Town and is a member of the International Association of Sports Museums and Halls of Fame.

- **Lloyd Bridges** (US): star of the television show *Sea Hunt* and responsible for introducing many viewers to the world of scuba diving.

- **Jacques-Yves Cousteau** (France): the best-known aquatic explorer in the world, Cousteau co-invented the aqualung and served as a television personality and expert on the world of marine life.

■ **Ben Cropp** (Australia): following his career as a spearfisherman, Cropp went on to work in the film industry and was known for his shark hunting. He later became an underwater cameraman, director, and producer.

■ **E.R. Cross** (US): compiled the world's first scuba diving safety training manual for sport divers.

■ **Dr. Jefferson C. Davis, Jr.** (US): one of the pioneers of dive medicine, Davis helped developed hyperbaric medicine and is known for the treatment of decompression sickness.

■ **Gustav Della Valle** (Italy): founder of ScubaPro, Della Valle introduced markets around the world to the equipment of scuba diving.

■ **Sylvia Earle, PhD** (US): recordholder for solo diving and the world's deepest woman diver, Earle is also the author of *Sea Change*, a 1995 book.

■ **Bernie Eaton** (UK): publisher and editor-in-chief of *Diver*, the UK publication with the largest circulation in the world of scuba diving.

■ **Emile Gagnon** (France): co-inventor of the aqualung with Jacques-Yves Cousteau.

■ **Al Giddings** (US): underwater director and cinematographer, Giddings has been awarded three Emmys.

■ **Hans and Lotte Hass** (Austria): With over 100 films on the submarine world, this pair have made contributions to the world of underwater photography, films, and science.

■ **Jack Lavanchy** (Switzerland): president of PADI Europe, Lavanchy popularized recreational scuba diving through Europe and North Africa.

■ **Jack McKenney** (Canada): one of the top underwater wildlife photographers and film producers, McKenney served as editor of *Skin Diver*.

■ **Bob Soto** (Cayman Islands): Soto brought recreational scuba diving to the Cayman Islands in 1957.

■ **Ron and Valerie Taylor** (Australia): first known for their spearfishing, the Taylors became known as filmmakers, working on films such as *Jaws*, *Jaws II* and *The Blue Lagoon*.

■ **Al Tillman** (US): founder of the National Association of Underwater Instructors (NAUI).

Grand Cayman

■ **Stan Waterman** (US): winner of five Emmy awards, Waterman is also known for his work in underwater films as director and producer.

Snorkeling

Snorkelers will find a good spot just south of **Smiths Cove Park**, along South Church Street. This free park has good snorkeling along the rocks on its north side; covered picnic tables and plenty of shade make it a popular lunch site. **Eden Rock** is also frequented by snorkelers. Another favorite is **Soto's Reef**, sometimes called Passion Reef, located behind Soto's Dive Shop (below the Lobster Pot restaurant on North Church Street). One of the top snorkel destinations is the **wreck of the *Cali*** (see above).

Submarine Trips

Atlantis Adventures offers the ***Atlantis XI*** submarine and ***Atlantis Deep Explorer*** research vessel (Harbour Drive, ☎ 800-887-8571 or 345-949-7700, www.goatlantis.com/cayman). If you're curious about what lies below the water's surface, the 48-passenger *Atlantis XI* is the perfect way to have a peek at Grand Cayman's underwater world. Swimmers and non-swimmers alike enjoy safe, air-conditioned, comfortable travel to 100 feet below the surface aboard the *Atlantis* on either the Expedition or the Odyssey adventure, with a narrated view of coral gardens, sponge gardens, the undersea wall, and more.

You can buy tickets at the headquarters located just south of the cruise ship terminal on Harbour Drive in downtown George Town. Tours operate six days a week. The dive takes 50 minutes, but the total tour time is one hour and 40 minutes. You'll board an open-air boat and travel out to the dive site just off George Town's shore. On the sub, bench seating runs along the length of the vessel, and all visitors have a porthole from which to enjoy the underwater scene.

After viewing the marine life, don't be surprised to see some human life forms approaching the submarine – these are the Atlantis divers. Wearing armored wetsuits to protect against fish nibbles, these divers feed clouds of hungry fish and provide good photo opportunities.

AUTHOR TIP

Bring along your camera on this fascinating tour, but load film with an ASA rating of 1000. Your flash is useless in the confines of the sub because it will reflect off the portholes. The ASA 1000 film is fast enough to capture the colorful images you'll witness without using a flash.

Atlantis also offers a night dive, a great opportunity to really see the fantastic colors of the coral reef and its inhabitants. Ticket prices are $72 per person; children under 12 are half-price.

A new adventure from Atlantis features a longer dive during which guests view scuba divers feeding fish; this cruise is priced at US $82 per person.

The company also offers a one-of-a-kind experience on their submersible research vessel, *Atlantis Deep Explorer*. Plunging down to a depth of 1,000 feet, the 22-foot sub carries two passengers and a pilot and is the only one of its type open to the public. Several times a day, the yellow vessel plunges down the Cayman Wall to depths far beyond the range of sports scuba divers.

The vessel has a large, three-foot-diameter convex window and the passengers sit side by side in front of this viewport. The view varies with the depth: from 200 to 400 feet below the surface are colorful sponges and corals in what's termed the "sponge belt." Hundreds of sponges blanket the vertical wall in forms ranging from 20-foot-long orange rope sponges to gigantic barrel sponges. From 650 to 1,000 feet, living formations give way to limestone pinnacles that house deep-sea creatures, such as stalked crinoids, porcelain corals and glass sponges. Termed the "haystack" zone, the haystacks or limestone blocks stand over 150 feet tall. Here, light no longer penetrates the sea and the research sub illuminates the dark water with powerful lights. The highlight of many trips is a visit to the *Kirk Pride*, a shipwreck that sits on a ledge at 800 feet. This 180-foot freighter sank in a storm in 1976 and its fate was unknown until the wreck was discovered by an *Atlantis* research submarine in 1985. Tickets are US $295-395 per person (depending on type of dive). Five dives are scheduled each day, Monday through Friday. The tour last about an hour, and advance reservations are strongly recommended.

As with the *Atlantis* submarine trip, bring along your camera, loaded with ASA 1000 film, for this excursion.

 AUTHORS' NOTE: *No children under three feet tall are permitted on these subs.*

Semi-Submarines

Nautilus: **The Undersea Tour**, ☎ 345-945-1355, nautilus@candw.ky, www.nautilus.ky. This cruise provides a one-hour tour aboard an 80-foot semi-submersible vessel to view the rich marine life of the bay. The sub goes out about three-quarters of a mile offshore and gives visitors a chance to view two shipwrecks and to watch a diver feed a variety of tropical fish. Travelers sit in a glass hull six feet beneath the surface but can go up on deck anytime during the trip. These one-hour tours are priced at US $35 per person and $15 for children. Tours depart from the dock at Rackham's Pub on North Church Street.

The *Nautilus* also offers the two-hour Captain Nemo's Adventure Tour, which begins with the one-hour undersea trip. The vessel then moors over a wreck or reef and visitors can walk about above or below deck, swim or snorkel. The afternoon tour is priced at $39 for adults, $19 for children.

Seaworld *Explorer*, South Church Street, ☎ 345-949-7700. Not a true submarine but actually a glorified glass-bottom boat, the Seaworld *Explorer* sits next to the *Atlantis* submarine. It is a good option for those who might feel a little claustrophobic about a submarine adventure, since it does not actually submerge. Visitors descend into a glass observatory and view marine life as well as two shipwrecks. The *Explorer* travels to the *Cali*, a schooner that hit the reef in 1944, and the *Balboa*, a freighter from Cuba destroyed by a hurricane. Today, the wrecks are encased in corals and filled with fish life. Tickets for the Seaworld *Explorer* are US $35 per person; children ages two-12 pay US $19. Tours last one hour.

Underwater Photography

Good underwater photos are the best souvenirs divers and snorkelers can bring home. If you're serious about underwater photography, consider a class taught by George Town's Cathy Church. **Cathy Church's Underwater Photo Centre and Galleries** also offers E6 film processing, underwater camera rentals, and Nikon repair. Open daily at Sunset House Hotel. For information, ☎ 345-949-7415 or visit the center's web site at www.cathychurch.com.

Another option is **Cayman Camera, Ltd.**, South Church Street, George Town, ☎ 345-949-8359. This shop sells underwater camera gear including inexpensive disposable cameras.

■ On the Water

Pirate Sails

 Yo ho ho, the pirate ship anchored off George Town's shores is friendly and lots of fun. The ***Jolly Roger***, which claims to be the only authentic replica of a 17th-century Spanish galleon in the Caribbean, offers several kinds of buccaneering fun. Take a pirate cruise (walk the plank if you don't set the sails!) and you can fire the cannon and witness a sword fight. Dinner cruises and sunset sails also offered (see page 127). Price is US $30 for the pirate cruise. Call for sailing dates (three times per week) and boarding times; reservations are needed. The ship departs from The Jewelry Factory across from the Hard Rock Café at George Town Harbour, ☎ 345-945-7245 or 945-SAIL, e-mail jolroger@candw.ky.

Take a pirate cruise aboard the Jolly Roger.

Tarpon Feeding

Watching the Tarpon Feeding is a Cayman must: you've got to take part at least once during your visit. Restaurants usually stagger their feeding times; each event draws huge tarpon (most three feet long) to compete for chunks of fish. You'll find tarpon feeding at **Rackham's Pub**, ☎ 345-949-3860, and the **Almond Tree**, ☎ 345-949-2893, both on North Church Street, and at **The Wharf**, ☎ 345-949-2231, just outside George Town on West Bay Road.

Beaches

George Town isn't known for its beaches (most of its coast is ironshore), but you will find a beach at **Club Paradise**, 96 South Church Street, ☎ 345-945-1444. Shaded with willowy casuarina trees, the beach has a bar and open-air restaurant; it's also home to Abanks' Divers (yes, like the one in *The Firm*).

Farther east, **Smith's Cove** is a beautiful, quiet beach tucked in a residential area south of George Town. To reach Smith's Cove, follow South Church Street.

■ In the Air

Aerial tours of Grand Cayman are available through Island Air with **Seaborne Flightseeing Adventures**. The 25-minute tour includes a look at Grand Cayman from a 19-passenger Twin Otter aircraft. Tours are scheduled only between December and June. Cost is US $56. For information or reservations, ☎ 345-949-6029.

Day-Trips

If you are making a repeat visit to Grand Cayman or you're booking a week on the island, you may want to consider a day-trip to Cayman Brac or Little Cayman. Less than an hour's flight northeast of Grand Cayman but worlds apart in terms of atmosphere, these small islands are tailor-made for travelers in search of bonefishing, secluded beaches, and nature appreciation.

Day-trips are easy thanks to frequent flights from **Island Air** (☎ 345-949-5252, fax 345-949-7044). Special day-trip rates from Grand Cayman to either Cayman Brac or Little Cayman are available for US $110. Several daily flights connect the islands. Return flights allow travelers to stay on the island until late afternoon, arriving back on Grand Cayman a little after 6 pm.

CAYMAN BRAC: Like its smaller sibling, Cayman Brac has its own special qualities, assets that include undersea walls, the most rugged terrain found in the Cayman Islands, caves that tempt exploration, birding, and much more.

DID YOU KNOW?

The island is named for the "brac," Gaelic for bluff, which soars 140 feet from the sea on the island's east end.

The bluff is the most distinctive feature of this 12-mile-long, one-mile-wide island located 89 miles east-northeast of Grand Cayman and just seven miles from Little Cayman.

The sheer bluff is visited by hikers and non-hikers alike, and is a favorite for birdwatching, one of the most popular activities. Here, the 180-acre **Parrot Reserve** is home to endangered Cayman Brac parrot. Only 400 of the birds remain in the wild on this island.

With a population of fewer than 1,300 residents, Cayman Brac is closer in pace to Little Cayman than its big brother, Grand Cayman. Residents, or Brackers, are known for their personable nature, and welcome vacationers to their sunny isle.

Among Cayman Brac's unique features are its many **caves**. The bluff is pocked with caves that frame beautiful seaside views. Several of the 18 caves on Cayman Brac have been explored and five are frequently visited by vacationers. **Rebecca's Cave**, east of Divi Tiara Hotel, is marked with signs. It is the best-known of the island's caves, and is named for a young child who died here during the Great Hurricane of 1932. Skull Cave, Peter's Cave, Bat Cave, and Great Cave present other challenges, some requiring steep climbs.

Without a doubt, undersea life is one of the island's biggest draws. One attraction is a Russian frigate deliberately sunk in September 1996. Renamed the **MV *Captain Keith Tibbets***, this 330-foot freighter was built for use by the Cuban navy. It lies approximately 200 yards offshore northwest of Cayman Brac. The bow rests in about 90 feet of water; the stern is just 40 feet below the surface. The sinking of the vessel was recorded by Jean-Michel Cousteau Productions in *Destroyer at Peace*, a documentary film. Although day-trippers cannot dive because of the return flight, several dive operators offer **snorkel trips**; check with **Brac Aquatics** (☎ 800-544-2722 or 345-948-1429), **Dive Tiara**, (☎ 800-661-DIVE or 345-948-1553) and **Reef Divers Brac Reef Beach Resort** (☎ 800-327-3835 or 345-948-1642, www.bracreef.com) for information.

Bonefishing is another top draw for many Cayman Brac vacationers. Guides lead anglers on half- and full-day excursions to seek bonefish in the shallows; deep-sea fishing is another popular option and groups of up to four can book a charter for a chance at a trophy catch. See the *Cayman Brac* chapter for more information about activities on the Island.

There are several rental car agencies that have vehicles available by the day, including **T&D Avis** (☎ 345-948-2847 or 800-228-0668), **Brac Rent-A-Car** (☎ 345-948-1515), **B&S Motor Ventures Cycle and Car Rentals** (☎ 345-948-1646, www.bandsmv.ky) and **Four D's Car Rental** (☎ 345-948-1599). Rental cars start about US $40 per day.

LITTLE CAYMAN: Visitors find that the island is indeed petite, spanning only 11 miles in length and two miles at its widest point. Perfect for a day-trip, the highlights of the isle can easily be seen in a day.

Little Cayman's chief draw is its eco-tourism: diving, fishing, and bird watching. While flying in and out on the same day rules out diving, **snorkelers** will find numerous chances to take a peek at what lies beneath the water's surface. The most famous site is **Bloody Bay Wall**, on the north side of the island. The wall is a short swim from shore and starts at a depth of only 20 feet.

Birders head to **Booby Pond Visitors Centre**. Operated by the National Trust, this 1.2-acre brackish mangrove pond is the home of the Caribbean's largest breeding colony of red-footed boobies and a breeding colony of magnificent frigate birds. Telescopes are available for use any time.

Vehicles are available from **McLaughlin Rentals** (☎ 345-948-1000, fax 345-948-1001, littlecay@candw.ky). Jeeps can be rented for US $52 per day; SUV's are US $58 per day. A Cayman Islands driving permit (CI $7, US $8.73, available at the agency) is also required. All vehicles come with (and must be returned with) a full tank of gas. And there's no need to worry about getting lost; only one road circles the island.

While driving on the island, you will soon see that, with under 170 permanent residents, the island's largest population consists of birds and iguanas. Over 2,000 Little Cayman rock iguanas live here, so "Iguana Crossing" and "Iguana Right of Way" signs are posted along the road to protect the large lizards.

For more information on island activities, see the *Cayman Brac* and *Little Cayman* chapters, beginning on pages 197 and 215 respectively.

Sights & Attractions

Cayman Islands National Museum, Harbour Drive, ☎ 345-949-8368, www.museum.ky. The best way to learn more about Cayman history and culture is to stop by this museum, just across from the cruise ship terminals. It is housed in the Old Courts Building, one of the few 19th-century structures left on the island. Twelve outdoor steps lead up to the second story of the building; these gave rise to a Cayman saying, "walking the 12 steps," which meant you were being taken to court. Over the years, this seaside building has served as a courthouse, jail, and meeting hall, and today it houses over 2,000 artifacts that recall the history of these islands. Created in 1979 by a museum law and opened in 1990, the museum collects items of historic, scientific, and artistic relevance.

Visitors enter on the ground floor and start with an eight minute slide show about the history of the islands. They then enjoy a self-guided tour of the museum, with displays on all aspects of Caymanian life. A bathymetric map displays the depth of the seas around the Cayman Islands, including the Cayman Trench at 23,750 feet below sea level. Other exhibits recall facets of natural history: mangrove swamps that create a rich birding environment; Caymanite, a semi-precious stone unique to the Cayman Islands; and displays on local marine life.

Some of the most fascinating exhibits recall the early economy of the Caymanians. An oral history program captures the history of the early turtlers who made a living capturing the now-protected reptiles. Exhibits show the tools of the early residents, including the muntle, a club used to kill fish when they were caught; the calabash, a versatile gourd that, once dried, had many uses; sisal switches used to beat mosquitoes away; and wompers, sandals worn on the east end, originally made from leather and later from old tires.

After your museum tour, you'll exit through the museum shop, a good source of Caymanian-made items. The shop, housed in the old jail with part of the old coral stone wall still exposed, has a good selection of books and maps of the Cayman Islands; if you don't have time for a museum tour, you can enter through the store for a little shopping.

The Cayman Islands National Museum, George Town.

Admission is CI $4 for adults, CI $2 for children and seniors. The museum is open Monday through Friday, 9 am to 5 pm; Saturday, 10 am to 2 pm. Those interested in Caymanian history can become museum members for as little as $10. Membership includes unlimited admission, invitations to previews and receptions, 10% discount in the museum shop, newsletter on events and exhibits, and volunteer opportunities. Members also have access to the museum library by appointment. For information, ☎ 345-949-8368 or fax 345-949-0309.

Clock Tower, Fort Street at Edward Street. Also known as the Town Hall clock, this landmark was constructed in 1939 in memory of Queen Elizabeth II's grandfather, King George V.

Elmsie Memorial Church, Harbour Drive just south of Fort Street. To see the real attraction of this historic church, you'll need to enter. Once inside, look up: the ceiling is built in the shape of a ship's hull. The reason: the church was built by a shipbuilder, Captain Rayal Bodden.

Post Office, Edward Street and Cardinal Avenue, ☎ 345-949-7001. A great spot to mingle with local residents is the main post office in George Town, located between the Royal Bank of Canada and the Bank of Nova Scotia. Grand Cayman has no postal delivery routes, so all mail is placed in the boxes of this open-air post office. Stop by the **philatelic bureau** – open 8:30 to 5:30, Monday through Friday, and 8:30 to 1 on Saturday – for

Caymanian stamps and first day covers. This building was also designed by Captain Bodden.

Public Library, Edward Street at Fort Street near the Clock Tower. This library is far more than a repository of books; it is also an architectural sight. The building was the creation of shipbuilder Captain Bodden and it's worth a trip inside to see the hammered ceiling decorated with shields of UK educational institutions.

Law Courts, Edward Street. Not far from the library stand the Law Courts, where barristers still plead their cases wearing traditional wigs.

Legislative Assembly, Fort Street. The assembly is home to the legislature and, if you are properly dressed, you may enter. Inside, you'll see many historic photos of Cayman's earlier days.

Stingray Brewery, Red Bay Road, past Prospect, ☎ 345-947-6699. This attraction is located east of town; to reach the brewery, follow Crewe Road or South Sound Road to Red Bay Road; continue east on Red Bay Road. You'll see the brewery on your right. This microbrewery produces a local wheat beer, which is sold throughout the island in stores, restaurants, and bars. The brewery is closed on Sundays.

Cardinal D's Park, off Courts Road, ☎ 345-949-8855. This small zoo is a good stop for families. Over 60 species of exotic birds, including Cayman parrots, whistling ducks, agoutis, blue iguanas, turtles, miniature ponies, emus, and more are on display. A petting zoo and snack bar make this attraction popular with kids. Open daily; admission is CI $5. Guided tours are available for groups of eight or more at 11 am and 2 pm.

Fort George, Fort Street and Harbour Drive. These ruins are all that remains of the fort that once protected this coastline. Built in 1790, the fort was often used to protect the island from pirates; in World War II, it was used as a base to watch for German submarines. Sadly, the fort was largely demolished a few decades ago by a developer. He was stopped by local residents before he could completely obliterate the historic monument.

Seamen's Memorial, Harbour Drive. Next to Fort George stands the Seaman's Memorial, which remembers the lives of 153 Caymanians who have been lost at sea.

DID YOU KNOW?

George Town was once called Hogsties and later The Hog Styes because of the pens where wild boars were contained. In the late 1700s, the community was given its more dignified name in honor of King George III.

Shopping

 George Town is the best place to shop in the Cayman Islands. Here, you'll find a good selection of duty-free china, perfumes, leather goods, watches, crystal, and more. Jewelry (mostly gold) is a popular buy and available at stores such as **24 K-Mon Jewellers** (Treasure Island Resort), **Savoy Jewellers** (Fort Street and Church Street), and **The Jewelry Center** (also on Fort Street). For china and crystal, check out the **Kirk Freeport Centre** (Albert Panton Street). **Caymanite**, a stone found only on the eastern edge of Grand Cayman's East End and the bluff on Cayman Brac, is sold throughout the islands mounted as jewelry. The semi-precious stone, a form of dolomite, ranges from a light beige to a beautiful amber color and is often mounted in a gold setting. Another popular island purchase is the **Tortuga Rum Cake**, available from the Tortuga Liquors (☎ 800-444-0625), made using five-year-old Tortuga Gold Rum. Sealed in a yellow and red box, the cake is the product of a 100-year-old family recipe. If you want to skip the cake, take home a bottle of Tortuga, Blackbear, or Cayman Gold Rum. **Black coral jewelry** is also a widespread commodity, but note that its harvesting depletes the sea's black coral supply. Only jewelers licensed to remove the coral may do so.

 AUTHORS' NOTE: *Without a certificate testifying that your purchase is from an approved seller, your black coral may be confiscated at Customs.*

Anything made with **turtle products** should also be avoided. All goods – including oils, steaks, shells, and jewelry – made from turtles and turtle shells have been banned by US Customs. Even passengers traveling through the US to other nations will have to surrender turtle products at US Customs.

Local products you won't have to worry about clearing through Customs are arts and crafts. Look for **birdhouses** made from coconuts, **brooms** woven from thatch, and **pepper sauce** distilled from fiery Scotch bonnet peppers to capture the spirit of the islands.

AUTHOR TIP

 Know your prices before you leave home; those "bargains" may or may not be such a good buy. Some of the really good deals are on Cayman-made items.

■ Malls

You'll find several malls in George Town. The newest is **Aqua World Duty Free Mall**, located next to the Hard Rock Café on the waterfront. The $8 million mall is home to 22 stores, including Blackbeards, Havana Cigars, Just for Kids, and Café Splash. Even non-shoppers will find plenty of reasons for a stop. The mall is home to a 12,000-square-foot saltwater aquarium filled with sharks, eels and rays; the sharks are fed daily and educational lectures on marine life take place between 11 and 1. Take a trip up the observation tower for a good photo opportunity of George Town.

Other malls in George Town include **Anchorage Centre**, Harbour Drive and Cardinal Avenue; **The Duty Free Centre**, Edward Street; **Cricket Square**, Elgin Avenue; and **Picadilly Centre**, Elgin Avenue.

■ Specialty Shops

Artifacts, Harbour Drive, ☎ 345-949-2442. This shop specializes in rare coins and coin jewelry. It also has a large inventory of silver, antique scientific instruments, West Indian maps, and Halcyon Days enamel works. It's fun to look around here and see their collection of shipwreck coins.

Bernard K. Passman's Black Coral, Fort Street, ☎ 345-949-0123. Black coral in the form of fine jewelry, sculpture and even cutlery sets are offered in this gallery. Passman was commissioned to create a black coral horse and corgi for Queen Elizabeth II and Prince Philip; his creations are considered works of art.

The Book Nook II, Anchorage Centre, ☎ 345-949-7392. This shop (along with its cousin of the same name on Seven Mile Beach) is excellent for its selection of both nonfiction and fiction books. You'll also find a good selection of Caribbean travel books at both.

Cayman Camera, Ltd., South Church Street, George Town, ☎ 345-949-8359. This store, just across the street from the submarine, has a good selection of fresh film and batteries and plenty of inexpensive underwater cameras (as well as serious photographic gear from Nikon, Hasselblad, Olympus, Minolta, Pentax and others).

Cayman Glassblowing, Anchorage Centre, ☎ 345-945-3122. We spent one afternoon at a table in the mall watching glassmakers create beautiful sculptures. Stepenn Zawistowski and his assistants make pieces in all sizes, from small collectibles to life-size marine life.

Cayman Islands National Museum, Harbour Drive, ☎ 345-949-8368. This shop is a good stop even if you don't have time for a tour of the National Museum (there's a separate entrance for the store). Housed in the old jail, part of an old coral stone wall is exposed, giving the shop an interesting feel. You can purchase postcards, souvenirs, maps, Caribbean books, and even Caymanite jewelry.

Smiths Cove, near George Town, is a good place to snorkel and dive.

Sunset on Seven Mile Beach, Grand Cayman.

Above: *Grand Cayman's Stingray City is one of the most popular places in the Caribbean.*

Opposite: *Parasailing off Seven Mile Beach, Grand Cayman.*

Below: *Sea turtles at the Cayman Turtle Farm.* (© Cayman Islands Department of Tourism)

Above: *Historic house and sand garden at the Botanic Park on Grand Cayman.*

Opposite: *East End signpost, Grand Cayman.*

Below: *A blue iguana at the Botanic Park.*

Above: *The Bluff on Cayman Brac.*

Opposite: *Point of Sand, Little Cayman.*

Below: *One of Cayman Brac's pristine beaches.*

Rum Point, Grand Cayman.

Grand Cayman's magnificent blowholes.

The Coach Factory Store, Anchorage Center, Cardinal Avenue off Harbour Drive, ☎ 345-949-5395. Just steps from the cruise terminal, this duty-free shop sells Coach leather goods direct from the factory.

Colombian Emeralds International, Harbour Drive, George Town, ☎ 800-6-NO-DUTY (666-3889), www.colombianemeralds.com. This popular Caribbean boutique, with locations in Antigua, Aruba, the Bahamas, Barbados, Grenada, St. Lucia, St. Martin, the USVI and others, sells not only emeralds but other fine gemstones. All purchases include certified appraisals, 90-day insurance and full international guarantees.

Diamonds Direct, Anchorage Centre, ☎ 345-945-6868. Diamonds are a shopper's best friend thanks to duty-free and tax-free prices at this store, which deals directly with mine sources in Africa and Russia.

Duty Free Ltd., South Church Street, ☎ 345-945-2160. This shop sits right on South Church Street just past where Harbour Drive becomes South Church. It sells all types of gold jewelry as well as treasure coins, gems, black coral, and watches. Paloma Picasso creations as well as Tiffany & Co. gifts are also available.

Heritage Craft Souvenirs and Gift Market, Harbour Drive and Goring Avenue, ☎ 345-945-6041. This shop specializes in Caribbean gifts and souvenirs including straw hats, local music, Caribbean coffees and teas, artwork, hammocks, wood carvings, and more. The shop is located opposite the National Museum, just steps from the Cruise Terminal.

Hobbies and Books, Piccadilly Centre on Elgin Avenue, ☎ 345-949-0707. This longtime Caymanian favorite hosts many author events. You'll find a large array of Caymanian guidebooks, cookbooks, and other items of local interest here as well as bestsellers and popular works.

Jeweler's Warehouse, Harbour Drive, ☎ 345-949-6597. This store has good prices on a variety of fine jewelry, from earrings starting under $100 and small strands of pearls for under $35 to fine gemstones with four-digit price tags.

Kirk Freeport, Cardinal Avenue, ☎ 345-949-7477. The Kirk Freeport name is a Cayman institution, well-known among those seeking duty-free gifts. The best known of the Kirk Freeport stores is Cardinal Avenue's Kirk Jewellers, the exclusive Rolex distributor in the Cayman Islands. The shop also stocks Tag Heuer, Omega, Breitling, Tudor, Gucci, Bvlgari, Fendi, and other lines. Fine jewelry from designers such as Bvlgari, Mikimoto, Soho, and Chaumet are popular purchases. Writing instruments and leather accessories from Cartier, Montblanc, Waterman, and A.T. Cross bring duty free prices. Other shops under the Kirk Freeport umbrella include the exclusive Cartier Boutique, which offers 18 karat jewelry, watches, leather goods, perfumes, and pens, and La Perfumerie I & II, featuring fragrances from around the globe including Chanel, Lancôme, Yves Saint Laurent, Givenchy, Clinique, and more. Mini facials and makeovers are also available.

Grand Cayman

London Jewellers Factory Store, Anchorage Centre, George Town, ☎ 345-949-9861. Fine gems and gold jewelry are the specialty of this outlet store, which sells many sample lines and production overruns at a discount price.

Savoy Jewellers, Queen's Court, ☎ 345-949-7454. A Caymanian favorite is Savoy Jewellers on West Bay Road in the Seven Mile Beach area. It sells an extensive collection of diamonds, Hèrmés watches, the St. Petersburg Collection of Fabergé eggs, Erté sculptures, and other finery. All jewelry is 18K gold and transportation from island hotels is available upon request.

Sterncastle Treasures, 49 South Church Street, ☎ 345-949-4944. This small corner shop, just steps from the new Aqua World Duty Free Mall and right on the waterfront, is a must if you're in search of shipwreck jewelry. The staff here is knowledgeable about all the pieces, which include gold doubloons set in exquisite gold settings. Even if you're not in the mood to buy, stop in and have a look at the shipwreck exhibit, with display from a wreck in the Florida Keys.

Underwater Photo Centre, South Church Street, ☎ 345-949-7415. More a lab and rental facility than a retail store, this shop has everything you'd need to start a hobby in underwater photography – including classes by renowned underwater photographer Cathy Church. The shop offers Nikonos repairs as well as rentals and E6 film processing.

Where to Stay

ACCOMMODATIONS PRICE SCALE
Prices listed are for a standard room for one night during high season (expect prices to be as much as 40% lower during the low season). The price scale refers to US $.
$ . . . . Under $100
$$ . . . . $100-$200
$$$ . . . . Over $200

■ Hotels & Resorts

Sunset House Resort, 390 South Church Street, ☎ 800-854-4767, 345-949-7111, fax 345-949-7101, www.sunsethouse.com, $-$$. Located just south of George Town, Sunset House is a favorite with divers. Just offshore lie both the reef and several shipwrecks, making this a virtual playground for those interested in underwater adventure.

There's nothing fancy about Sunset House – it's designed for those whose vacation centers around the time spent in the water, not necessarily on land. The 59 guest rooms include standard accommodations overlooking the courtyard and deluxe rooms with ocean or garden views. Two suites are also available.

Divers and those who want to learn can utilize the full-service dive operation, which offers resort courses, certification courses, check-out dives, and advanced instruction. When you're suited up and ready to go, it's just a matter of stepping off the shore ladder and into the aqua-playground. For more distant dives, one of six custom boats will take you on two-tank dives around the island while *Manta*, a catamaran, takes experienced divers on all-day, three-tank dives.

Facilities include a restaurant featuring local and continental cuisine, gift shop, oceanfront bar, freshwater swimming pool and hot tub, full-service dive shop, six dive boats, and the Sunset Underwater Photo Centre, which offers half-day to week-long photography courses.

Recently, the Sunset House sank a bronze mermaid in the waters just offshore; perfect for scuba divers learning buoyancy, for underwater photographers, and for snorkelers.

Seaview Hotel, South Church Street, ☎ 345-945-0558, e-mail seadive@candw.ky, $. Since 1952, this small hotel has attracted divers and travelers looking for a central location. The hotel is home to the Seaview restaurant, which is open for lunch and dinner daily. Rooms include air conditioning and private baths. You'll find a dive center on site as well as a pool.

■ Guest Houses

Erma Eldemire's Guest House, South Church Street, ☎ 345-949-5387, fax 345-949-6987, $. Located one mile south of George Town, this guest house is a 10-minute walk from Smith Cove. It's been in operation since 1970, and is family operated and cozy.

Rooms include private bath, air conditioning, and ceiling fan. Guests have access to a refrigerator and hot plate (studios and the one apartment have private kitchen facilities). Daily maid service, except on Sunday. Credit cards and checks are not accepted. A three-day deposit is required with reservation.

Where to Eat

DINING PRICE SCALE		
The scale below indicates the approximate cost of a meal for one person, including drink and gratuity. The price scale refers to US $.		
$	Under $15 per person	
$$.	$15-$30 per person	
$$$	$31-$40 per person	

■ American

 Blue Parrot, South Church Street at Coconut Harbour, ☎ 345-949-9094, $-$$. Not necessarily the place to go for a quiet dinner, this restaurant boasts the island's largest TV screen. Order up grilled seafood, sandwiches, and salads for lunch and dinner.

Hard Rock Café, South Church Street, ☎ 345-945-2020, $$. Located right across the street from the *Atlantis* submarine, this popular eatery serves up all the usual Hard Rock favorites: sandwiches, burgers, salads, and more. It's all dished up with plenty of music and enjoyed in a building filled with musical memorabilia.

■ Asian

Country and Western Restaurant, Red Bay Road just past the Lion's Centre, ☎ 345-945-4079, $$. You wouldn't know it from the name, but this restaurant specializes in Chinese and Caymanian dishes. Nearly three decades in business, the restaurant is open for lunch and dinner. Chinese favorites include chicken fried rice, beef chop suey, sweet and sour chicken, and more.

Ching Chinese, North Sound Road Industrial Park in Mirco Centre, ☎ 345-945-5277, $$. This indoor restaurant has been a Cayman favorite for seven years. The menu's varied and includes shrimp with black bean sauce, sweet and spicy fish, pepper steak, Peking duck (with 24-hour notice), shrimp lo mein, and vegetarian dishes. Delivery is available.

■ Bars & Pubs

The Landmark British Pub, Cardinal Avenue and Harbour Drive, ☎ 345-949-2582, $$. This pub has all the traditional grub: cottage pie, Cornish pasties, fish and chips, steak and kidney pie, jacket potatoes, and even a traditional English fry-up. For some island taste, try the chicken curry.

Ports Of Call Beach Bar, at The Wharf on West Bay Road, ☎ 345-949-2231, $$. Located right on the water's edge, the open-air bar boasts an uninterrupted view of the setting sun. A school of huge tarpon usually lingers below the deck, waiting for scheduled handouts, and live music is offered most evenings.

Rackham's Pub and Restaurant, North Church Street, ☎ 345-949-3860, $$. This open-air bar is a great place to start the evening; the casual restaurant makes the perfect place to move on to dinner, just steps away. The menu offers everything from burgers to dolphin (not the Flipper variety), lobster and shrimp. Don't miss the tarpon feeding at 7 pm!

■ Caribbean

Billy's Place Restaurant, North Church Street at Eastern Avenue, ☎ 345-949-0470, $. Sample local favorites, such as fish Cayman-style, jerk conch, conch stew, jerk pork, curry chicken, curry goat, oxtail, and stew beans, at this inexpensive eatery. Start with samosa, an appetizer of flaky pastry stuffed with peas and potatoes and served with mint and mango chutney. Jerk burgers, jerk pizza, and Indian favorites, such as curried shrimp and chicken tikka (chicken marinated in lemon juice, yogurt, garlic and Indian spices), round out the menu. Open for lunch and dinner Monday through Saturday; dinner only on Sundays. Picnic tables beneath shady trees offer al fresco dining. Take-out service is available.

■ Continental

The Brasserie, Cricket Square, Elgin Avenue, ☎ 345-945-1815, $$-$$$. This elegant restaurant is a favorite with local residents, especially those who work in the surrounding office buildings. You'll enter through the bar, with its warm mahogany tones; the dining room lies to the right. The menu is accompanied by an extensive wine list (ask for assistance from the knowledgeable waitstaff if you have any questions about the staggering array of options) then move on to favorites such as tomato and mozzarella salad, smoked duck breast, or penne pasta with grilled zucchini. This restaurant is the perfect choice when you're ready to get away from the hustle and bustle of beachside dining. Reservations suggested.

■ Fine Dining

Grand Old House, South Church Street, ☎ 345-949-9333, $$$. Located on South Church Street, the Grand Old House is one of Grand Cayman's most lauded restaurants and winner of many awards. It's situated in a 1908 building that was once the centerpiece for a coconut plantation and was later used as a hospital during World War II. Today, the restaurant features some of the finest dining on the island, with a menu that includes entrées such as tenderloin of Black Angus beef; New Zealand baby rack of lamb; pork with mushrooms, chardonnay cream sauce and roasted potatoes; baked filet of dolphin; potato-crusted tuna; and broiled Caribbean lobster tail. Specialties of the house include shrimp "Grand Old House," baked with fresh local herbs, white wine and hollandaise sauce; turtle steak Cayman style; and pan-fried crispy duck breast in Cointreau accompanied by a sweet potato. There's an extensive wine list.

■ Italian

Casanova Ristorante, Old Fort Building, ☎ 345-949-7633, $$$. Specializing in romantic dining, this restaurant is decorated with Italian artwork. An extensive menu offers penne pasta sautéed with Caribbean lobster, linguine with clams, potato dumplings with homemade pesto sauce, veal piccata, and many seafood dishes. Open for lunch Monday through Saturday; dinner nightly. Reservations suggested.

■ Seafood

Almond Tree, North Church Street, ☎ 345-949-2893, $$$. The Almond Tree may just win the award as the most romantic restaurant on Grand Cayman by our standards. We recently had dinner at this seaside eatery and can't wait to return. Tables are set upstairs for a great view of the water and the city's lights; other tables are on small decks out on the ironshore seaside; one large table is located in a gazebo perched over the water (if you get this table, however, be warned that you'll have lots of company at tarpon feeding time!). Meal choices here range from Caribbean lobster to coconut shrimp.

Crow's Nest, South Church Street, ☎ 345-949-9366, $$-$$$. West Indian favorites fill the menu here. Dine in the breeze of the ceiling fans of this Caymanian cottage. Start with conch fritters or a jerk chicken sampler and then enjoy red bean soup or conch chowder. Entrées include Jamaican chicken curry, turtle farm steak topped with a peppery vermouth cream sauce, and red snapper, mahi mahi, mako shark, or swordfish prepared grilled, pan-fried, or blackened. Open for lunch and dinner; reservations recommended.

Lobster Pot, North Church Street, ☎ 345-949-2736, $$$. This second-floor restaurant, built with a view of the George Town Harbour, serves seafood accompanied by an extensive wine list. Lobster and surf and turf are favorites, as well as grilled salmon filet, mango chicken, Cayman turtle steak, seafood curry, and cracked conch. Save this one for a special night out; prices are high, even by Cayman standards. A children's menu is available here; if you bring the kids, don't miss tarpon feeding time between 6:30 and 6:45. The restaurant is open for lunch on weekdays only and dinner nightly. Reservations are recommended.

Smuggler's Cove Caribbean Café and Grill, North Church Street, ☎ 345-949-6003, $$$. This oceanfront restaurant is open for dinner only. A favorite with couples, the waterfront location offers both indoor and outside dining. Seafood dishes are king here, including coconut shrimp, red snapper, lobster ravioli, grilled lobster, and baked Chilean salmon with crab. Daily specials include seasonal seafood as well as game, lamb, and veal dishes. Reservations are recommended.

The Wharf, West Bay Road, ☎ 345-949-2231, $$$. Just past George Town at the start of the beach, The Wharf is a favorite with couples. This seaside restaurant and bar is open for lunch on weekdays and dinner nightly, featuring continental and Caribbean cuisine. Located right on the water's edge, the open-air bar offers an uninterrupted view of the setting sun. A school of huge tarpon gathers below the deck, waiting for scheduled handouts. Live music is offered most evenings. Reservations are recommended here. Open for dinner nightly, this restaurant also offers a children's menu.

Nightlife

■ Dancing

If you like country music, you can do a little boot scootin' at **Country and Western Restaurant** (Red Bay Road just past Lion's Centre, ☎ 345-945-4079). Dancing is on weekends only.

■ Mystery Theater

The *Nautilus* offers a unique tour on Thursday evenings. The Murder Mystery Theater is scheduled from 6:30 to 8 pm and includes a professional actor who interacts with the audience in trying to solve a "murder" on board. Unlimited hors d'oeuvres as well as beer, wine, and rum punch are available throughout the evening. These tours are priced at $47.50 for adults, US $25 for children. Call ☎ 345-945-1355 for reservations.

■ Night Submarine Dive

Atlantis offers a night dive; it's a wonderful chance to look at the vivid colors that are only seen during the night hours. ☎ 800-887-8571 or 345-949-7700.

■ Sunset Comedy Cruise

The *Nautilus* offers a weekly sunset comedy cruise with The Big Kahuna (see page 153); food and beverages are included. These cruises are priced at US $47.50 for adults, US $25 for children. Call ☎ 345-945-1355 for reservations.

■ Sunset Sails

Sunset sails are a good way to end the day and are offered by several operators. They're especially popular with couples.

Jolly Roger, ☎ 345-945-7245, e-mail jolroger@candw.ky. The *Jolly Roger*, an authentic replica of a 17th-century galleon, offers sunset cruises several nights per week. The boat leaves at dusk and sails for 2½ hours. The sunset cocktail cruise includes a snack as well as a complimentary open bar with beer and mixed drinks. Sunset sails are US $40 per person. On nights when there is no sunset cruise, the *Jolly Roger* offers a dinner cruise, which starts with rum punch and features a Cayman-style dinner (your choice of fish or beef); there's also an open bar with beer and mixed drinks. Dinner cruises run US $60. There is a US $5 per person charge for the return transportation to your hotel. Tours depart from The Jewelry Factory, across the street from the Hard Rock Café in George Town Harbour.

Cockatoo, Parrots Landing, George Town, ☎ 345-949-7884. This catamaran offers sunset sails from 5 pm to 7 pm for CI $20. Cost includes fruit punch; BYOB.

■ Nightclubs & Sports Bars

Durty Reid's, Red Bay Plaza, ☎ 345-947-1860. This sports bar says it has "warm beer, lousy food, and surly help." Have some jerk chicken or pork and judge for yourself!

East of George Town

For all the glitz of Seven Mile Beach and the high finance of George Town, the land east of the capital city is simple and countrified, charming visitors with a true Caribbean atmosphere. Condos are few and far between, sandwiched instead by miles of unimproved land and small Caymanian cottages. Cattle graze in the fields, beaches stretch for miles without a watersports operator in sight.

East of George Town lies the bulk of Grand Cayman. A single road leads along the South Sound to the communities of **Spotts** and **Savannah**, home of Pedro St. James Historic Site.

Farther east lies **Bodden Town** (the original capital city of the Cayman Islands), and miles of land unchanged by progress. This main highway changes names continually – it's called Jackson Road, Poinciana Road, Shamrock Drive, Church Street, Eastern Highway, A2, A3, A4, and more. Just stay on the main road and continue east; you won't get lost.

The highway winds past several good swimming areas, including a public beach in **Spotts** and another in **Breakers**. Just past Breakers, you'll have a choice: continue east to the easternmost portion of the island, or turn north. If you turn north on Frank Sound Road, you'll pass the **Mastic Trail** and the **Queen Elizabeth II Botanic Park**, both excellent attractions for those interested in the flora and fauna of the island. The road continues to **Old Man Bay** and meets up with the main road again along the northern stretch of the island.

If you don't turn north on Frank Sound Road, you can follow the main road alongside some of the most rugged shoreline on Grand Cayman. Just before the road begins its northern turn on the easternmost stretch of the island, it passes an attraction called the **blowholes**, where the sea spews forth between the rocks with each wave.

Continuing east toward the sea you'll see the sites of two of the island's most famous shipwrecks: the **Wreck of the Ten Sails** (1794) and the *Cumberland Transport* (1767). Pull over at the Wreck of the Ten Sails Monument in the community of Gun Bay.

In this region, even non-divers can see the remains of another shipwreck sticking right out of the water. The *Ridgefield*, a former WW II ship, wrecked at this site on December 1962.

Turning north, the road continues past a largely undeveloped stretch of island covered in dense, low-growing woodland. The easternmost reaches are treasured by windsurfers, who seek out this point for its stronger winds.

Traveling on either road, you can reach the north side and turn back west to **Rum Point**, a remote but active area filled with opportunities for watersports and dining (a ferry from Seven Mile Beach brings visitors to this remote beach). This is definitely the most "happening" spot east of George Town, a miniature version of Seven Mile Beach (without the hotels).

South of Rum Point lies **Cayman Kai**, one of the most lavish residential areas in Grand Cayman. This peninsula is lined with expensive homes and villas.

Grand Cayman

DID YOU KNOW?

"Going country" or "going to the tropical side" means a trip to the East End residential section.

Adventures

■ On Foot

Hiking

The **Mastic Trail**, Frank Sound Road, ☎ 345-945-6588. The 200-year-old Mastic Trail, a former footpath used by locals to herd cattle from the North Side to the south coast, has been renovated and is open for guided tours through a two-million-year-old woodland area. The trail is a project of the National Trust for the Cayman Islands and winds through the Mastic Reserve.

The two-mile trail travels through swamps, woodland, and farming areas, with changing fauna and flora along the way. One of the most interesting places is a region filled with fine red soil called "red mold." The dirt contains minerals found in the ancient rocks of Africa and scientists believe that, through the years, dust from the Sahara Desert blew across the Caribbean and accumulated here (it's not uncommon for hazy days to be attributed to sand blowing off the distant desert).

Many visitors experience the trail with the expert guidance of **Silver Thatch Excursions** (☎ 345-945-6588, fax 345-949-3342, e-mail silvert@ hotmail.com). The company's founders, Geddes and Janet Hislop, identify birds along the way, often sighting the Grand Cayman parrot, Caribbean dove, West Indian woodpecker, Cuban bullfinch, smooth-billed ani, and the colorful bananaquit.

The hike also travels past 100 different types of trees, including black mangroves that grow from the brackish water, elegant royal palms, and tall mahogany trees. Fruit trees, first planted by early residents, include mango, tamarind, and calabash. Orchids bring color to the trees during the spring season, probably the best time of year to experience this eco-tourism attraction. Look for the wild banana orchids (the Grand Cayman version has cream-to-white blossoms with purple lips, and the variety seen on the sister islands is pale to bright yellow with a purple center).

The walk takes in several environments – from the mangrove swamp to dry woodlands to an ancient forest – as it travels south to north. The forest contains over 100 species of trees and 550 other plant varieties. The trail was named for the mastic tree, once used by islanders for its lumber. Today, a tall mastic tree can still be seen at the halfway point of the trail.

Silver Thatch Excursions' guided tours along the Mastic Trail are US $50 per person (children 12 and under are half-price on all tours). Reserva-

East of George Town

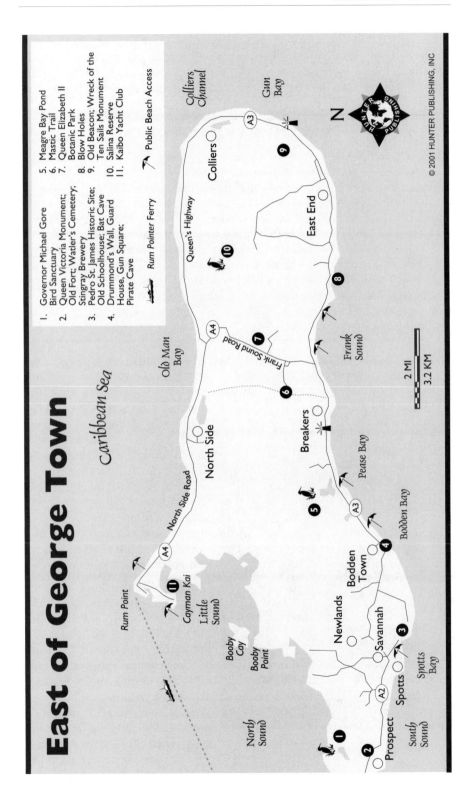

1. Governor Michael Gore Bird Sanctuary
2. Queen Victoria Monument; Old Fort; Watler's Cemetery; Stingray Brewery
3. Pedro St. James Historic Site; Old Schoolhouse; Bat Cave
4. Drummond's Wall, Guard House, Gun Square; Pirate Cave
5. Meagre Bay Pond
6. Mastic Trail
7. Queen Elizabeth II Botanic Park
8. Blow Holes
9. Old Beacon; Wreck of the Ten Sails Monument
10. Salina Reserve
11. Kaibo Yacht Club

Rum Pointer Ferry

Public Beach Access

© 2001 HUNTER PUBLISHING, INC

Grand Cayman

tions, which may be made via e-mail, are required for all tours and must be made 24 hours in advance. There is a minimum of two persons per tour; groups of four or more receive a 10% discount. Participants on all tours are provided with snacks, including traditional Caymanian foods and beverages.

CONSERVATION EFFORTS

The purchase of the ancient forest seen along the Mastic Trail is just one project of the **National Trust**. Today the development plan includes protection of the Central Mangrove Wetland, 8,500 acres that flood during the wet seasons and are an important part of the natural Grand Cayman landscape. Over 7,000 acres of this wetland are privately held. To preserve this region, the National Trust is working to acquire parcels of the wetland and to conserve the region, which is home to whistling ducks, parrots, snowy egrets, and hickatees. The National Trust is encouraging donations for this project and can be reached at the National Trust for the Cayman Islands, PO Box 31116 SMB, Grand Cayman; ☎ 345-949-0121.

To reach the Mastic Trail, take Frank Sound Road north. Just past the fire

Towering trees form a canopy along the Mastic Trail.

station, take the first road left. Stay left and follow that dirt road 0.7 mile across several cattle guards (if you head north on Frank Sound Road and reach the Botanic Park, you've gone too far). A small parking area beside the Mastic Trail sign marks the trailhead. It can be hiked without a guide, although plants are not marked and the trail is not a loop, so plan to turn around and retrace your steps.

Queen Elizabeth II Botanic Park, Frank Sound Road, ☎ 345-947-3558, www.botanic-park.ky. This is one of the best attractions on Grand Cayman, both economically and educationally. The park's main features are the Woodland Trail, the Heritage Garden, and the Floral Colour Garden. Each offer distinct experiences. The trail emphasizes Cayman flora and fauna in a natural setting, while the gardens showcase tropical plants from around the globe in a beautiful setting.

The Woodland Trail, just under a mile long, is a must-see for anyone interested in Cayman plants. Budget at least half an hour for the walk. More time will allow you to read the informative exhibits and look for turtles in the swampy undergrowth. Stop and listen for the call of a Cayman parrot in the trees.

The trail winds through several types of environments. One of the wettest is a swamp filled with buttonwood, one of the few trees that can live with its roots continually submerged in water. The swamp provides humid-

Visitors find peaceful spots at the Queen Elizabeth II Botanic Park.

Grand Cayman

ity for bromeliads and orchids. On the other end of the spectrum, cactus country illustrates the dry regions of the Cayman Islands, and it's home to large century plants (agave) and cacti. One habitat is similar to that found on Little Cayman and includes flora found on the tiny sister island.

Birders should bring along binoculars for this walk. Commonly seen species include the Grand Cayman parrot, the northern flicker, vitelline warbler (a small yellowish bird found only in the Cayman Islands and on Swan Island), the zenaida dove, and the bananaquit.

Butterflies are another common sight. The caterpillars of the Cayman swallowtail (*Papilio andraemontaibri*) feed on lime trees; the white peacock (*Anarte jatrophae jamaicensis*) is the most commonly spotted along the trail.

Watch the shadowy undergrowth and you may spot some of Grand Cayman's most reticent residents as well. The agouti *(Dasyprocta punctata)*, a shy rodent, is occasionally seen. Other residents include the hickatee *(Trachemys decussata)*, a freshwater turtle found in the brackish ponds of the Cayman Islands and Cuba. The Grand Cayman blue iguana (*Cyclura Nubila Lewisi*) or the Cayman anole lizard (*Anolis conspersus*), with a blue throat pouch, are also seen. Grass snakes (*Alsophis cantherigerus*) feed on frogs and lizards, but are harmless to humans.

After a walk along the Woodland Trail, take time to visit the beautiful showplace gardens (see *Sightseeing*, page 145). The park is open 9 am to

5:30 pm daily. Admission is US $7.50 for adults, US $5 for kids 6-12, and children under age six are free.

Silver Thatch Excursions, ☎ 345-945-6588, fax 345-949-3342, silvert@ hotmail.com also offers guided hikes through the Queen Elizabeth II Botanic Park along either an historic or an environmental route. Both routes are priced at US $45 per person and include admission to the Botanic Park.

Golf

The new **Sunrise Family Golf Centre**, ☎ 345-947-GOLF, fax 345-946-0508, e-mail Sunrise1@candw.ky, is an executive walking course located nine miles east of George Town. The family-oriented facility includes a clubhouse with a pro shop, putting green and a driving range. Fee for nine holes is CI $17 (about US $21) or 18 holes for CI $25.50 (about US $32); juniors pay CI $10 (US $12.47). Clubs and pull carts are available for rent.

■ In the Water

Scuba

 While Stingray City (see page 140) may be deemed the world's best 12-foot dive, the waters off the east end of the island offer plenty of other dive sites for all experience levels. For a list of Grand Cayman's dive operators, see pages 71-73.

Oriental Gardens: Located off the reef at South Sound, just east of George Town, this dive lies 30 to 60 feet below the surface and is highly recommended for beginning divers. Like a little bonsai forest, the area is dotted with staghorn coral and is a good site for underwater photographers. Includes some swim-throughs.

Julie's Wall: Set east of where Frank Sound Road intersects with the main road, this dive site is 60 to 100 feet below the surface. This is an intermediate-level dive. The wall is home to black coral formations and rays are often spotted here.

The Maze: Located on the South Channel (not far from the Wreck of the Ten Sails), this is a honeycomb of tunnels that form a veritable maze. Best suited to intermediate and advanced divers, the site is 60 to 100 feet, but some of the passages lead far beyond that.

Snapper Hole: A 30- to 60-foot dive, this is a favorite with beginners, but still offers tunnels, plenty of marine life, and even an anchor from an 1872 shipwreck. The site is on the east end outside the reef that forms Colliers Bay.

Tarpon Alley: This wall dive of 60 to 100 feet is near Stingray City, just outside the North Sound. A favorite with underwater photographers, the alley has drop-offs, canyons and, of course, huge schools of shiny tarpon.

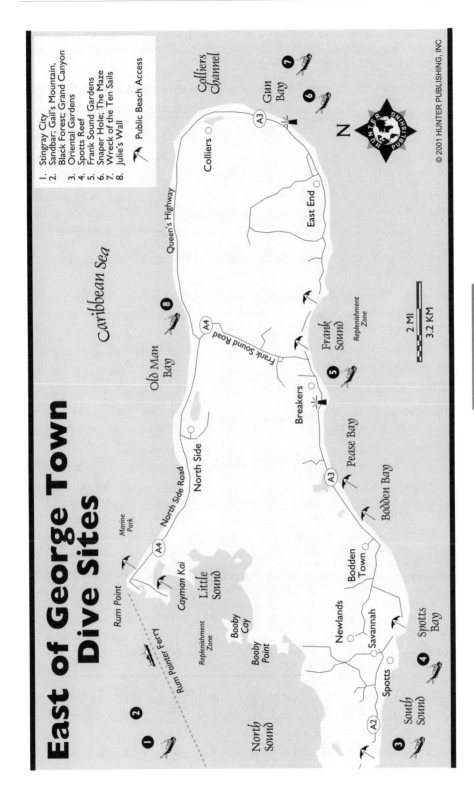

East of George Town Dive Sites

Caribbean Sea

1. Stingray City
2. Sandbar; Gail's Mountain, Black Forest; Grand Canyon
3. Oriental Gardens
4. Spotts Reef
5. Frank Sound Gardens
6. Snaper Hole; The Maze
7. Wreck of the Ten Sails
8. Julie's Wall

Public Beach Access

© 2001 HUNTER PUBLISHING, INC

Grand Cayman

2 MI
3.2 KM

North Sound

Rum Point

Rum Pointer Ferry

Replenishment Zone

Booby Point

Booby Cay

Little Sound

Cayman Kai

Marine Park

A4

North Side Road

North Side

Old Man Bay

A4

Frank Sound Road

Queen's Highway

Colliers

Colliers Channel

East End

A3

Gun Bay

Breakers

Frank Sound

Replenishment Zone

Pease Bay

Bodden Bay

A3

Bodden Town

Newlands

Savannah

Spotts

Spotts Bay

South Sound

A2

Eagle Ray Pass: East of Tarpon Alley and across from the main channel into the North Sound, Eagle Ray Pass is named for the rays that are often sighted here. This wall dive runs 40 to 100 feet.

Grand Canyon: Situated near the Sandbar west of Rum Point, this 80- to 110-foot wall dive is for intermediate and advanced divers.

Snorkeling

The east end is home to several good snorkel sites other than Stingray City's the Sandbar and the Coral Gardens.

Wreck of *Geneva Kathleen*: This wooden hulled schooner was wrecked in a 1929 hurricane. Today the wreck is a favorite with snorkelers because of its depth (just seven feet) and the artifacts that are scattered around the site. "Look, don't touch" when it comes to the artifacts, however; these are protected and cannot be taken from the site. Be careful of strong currents in this area.

Morritt's Tortuga Club: Morritt's is a favorite with windsurfers but just off the dock, snorkelers find an excellent site inside the reef. Look for good coral growth as well as plentiful marine life.

Rum Point: The calm, clear waters right off Rum Point are a favorite with many family snorkelers. You'll find some coral formations here.

Sunset Reef East: The site features large coral heads.

Half Moon Bay: On the south side of the island, this shallow site is often home to eels and crabs.

Turtle Inn, Bodden Town: This inn is home to good snorkeling just offshore. Check the accommodations section below for contact information.

You'll find a large number of snorkel operators (see page 139); a unique trip is the Eco-Adventure offered by **Ocean Frontiers** (☎ 800-544-6576 or 345-947-7500, www.oceanfrontiers.com). The two-hour trip starts at Kaibo Yacht Club near Rum Point and travels to tour the mangrove forest; both snorkeling and birdwatching are combined for a look at what lies above and below the water on this excursion. The rate is US $39.

If wrecks are your thing, Ocean Frontiers also offers a special wreck snorkel tour exploring up to five wreck sites (weather permitting). Snorkelers visit the Wreck of the Ten Sails, including the HMS *Convert*, the *Ridgefield*, the *Marybelle*, the *Methuselam*, the *Geneva Kathleen*, the *Romundi* and more. The tour lasts two hours and costs US $29.

ADVENTURE TALKS: OCEAN FRONTIERS

We talked with Steve Broadbelt about the snorkel adventures available through Ocean Frontiers.

■ *How does the east end of Grand Cayman rate as a snorkel site?*

The sites are the most remote and least visted on the island: they are healthy and vibrant reefs full of tropical fish and lush corals.

■ *How does your Eco-Adventure introduce travelers to Cayman's wildlife both above and below the water?*

Our expert staff give extended briefings prior to entering the water also using ID slates and books to help identify what's down there.

■ *What can you tell us about your other tours?*

We also offer Scuba diving tours on our deeper reefs and drop-offs. We offer Night dives and also a Shark Awareness Dive.

■ *What sets your operation apart from others on the island?*

The staff and guides are the best on the island. Our boats and equipment are state of the art. And the environment is untouched and pristine. We operate with small groups and offer personal service.

Rum Point: The northern tip of the east end is Rum Point, a peninsula that's home to willowy casuarina trees, chalky sand, aquamarine waters, and a club with just about every imaginable watersport. This point is home to the prettiest waters in the Cayman Islands – don't forget your camera!

DID YOU KNOW?

No one's quite sure how Rum Point got its name, but many believe a ship filled with rum wrecked here.

Over $5 million was spent to improve this getaway spot. It offers a full-service dinner restaurant, casual lunch eatery and bar, decks and walkways, plenty of comfy hammocks and picnic tables, a gift shop, and more.

You can arrive at Rum Point by car (about an hour's drive from George Town). To reach Rum Point, travel east from George Town on A2 (Crewe Road, which becomes Red Bay Road). Continue east on Red Bay Road through the communities of Savannah and Bodden Town, where the road becomes A3. Go east past the town of Breakers for about a mile. Turn left (north) on Frank Sound Road or A4. Continue north to a Y intersection at Ironshore Flat. Bear left on A4 along the north coast for about seven miles. A4 will become Rum Point Drive; follow the signs to Rum Point.

You can also reach Rum Point on the *Rum Pointer* ferry, which departs from the Hyatt Regency Grand Cayman. This 120-passenger ferry travels to Rum Point in about 40 minutes. For ferry reservations, ☎ 345-949-9098. Ferry tickets are about US $15 round-trip. If you're at Rum Point at dusk, don't miss the tarpon feeding off the docks.

Grand Cayman

RUM POINTER FERRY SCHEDULE

Check with *Rum Pointer* ferry (☎ 345-947-9412) for the most up-to-date schedule. At press time, this schedule was in effect.

DEPARTS HYATT	DEPARTS RUM POINT
9:30 am	11 am
noon	1 pm
2:30 pm	4 pm
5:30 pm	6:30 pm
7:30 pm	8:30 pm
9:30 pm	10:30 pm
On Sundays, the ferry takes an abbreviated schedule:	
9:30 am	11 am
noon	1 pm
2:30	6 pm

The pier at Rum Point.

Rum Point is also home to the Barefoot Man, a.k.a. George Nowak. The musician whose name is synonymous with Cayman music (you may have seen him in *The Firm*) plays at Rum Point on Monday and Friday nights from 5-10 pm at the Rum Point Restaurant and 2-6 on Saturdays on the beach.

Shark Dive

The **Cayman Diving Lodge,** ☎ 800-TLC-DIVE or 345-947-7555, fax 345-947-7560, www.caymandivelodge.com, offers a unique Shark Dive. Caribbean reef sharks up to seven feet long are spotted on these guided dives off Jack McKennedy's Canyon.

Lunch & Snorkeling Trips

One opportunity to learn more about Caymanian life is on a North Sound Beach Lunch & Snorkeling Trip, which is offered by numerous operators. This trip also features snorkeling at either Stingray City or the Sandbar (depending on visibility and water conditions) and Coral Gardens. The crew dives for pink queen conch, a shellfish that's then prepared as an appetizer, sliced and marinated in lime juice, onion and seasonings. Everyone goes on shore at Cayman Kai for a Caymanian lunch of peas and rice, potato or breadfruit salad, and local fish or spicy chicken. Part of the fun is talking with the captain and crew about Caymanian life. These trips cost about US $50 per person and run from 9 am to 3 or 4 pm.

Grand Cayman

LUNCH & SNORKEL TRIP OPERATORS

Bayside Watersports . . . . ☎ 345-949-1750

Black Princess Charter . . . . ☎ 345-949-0400 or 949-3821

Charterboat Headquarters . . . . ☎ 345-945-4340

Best Value Charters . . . . ☎ 345-949-1603

Captain Crosby's/C&G Watersports . . . . ☎ 345-947-4049

Captain Gleason Ebanks . . . . ☎ 345-916-1502 or 945-2666

Captain Marvin's Watersports . . . . ☎ 345-947-4590

Cayman Delight Cruises . . . . ☎ 345-949-6738/8111

Dallas Ebanks Watersports . . . . ☎ 345-949-1538/916-2707

Ernie Ebanks Watersports . . . . ☎ 345-949-1538/916-2707

Fantasea Tours . . . . ☎ 345-949-2182

Frank's Watersports . . . . ☎ 345-947-5491

Jackie's Watersports . . . . ☎ 345-947-5791

Oh Boy Charters . . . . ☎ 345-949-6341

Stingray City Charters . . . . ☎ 345-949-9200

■ On the Water

Stingray City

The top watersports attraction in the Cayman Islands, Stingray City, is in the mouth of the North Sound, halfway between West Bay and East End. Here, fishermen once cleaned their catch, attracting large southern Atlantic stingrays, who are now accustomed to being handled by participants in daily snorkeling excursions.

In 1987, *Skin Diver* magazine deemed this site "Stingray City" and since that time there's been no looking back. Stingray City is visited by many watersports operators, who offer half- and full-day excursions with stops at both deep and shallow spots. Operators depart from locations all along the island for this adventure. The site is now one of the most popular in the Caribbean; often called "the world's best 12-foot dive," it can be enjoyed by both snorkelers and scuba divers.

Divers at Stingray City.

Truly, this is one experience not to be missed. We have done the Stingray City experience several times using different operators and have never been disappointed. The trip out on the North Sound to the site is quick and scenic, but nothing can quite prepare you for the experience of petting, feeding, and being caressed by the stingrays. After mooring, some vacationers are a little cautious about heading into the waters (the stingrays are far less shy). We've noticed that all but the most nervous swimmer enjoys this experience.

On the shallow stop, the Sandbar, visitors stand (as still as possible to prevent kicking up sand and lowering visibility) while the stingrays swoop by, often brushing participants like large rubbery Frisbees. Trips cost US $35-$55 per person and typically include three stops, the deepest of which is Stingray City at about 12 feet, followed by the shallower Sandbar, about three feet deep.

FEEDING THE RAYS

Don't miss the chance to feed the rays some squid. Just pinch the squid between your fingers, arch your fingers back like you're about to slap someone, and put your hand down in the water: the greedy stingrays will do the rest. (If you don't arch your fingers back, the rays might suck up your fingers and give you a little scare. They don't have teeth, but their lips are a firm cartilage that will give you a jolt.) Typically about 30 stingrays frequent the area, so you're just about guaranteed the opportunity to pet and swim alongside these beautiful creatures.

After feeding the stingrays, most operators then take snorkelers over to **Coral Gardens**, a beautiful snorkeling area with several large coral heads, fans, and abundant marine life.

Stingray City Boat Tours

If you're not a swimmer or are traveling with small children, you'll still find opportunities for viewing the residents of Stingray City. Several operators offer the chance to get a view of the rays without ever getting wet.

Red Sail Sports, Rum Point, ☎ 345-949-8745. From the Red Sail location at Rum Point, you can take a glassbottom boat ride to the Sandbar six days a week. It's a 20-minute ride to the site; once there, snorkelers can explore the area in the water while others remain on board and view the rays through a glass port. Kids under three enjoy this excursion without charge; cost without snorkel gear is US $30 ($40 with snorkel gear).

STINGRAY CITY TRIP OPERATORS

These excursions leave from all over the island (most along Seven Mile Beach) and many include free shuttle service from hotels and condos.

Abanks Diving . . . . ☎ 345-945-1444
www.abanks.com.ky

Ambassador Divers . . . . ☎ 345-916.8839
www.ambassadordivers.com

Aqua Adventures . . . . ☎ 345-949-1616

Aqua Delights . . . . ☎ 345-945-4786

Aquanauts Diving . . . . ☎ 888-786-6887
or 345-945-1990, www.aquanautsdiving.com

Bayside Watersports . . . . ☎ 345-949-1750

Grand Cayman

Bob Soto's Diving Ltd.................. ☎ 800-BOB-SOTO
or 345-949-2871, www.bobsotosdiving.com.ky

Divers Down .... ☎ 345-945-1611
www.diversdown.net

Divers Supply .... ☎ 345-949-7621

DiveTech .... ☎ 345-949-1700
www.divetech.com

Don Foster's Dive Cayman Ltd. .... ☎ 800-83-DIVER
or 345-945-5132, www.donfosters.com

Fisheye of Cayman....................... ☎ 800-887-8569
or 345-945-4209, www.fisheye.com

Ocean Frontiers .... ☎ 800-544-6576
or 345-947-7500, www.oceanfrontiers.com

Ollen Miller's Sun Divers .... ☎ 345-947-6606

Peter Milburn's Dive Cayman .... ☎ 345-945-5770
www.petermilburndivecayman.com

Red Baron Charters .... ☎ 345-945-4744

Red Sail Sports......................... ☎ 800-255-6425
or 345-945-5965, www.redsail.com

Seasports.............................. ☎ 345-949-3965

Sunset Divers .... ☎ 800-854-4767
345-949-7111, www.sunsethouse.com

Tortuga Divers .... ☎ 345-947-2097

Treasure Island Divers.................. ☎ 800-872-7552
345-949-4456, www.tidivers.com

Windsurfing

The **east end** is a top windsurfing area because of its stronger winds. Trade winds of 15 to 25 knots blow during the winter months, dropping to 10 to 15 knots in the summer. Windsurfers find plenty of action inside the reef, while others choose to go out through the channel (be cautious of sharp coral when going through the channel). **Collier's Channel** is a good point to take the waves.

At Morritt's Tortuga Club (as well as close to Seven Mile Beach, near The Links of SafeHaven), **Cayman Windsurf** caters to both beginner and advanced windsurfers. Learn the sport, improve your knowledge, or just rent a craft and enjoy slicing through the water with the breeze. Beginners have four miles of reef-protected calm waters in which to learn and advanced practitioners can sail out through Collier's Channel. Prices average about US $35 for one-hour rentals; lessons run about US $45. For more details, call Cayman Windsurf, ☎ 345-947-7492 or fax 345-947-6763.

■ On Wheels

The **east end** is excellent for cycling and scooter riding. A flat grade and little traffic make for a leisurely ride. **Cayman Cycle Rentals** (☎ 345-945-4021) has a shop at Treasure Island Resort, the Hyatt Regency Grand Cayman, and Coconut Place; scooters average about $25 per day. A temporary Cayman islands license, available from the rental agency, is required to drive a scooter and riding experience is necessary. For more on cycling, contact the **Cayman Islands Cycling Association**, Box 456, George Town, Grand Cayman, BWI, ☎ 345-949-8666.

Eco-Travel

■ Birding

The best birding on Grand Cayman is found in this region, from the **Mastic Trail** to the Woodland Trail at the **Botanic Park** to **Meagre Bay Pond**, east of Bodden Town. Set off the main road, the large pond was once a popular hunting site and was abandoned by the teal and mallard that once populated the region in the early 1900s. However, the pond is now designated an Animal Sanctuary by the government and hunting is prohibited. Today, the bird population is beginning to increase once again.

Another top birding spot is the **Governor Michael Gore Bird Sanctuary**. Located about three miles east of George Town in Spotts, this site has an observation blind.

The only operation of its kind on Grand Cayman, **Silver Thatch Excursions** (☎ 345-945-6588, fax 345-949-3342, e-mail silvert@hotmail.com) offers specialized birding trips for US $50 per person. These trips include visits to birding sites such as the Governor Michael Gore Bird Sanctuary, a haven for waterfowl, as well as Meagre Bay Pond, Queen Elizabeth II Botanic Park, and the Willie Ebanks Farm, to view endangered West Indian whistling ducks. Company founders Geddes and Janet Hislop also offer private birding tours at US $40 per hour.

■ Bats

Look for bats at the **Bat Cave**, outside Savannah at Spotts Bay. The cave is a little tough to find. If you're driving west on the way to George Town, take the first left on a dirt road past Pedro St. James. Follow the dirt road to the sea, turn left and follow the cliff to a sandy beach. Climb down 10 feet to the small entrance of the cave (you'll have to crawl inside). If you can't find it, just stop and ask in Savannah.

Cultural Excursions

■ Savannah

The small town of Savannah, east of George Town on A2, is best known as the home of **Pedro St. James**, an 18th-century great house that became known as the "birthplace of Cayman democracy" (see page 146). The town is well worth a visit. Pedro St. James, called Pedro Castle by residents, has been beautifully restored and is of interest to history buffs as well as nature lovers thanks to its bluffside perch.

■ Bodden Town

History buffs can take a self-guided tour of Bodden Town, the city that served as the original capital of the Cayman Islands. Bodden Town is home of several historic sites. The **Queen Victoria Monument**, a place where men met to discuss politics in the 20s and 30s, is located at Church Street (the main road) and Old Monument Road.

Turn onto Old Monument Road and continue north to Mijall Road; off Mijall Road stands a site called **Slave Wall** or **Drummond's Wall**. No one knows just when this stone wall was constructed, but it is believed that an enslaved man named Drummond supervised the building of a portion of this wall.

Continuing east along Church Street to Cumber Crescent is **Gun Square**, where two 18th-century cannons once guarded the channel. Today those cannons point downward.

The Lighthouse at Breakers.

Farther east is **Meagre Bay Pond**, once a hunting ground and now a sanctuary for the many birds that make this pond their home.

The rich history of the Cayman Islands is sometimes overlooked by travelers enjoying the many shopping and watersports opportunities. Two historic tours are offered by Silver Thatch Excursions (see page 143 for contact information).

The **Eastern Experience** takes travelers to East End on Grand Cayman. Participants view an old lighthouse and see the Wreck of the Ten Sails Monument, recalling the seafaring days of the Cayman Islands. The tour also stops at Old Prospect, site of the first fort, and Watler's Cemetery. In Bodden Town, participants go on a walking tour to see early Caymanian architecture and then travel on to the blowholes at Breakers.

A second historic tour starts with a walking tour of **West Bay**, including a stop at Old Homestead to learn more about early Cayman life. Travelers then head to George Town for a walking tour of the capital city and a visit to the site of Fort George and Elmslie Memorial Church, built by a shipwright with a ceiling constructed to resemble a schooner's hull. The grave markers in the adjacent cemetery resemble houses, a typical style on the islands. The tour continues on to Old Prospect and the Old Savannah Schoolhouse.

Sightseeing

 Queen Elizabeth II Botanic Park, Frank Sound Road, ☎ 345-947-9462, www.botanic-park.ky. Situated about 25 minutes from George Town, the Queen Elizabeth Botanic Park is a 65-acre area filled with native trees, plants, and wild orchids, as well as birds, reptiles, and butterflies. For more about the park's Woodland Trail, see page 133.

The Visitors Centre, Heritage Garden and Garden of Flowering Plants are the newest additions to the gardens. The two-story **Visitors Centre**, built in traditional Caymanian architectural style, includes displays on natural history and botanical art, and small flower shows. Near the waterfall at the back of the center is a snack bar, which serves sandwiches, patties, ice cream and juices.

Visit the **Heritage Garden** for a look at Cayman history. A Caymanian house from the East End has been restored and filled with donated furniture. The three-room structure was originally a family home where nine children were raised; today the yard is filled with the plants and fruit trees that a Caymanian family would have raised earlier this century. A cistern collects valuable rainwater and a separate kitchen keeps the heat of the stove and fire danger separate from the house. Beside the home, cassava, sugarcane, plantains, bananas, and sweet potatoes are grown in small open pockets in the lowland forest. Fruit trees are grown in soil found among the ironshore, much as they would have generations ago. Medicinal plants commonly grown around a Caymanian house, such as aloe vera, are found here.

The **Garden of Flowering Plants** is the most traditional botanical garden area here, with two acres of floral gardens arranged by color. Pink, purple, orange, silver, and a whole rainbow of tones blossom with color and fragrance year-round. Overlooking the gardens and a small pond that features six-foot Victoria water lilies, a teahouse has been constructed.

The gardens are open 9 am to 5:30 pm, daily. Admission is US $7.50 or adults, US $5 for kids six-12, and children under six are free.

Pedro St. James National Historic Site, Savannah, ☎ 345-947-3329, www.pedrostjames.ky. To reach the site, take Red Bay Road (A2) east from George Town to Savannah. Turn right on Pedro Castle Road; you'll see the site on your right.

One of East End's top attractions is also its oldest. Pedro St. James Restoration Site, an 18th-century great house, is called the "Birthplace of Democracy in the Cayman Islands." Called Pedro Castle by local residents, the historic structure is situated in the community of Savannah, east of George Town.

The oldest known stone structure in the Cayman Islands, Pedro St. James was first built for William Eden, an early settler. In 1831, the house was the site of an historic meeting when residents decided that the five districts should have representation in the government. Four years later, a proclamation declaring the emancipation of all slaves was read at Pedro St. James and several other sites in the islands.

The restoration of the great house to its 1820s condition was a major undertaking, a US $7.5 million project. The site is at the center of a 7.65-acre landscaped park atop the 30-foot Great Pedro Bluff. For the past several years, historic research into the site has been conducted. Today, the three-story great house is home to a 49-seat theater as well as a café.

Your visit begins in the theater with a 25-minute multimedia show explaining the significance of Pedro St. James. Shows begin on the hour and are must-sees; the high-tech presentation is a valuable lesson in Caymanian history. The special effects will hold children's attention (although they might be a little scary for the very young).

After the multimedia show, you can take a self-guided look at the three-story home. For all its historic significance, the home has a sad history as well. At the foot of the exterior stairs, a young girl who lived in the home was struck and killed by lightning; the resulting fire burned much of the original structure. After the fire, the two families who resided at Pedro St. James thought the house was unlucky and they built homes near the ruins. These structures can still be seen along with an outdoor cookhouse.

You'll find some hiking here as well. The Ironshore Trail is a wide trail that's popular with many visitors. It's lined with native plants, and provides a good view of the Great Pedro Bluff.

Pedro St. James National Historic Site.

DID YOU KNOW?

Many Caymanians refer to Pedro St. James as Pedro Castle. The name harks back to the 1950s when a private investor tried to transform the site into a tourist accommodation.

Pirates Cave, Shamrock Drive, Bodden Town, ☎ 345-947-3122. A less scenic and more touristy stop (but nonetheless fun) is at the Pirate Cave in Bodden Town. Reputed to have been used by pirates to hide their treasure and supposedly linked by tunnels to similar caves in the reef, the cave is now open for self-guided tours. You'll first view a blue iguana and Cayman parrot, as well as a traditional Cayman cottage, then head underground for a look at the cave. Across the street, alleged pirate graves, carved by slaves from rock in the shape of small houses, make an interesting site. Open daily 9 am to 5 pm. Admission is CI $5 for adults, CI $4 for children under age 12.

Stingray Brewery, Red Bay Road, ☎ 345-947-6699. This microbrewery produces Stingray Beer, sold throughout the islands, and offers a tour of the brewery. Located just east of the intersection of Crewe Road and South Sound Road (on the right side of the road if you are traveling east). Closed Sunday.

Blowholes. On the main road between Frank Sound and East End, east of the turnoff for Frank Sound Road, lies this roadside attraction. Park and walk down to the rugged coral rocks that have been carved by the rough waves into caverns. As waves hit the rocks, water spews into the air, creating one of the best photo opportunities on the island. You'll access the blowholes from a free parking area just off the main road; follow the wooden stairs down to sea level. Don't stand too close to the edge of these formations! The water shoots strongest when the waves are large (and the calmest days have no action at all), with sprays reaching 20 to 30 feet in the air. Wear good shoes for this excursion; the ironshore is sharp and footing isn't solid.

Wreck of the Ten Sails Monument, Gun Bay in East End. The history of the Wreck of the Ten Sails is recalled at this monument opened by Queen Elizabeth II on her visit to the island in 1994. Cayman's most famous shipwreck wasn't actually one wreck, but 10. The Wreck of the Ten Sails occurred on February 8, 1794 when a fleet of 10 British ships, sailing from Jamaica, hit the reefs of Gun Bay. When the lead ship ran into trouble on the reefs, it put up its signal flags to warn the other ships. Here the story becomes somewhat of a mystery; it is unknown whether the ship hoisted the wrong flag or whether the flag was misread by the other ships but, tragically, the other vessels, one by one, wrecked on the reef. Residents rowed out to the reef and saved almost every sailor. Legend has it that, because of the heroic rescue by the residents, King George III gave the islands tax-free status. This part of the legend is untrue.

Shopping

Shopping is pretty limited on this end of the island, although you'll find some souvenir shops at Rum Point. One good option for travelers heading all the way east is the **Wreck View Art Gallery**, located in East End opposite the Portofino restaurant. This gallery features local wood carvings made of driftwood, mahogany and coconut as well as original paintings. Open Sunday through Friday; ☎ 345-947-6604 or 947-6512.

Where to Stay

■ Hotels & Resorts

 Cayman Diving Lodge, East End, ☎ 800-TLC-DIVE, 345-947-7555, fax 345-947-7560, www.caymandivelodge.com, $$-$$$. Located 35 minutes east of George Town, this all-inclusive diving lodge is dedicated to enthusiasts, those whose vacation will focus on what lies beneath the waters. The lodge includes 11 guest rooms with air conditioning, as well as a restaurant, bar, and gift shop. Two dive boats run to offshore wall dives and caves. The resort also offers a unique shark dive (see page 139).

Cayman Kai Resort, Cayman Kai, just south of Rum Point, ☎ 345-947-9055, fax 345-947-9102, $$. Cayman Kai is in one of the island's most elegant, secluded areas. Just a short drive from Rum Point, it's also fairly close to the action if you prefer things to be a little busy. The 20 guest rooms at this small resort include air conditioning, ceiling fans, TV, kitchenettes, and screened patios. The resort has a beach bar, dive shop, and tennis.

Morritt's Tortuga Club, East End, ☎ 800-447-0309, 345-947-7449, fax 947-7299, www.morritts.com, $$. A favorite with divers and windsurfers, this East End resort is set right on the beach. Amenities include air conditioning, ceiling fans, phones, TV, kitchenettes, pool, Jacuzzi, restaurant, bar, dive shop, scuba trips, snorkeling, sailing, windsurfing, fishing, and more. Recently completed is Morritt's Grand Resort, a timeshare property adjacent to the existing resort (see *Condos & Villas*, below).

North Side Surf Inn, North Side, ☎ 345-947-1431, fax 345-947-0704, www.northsidesurfinn.com, $. Located about halfway between Rum Point and the intersection of Frank Sound Road on the North Side, this small inn offers 10 guest rooms right on the beach. All rooms have air conditioning; dive packages are also available. One special attraction of this small inn is the **Red Ginger** restaurant; its cuisine brings many visitors, both locals and travelers alike, out from George Town and Seven Mile Beach (see page 151).

Grand Cayman

Royal Reef, Colliers Bay in East End, ☎ 888-452-4545, www.royalresorts.com, $$$. This is a new timeshare facility that is also open to the general public. The first building phase consists of 30 two-bedroom, two-bath villas, to be followed by 50 more units in the near future. Each of the villas has all the features you'll need for a home away from home, including a completely furnished kitchen, dining room, living room, and more. Full maid service is also included. Some of the units have beach views. The resort has a mini-market, car rental desk, beauty salon and spa, and social activities for adults and children. the resort's pool has a swim-up bar, and overlooks the ocean. "The Royal Resorts have always been five-star properties and that's perfect for the Cayman Islands because it's a five-star destination all the way," says Deborah Batteiger, the resort's promotions coordinator.

■ Condos & Villas

Cayman Villas, Airport Road, ☎ 800-235-5888, 345-945-4144, fax 345-949-7471, www.caymanvillas.com, $-$$$. Well known for their luxurious listings on Seven Mile Beach, Cayman Villas also offers exclusive properties in Cayman Kai. "Cayman Villas specializes in beachfront condos and private houses ranging from economy to deluxe, from studios to seven bedrooms," says Penny Cumber, managing director. "Most private houses are at Cayman Kai, but there are many other quiet beaches around Grand Cayman, Cayman Brac and Little Cayman on which we also have villas. Guests can have their own private beach and still be in the midst of all the action." Some popular economy properties managed by Cayman Villas include Kai Sound, a studio cottage on the beach, and Gemini, a duplex with one-bedroom, one-bath cottages at Cayman Kai.

Villas appeal to many types of travelers. Cumber says that the different properties offer variety to suit all tastes: honeymooners rent the quiet private houses and condos or a place close to action; families with young children prefer houses/condos all one level; families with older children take houses within walking distance of watersports; large family reunions or a large gathering of friends rent condos or houses close to each other; while wedding parties and guests in stay in nearby villas. Honeymooners and those celebrating a special occasion receive a complimentary bottle of champagne.

Morritt's Grand Resort, East End, ☎ 800-447-0309, 345-947-7449, ext. 5930 or 5941, fax 345-947-3544, www.morritts.com, $$$. This timeshare resort located next to Morritt's Tortuga Club offers deluxe one- and two-bedroom units, its own beach, and a swimming pool overlooking the Caribbean Sea.

■ Small Inns

Turtle Nest Inn, Main Road (A3), Bodden Town, ☎ 345-947-8665, fax 345-947-6379, www.turtlenestinn.com, $$. Although this inn is located on the main street in Bodden Town, it offers a beautiful beach with plenty of tranquillity. The Spanish-style hotel is a two-story building with cool tile floors and bright Caribbean color bedspreads and rattan couches. Guest accommodations are one-bedroom apartments, each with fully equipped kitchens. Each room includes both a queen-sized bed and a double pull-out couch as well as TV, VCR, digital phone, ceiling fans, and central air conditioning. There's a gas barbecue on the beach for guest use, a laundry room, a freshwater pool, and twice-weekly restaurant.

Where to Eat

DINING PRICE SCALE
The scale below indicates the approximate cost of a meal for one person, including drink and gratuity. The price scale refers to US $.
$ . . . . Under $15 per person
$$ . . . . $15-$30 per person
$$$ . . . . $31-$40 per person

■ American

 **Wreck Bar and Grille**, Rum Point, ☎ 345-947-9412, $-$$. Dine on burgers, club sandwiches, patties, conch fritters, BBQ chicken salad, fisherman's salad, and jerk pork sandwiches in the comfort of your bathing suit. Table service to the beachside picnic tables makes this an enjoyable way to lunch on a relaxing Rum Point day. On Saturday afternoons, enjoy a buffet lunch here for CI $12, including jerk chicken, ribs, rice and peas. The Barefoot Man entertains at the Wreck bar from 3-6 on Saturdays so grab a table close to the bandstand.

Reef Point Restaurant and Lounge, Bodden Town (east of Pirate Cave), ☎ 345-947-2183, $-$$. This eatery sits right on the main road. It serves local dishes as well as pizza and snacks, and is well known for daily shark feedings at 6 pm; toothy visitors up to six feet long come by for an evening snack.

■ Caribbean

Red Ginger, North Side Surf Inn, North Side, ☎ 345-947-1431, $$-$$$. You wouldn't think that you'd find one of the island's best-loved restaurants this far out on the North Side, but Red Ginger is definitely a favorite with locals in the know. When you see the long line of cars parked along the road, you'll know that reservations are a must. The casual restaurant has a view of the waves but the menu offers plenty of distraction: grilled beef tenderloin, poached Chilean salmon, jerk lamb chops, pan-fried turtle medallions, potato gnocchi, baked eggplant gâteau, and more. Take-out is available, and you'll find a children's menu as well.

The Edge, Bodden Town, ☎ 345-947-2140, $. Open for breakfast, lunch, and dinner, this casual restaurant serves Caribbean favorites as well as American fare. Located just east of the Turtle Inn, you can't miss The Edge: just look for the thatched roof. Dine outside beneath umbrellas for a view of the water. Take-out dishes are available, as is a kids' menu.

■ Eclectic

David's Restaurant, Morritt's Tortuga Club, East End, ☎ 345-947-7449, ext. 5939, $$. This restaurant, with both indoor and outdoor seating, serves a menu that's varied nightly. On Monday, the beach barbecue features jerk pork and barbecued chicken. Tuesday is comedy night and brings a three-course dinner, while Wednesday diners choose from stir fry, seafood or fajitas. Thursday means Caribbean dishes, and Friday features an à la carte menu. Steak is featured Saturday nights; snapper and an à la carte menu are offered Sundays. Reservations recommended.

■ Italian

Portofino Restaurant, East End near Morritt's Tortuga Club, ☎ 345-947-2700, $$. This casual restaurant serves a popular Sunday buffet as well as a wide array of Italian dishes. Don't miss the view of the Wreck of the Ten Sails and the remains of the *Ridgefield*, easily visible from the shoreline.

■ Seafood

Cecil's, Kaibo Yacht Club, Cayman Kai, ☎ 345-947-9975, $$$. Free ferry service from SafeHaven takes diners from the Seven Mile Beach area to this east side restaurant in just over 15 minutes. Once here, you'll be rewarded with views of the North Sound, all enjoyed with dishes that range from Caribbean to Cajun. Start with oysters Rockefeller, Creole barbecue shrimp, Louisiana crab cakes, or calamari. Entrees include pan seared tuna with honey ginger sesame sauce, Caribbean lobster tail stuffed with seafood, pan-seared catfish with Louisiana crawfish sauce, and Black Angus filet mignon. The restaurant is open Tuesday through Sunday for dinner; call for ferry times as well as reservations.

The Lighthouse, South Side, ☎ 345-947-2047, $$. Don't worry about missing this restaurant: just look for the first lighthouse on your right as you head out from George Town. This fun eatery serves lunch and dinner either indoors or outside. Along with a menu featuring seafood – conch chowder, jerk shrimp pitas, and seafood Caesar salads – several Italian dishes are offered as well.

Rum Point Restaurant, Rum Point, ☎ 345-947-9412, $$-$$$. Open for dinner only, this eatery features island favorites like shrimp, lobster, and conch, as well as pasta dishes, prime rib, and chicken. The Barefoot Man performs on Friday and Monday nights so be sure to make reservations.

Nightlife

 Nightlife is quiet on the eastern half of the island with many vacationers choosing an early-to-bed, early-to-rise routine to partake in an early morning dive. One good option on the East End is comedy night at **David's Restaurant** at Morritt's Tortuga Club (☎ 345-947-7449, ext. 5939). No kids are permitted at this show, which features a favorite local comedian, the **Big Kahuna**. Live music is offered at the restaurant on Wednesday nights, and Thursday brings a Caribbean night with limbo dancers and a fire eater.

The **Barefoot Man** is another major attraction. A longtime favorite on Grand Cayman, performing for many years at the old Holiday Inn, the Barefoot Man performs his fun calypso tunes at **Rum Point Restaurant** on Monday and Saturday nights from 5-10 pm; call ☎ 345-947-9412 for reservations.

An early evening activity is the nightly **shark feeding** at Reef Point restaurant (☎ 345-947-2183). Sharks are fed about 6 pm and you'll be amazed at the size of some of these creatures!

Seven Mile Beach

This beautiful swath of white sand separates a five mile strip of hotels, condominiums, and restaurants from an aquamarine sea (since the beach measures just five miles, the name "Seven Mile Beach" is somewhat of a misnomer). Dotted with casuarina trees, this beach is the most popular spot on the island. Come here to watch and be watched, to enjoy an island concoction or to slather on oil and bake yourself into tropical bliss. Watersports operators line the way, offering everything from scuba trips to parasailing to windsurfing.

Seven Mile Beach runs from south to north along Grand Cayman's western edge, stretching from George Town to the North West Point. Along this stretch, the land is only about a mile wide, between the waters of the West Bay and the North Sound. To the east, the shoreline of the North Sound is uneven, at some points etching into the land with salt creeks and small harbors. Much of the eastern reaches of the Seven Mile Beach area are covered by swampy vegetation. The largest harbor along this stretch of the North Sound is **Governors Harbour**, where Governors Creek creeps into the land in a maze of natural and man-made canals. Today it's lined with luxury lots and lavish homes, as well as the **Cayman Islands Yacht Club**.

The resort areas of Seven Mile Beach face the West Bay and look toward the **Main Drop-Off**, an area of the ocean that plummets to great depths. Protected marine parks (see pages 26-27 for a description of the marine park preservation laws) run parallel to the shore, safeguarding delicate coral reefs and marine life. In some ways the strip of sand seems much longer than its five miles because of the numerous businesses packed along its expanse. The beach is public and you'll find access points scattered all along, sometimes sandwiched between condominium developments. One of the best access points is the **public beach park**, tucked north of the Westin Casuarina Hotel. With plenty of parking (other beach access areas offer parking on the shoulder of busy West Bay Road), this is one of the best options for enjoying Seven Mile Beach if you're not staying at one of the area properties. The park includes shaded pavilions, restrooms with changing rooms, and a small playground for the kids. Squeaky clean and, like the rest of the island, devoid of beach vendors, the park is a wonderful place to spend an afternoon.

TOP SEVEN REASONS TO VISIT SEVEN MILE BEACH

For many travelers, Grand Cayman is synonymous with Seven Mile Beach, a stretch of powdery sand lined not just with palms and casuarina trees, but also with enough fun to keep even the most restless traveler busy. The heart of the Caymanian tourism business, this is one of the most popular beaches in the Caribbean. Regardless of your interests, you'll find plenty of reasons to recommend Seven Mile Beach.

GREAT RESORTS. Grand Cayman is known for its condominiums, but the island is also home to several grand resorts. Clients looking for full-service accommodations with amenities ranging from business centers to spas to fitness facilities will find them along Seven Mile Beach.

SCUBA DIVING AND SNORKELING. Grand Cayman is a capital in the world of scuba diving and Seven Mile Beach sits at

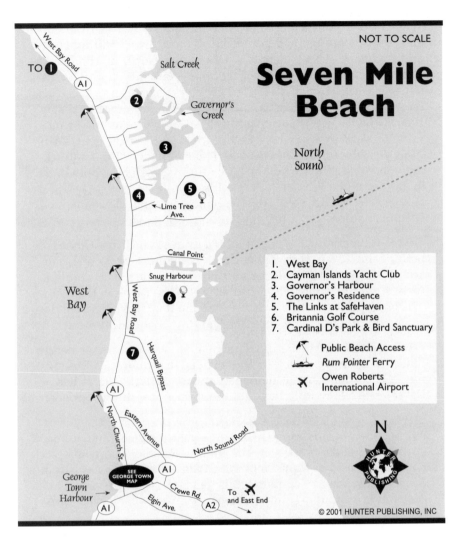

NOT TO SCALE

West Bay Road

TO ❶

Salt Creek

Seven Mile Beach

A1

❷

Governor's Creek

❸

North Sound

❹   ❺

Lime Tree Ave.

Canal Point

Snug Harbour

West Bay

West Bay Road

❻

1. West Bay
2. Cayman Islands Yacht Club
3. Governor's Harbour
4. Governor's Residence
5. The Links at SafeHaven
6. Britannia Golf Course
7. Cardinal D's Park & Bird Sanctuary

Public Beach Access

Rum Pointer Ferry

Owen Roberts International Airport

❼

Harquail Bypass

A1

North Church St.

Eastern Avenue

North Sound Road

N

SEE GEORGE TOWN MAP

A1

George Town Harbour

Crewe Rd.

To and East End

Elgin Ave.

A2

A1

© 2001 HUNTER PUBLISHING, INC

Grand Cayman

the hub of the action. Here, dive enthusiasts of all skill levels will find instruction, equipment rentals, and dive operators running trips to sites around the island. Several good dive sites are right in the area, including the Wreck of the *Oro Verde*, a ship used by drug smugglers and scuttled in 1980. The site is a favorite wreck for beginning divers because of its shallow position.

Numerous snorkel excursions are also offered by many operators; the most popular goes to **Stingray City**. Trips often include drinks and lunch following the snorkeling adventure.

SHOPPING. Although not as extensive as the shopping in George Town, there are plenty of diversions along West Bay Road. **Coconut Place**, **West Shore Center**, and **Galleria Plaza** are some of the top shopping areas. The Marriott, Westin Casuarina, and

Treasure Island Resort each have numerous shops featuring jewelry, resort clothing, and gift items. Jewelry lovers will find several excellent shops, including **Chests of Gold**, at the Hyatt Regency and the Westin, offering numismatic jewelry set in 18-karat gold. **Venture Gallery**, in the West Shore Center, also has an enormous selection of rare coins and coin jewelry. **Mitzi's**, in Bay Harbor Center, specializes in fine jewelry, including beautiful gold work by Carrera y Carrera, all in 18 karat gold. **24-K Mon Jewelers**, with locations at Treasure Island Resort, Buckingham Square (in front of the Hyatt Regency), and Cayman Falls (across from the Westin), offers coins, diamonds, gemstones, and gold jewelry. Black coral, pearls, hand-enameled cloisonné, and custom creations are other specialties.

GOLF. Golfers are challenged at two courses on Grand Cayman, both in the Seven Mile Beach area: **The Links at SafeHaven** and the Jack Nicklaus-designed **Britannia** course (Britannia is the world's first course designed for use of the Cayman ball). Under development at this writing is a nine-hole Greg Norman-designed private course at the **Ritz-Carlton Grand Cayman**.

FINE DINING. After a day of shopping, watersports, or beach fun, many travelers look to the island's fine dining as the evening's entertainment. Caymanian cuisine reflects the riches of the sea and Seven Mile Beach offers several fine dining options.

SUNSET AND DINNER CRUISES. Another good option for romantically-minded travelers are the many sunset and dinner cruises that sail along Seven Mile Beach. Red Sail Sports offers a sunset cruise from Rum Point on Sundays and other days from Seven Mile Beach. Complimentary appetizers are served; a full cash bar is available. Dinner cruises are also available with three courses.

NIGHTLIFE. The best nightlife on the island is found along Seven Mile Beach, from comedy clubs to discos.

Adventures

■ On Foot

Golf

The Links at SafeHaven, (Derek Nash, Golf Pro), PO Box 1311 GT, Grand Cayman, ☎ 345-949-5988, fax 345-949-5457, is the only championship 18-hole golf course in the Cayman Islands. This par 71 course has tournaments scheduled throughout the year; call

Seven Mile Beach.

for current list. Rates average US $100 for 18 holes, US $65 for nine holes. Shoe and cart rental are available (golf carts are mandatory and operators must be at least 17 years old and have a valid driver's license; cart rental runs US $20 per person). Men are required to wear shirts with collar and sleeves; women must wear a shirt to cover shoulders. Golf carts are mandatory and operators must be at least 17 years old and have a valid driver's license. Services at the course include a golf pro for lessons, golf shop, putting greens, chipping and bunker practice areas, aqua driving range, open-air patio bar, and The Links Restaurant for lunch and dinner (reservations suggested; ☎ 345-949-5988).

AUTHOR TIP

The goal of most golfers may be to drive the ball as far as it can go, but that task becomes a little more difficult with the Cayman ball. Designed to go only half as far as a regular ball, this tricky orb makes the best use of the small course area on the island.

At the Hyatt Regency Grand Cayman, the **Britannia** course (Robert Cummings, Golf Pro, PO Box 1588 GT, Grand Cayman, ☎ 345-949-1234, fax 345-949-8528) was designed by Jack Nicklaus. This links-style course, with the challenges of its seaside location, includes blind tee shots, pot bunkers, and two-tiered greens. On the fifth hole, golfers shoot over the Caribbean waters. This course can be played as a nine-hole championship course, an 18-hole executive course, or an 18-hole Cayman ball course. The course is available for regulation play (par 70) on Tuesday, Thursday, Saturday and Sunday afternoons. Players can book times on Monday, Wednesday, Friday and Sunday mornings for executive play (par 57). Rates are US $60 for nine holes or $100 for 18 holes for regulation play; US $75 for 18 holes, executive play. For advance starting times, ☎ 345-949-1234. Tournaments are scheduled throughout the year; call for a current list.

When completed, the new **Ritz-Carlton Grand Cayman** will be home to a nine-hole Greg Norman-designed private golf course. For an update on the completion of the course, call ☎ 800-241-3333 or see www.ritzcarlton.com.

Bowling

For bowling buffs, Grand Cayman is now home to the **Stingray Bowling Centre and Arcade** (☎ 345-945-4444, fax 345-949-6900, www.stingraybowling.com). Located on West Bay Road just north of the Strand Shopping Centre, the 10-lane facility features family bowling, an arcade, a pro-shop, snack bar, and more. The cost is CI $4 (about US $5) per game, CI $3 (about US $3.75) for adult rental shoes, and CI $2.50 (about US $3.10) for junior shoe rental. Children under 12 must be accompanied by an adult. The center is open Monday through Thursday from 11:30 am until 11:30 pm, Friday from 11:30 am until 1 am, and weekends from 11:30 am until midnight.

Miniature Golf

Miniature Golf, West Bay Road in front of the Hyatt Regency, Seven Mile Beach, ☎ 345-949-1474. Don't have the time or skills to tackle one of Cayman's golf courses? This fun mini-golf course might be a good alternative (and it's very popular with the younger travelers). The course has a jungle theme complete with elephants and even a waterfall.

■ In the Water

Scuba

 Just beyond the sand, much of Seven Mile Beach drops off into spectacular dive sites. For a list of dive operators on Grand Cayman, see pages 71-73.

Spanish Anchor: This dive site, located at the northern end of Seven Mile Beach, is named for the old anchor that's seen embedded in coral here.

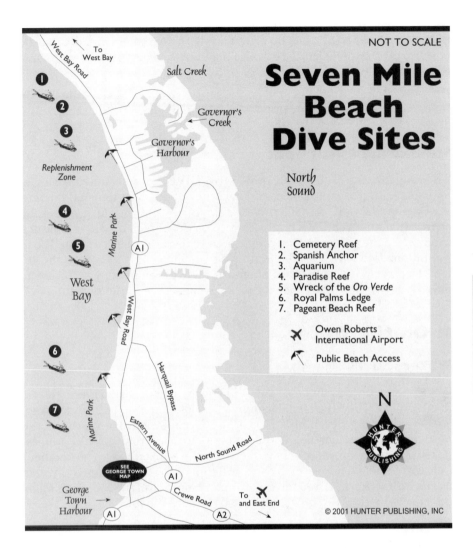

NOT TO SCALE

Seven Mile Beach Dive Sites

To West Bay

West Bay Road

Salt Creek

Governor's Creek

Governor's Harbour

North Sound

Replenishment Zone

Marine Park

A1

West Bay

West Bay Road

1. Cemetery Reef
2. Spanish Anchor
3. Aquarium
4. Paradise Reef
5. Wreck of the *Oro Verde*
6. Royal Palms Ledge
7. Pageant Beach Reef

✈ Owen Roberts International Airport

⛏ Public Beach Access

Marine Park

Harquail Bypass

Eastern Avenue

North Sound Road

N

SEE GEORGE TOWN MAP

A1

George Town Harbour

A1

Crewe Road

To and East End ✈

A2

© 2001 HUNTER PUBLISHING, INC

Grand Cayman

The Aquarium: With a name like The Aquarium, this 30- to 50-foot dive has to be good. Look for a wide variety of fish off the upper end of Seven Mile Beach. Goatfish, snapper, parrotfish, and more await on this beginner's dive.

Paradise Reef: Just north of the wreck of the *Oro Verde*, this 40- to 50-foot dive is the home of "Fang," a large dog snapper seen by many divers.

Wreck of the *Oro Verde*: About half a mile off the beach at Villas of the Galleon, the *Oro Verde* is a favorite with beginners because of its shallow position (25 to 50 feet). The ship was used by drug smugglers (*Oro Verde* means "green gold" in Spanish, so we'll let you draw your own conclusions about its cargo) and in 1980 was scuttled. Today, the gold is surrounded by rich marine life; the high that divers get from the myriad colors is a completely legal one.

Royal Palms Ledge: This shallow area, offshore from the Royal Palms Beach Club (page 181), is a favorite with both snorkelers and divers; the reef starts at 46 feet. This site is also popular with night divers who come for a view of shrimp and squid.

Pageant Beach Reef: Located on the southern end of Seven Mile Beach, this spur and groove site can be accessed from shore by snorkelers and divers.

Submarine Excursions

SEAmagine, ☎ 877-252-6262 or 345-916-DIVE, www.seamagine.com, e-mail marketing@seamagine.com. This is one of the most unusual tours in the Cayman Islands, sort of a private submarine that you can even get the chance to maneuver. Each trip takes two passengers in a glass bubble of a cabin while the pilot is on the *outside* of the cabin in scuba gear. You'll be in communication with the pilot at all times as he points out fish on the 40-foot-deep reef. The tour takes about an hour to complete; you'll need to make reservations to arrange for pickup along Seven Mile Beach.

■ On the Water

Watersports

 Non-divers can enjoy the undersea world aboard a glass-bottom boat. The **MV *Reef Roamer*,** a 34-foot, 26-passenger vessel, travels along Seven Mile Beach. It offers a look at both natural and man-made attractions below the water's surface, from colorful tropical fish and coral to shipwrecks usually viewed by scuba divers. The one-hour tour costs US $25; for reservations, ☎ 345-947-4786. For more active fun on the water's surface, rent a WaveRunner from one of the operators along the beach. Prices average about US $40 for a half-hour.

Sailing

Many watersports operators run sailing trips out to Stingray City (see pages 141-142). One of the largest is **Red Sail Sports Grand Cayman** (☎ 800-255-6425, www.redsail.com), located at the Hyatt Regency, Westin Casuarina, and Marriott. Along with a full menu of water toys, from Hobies to water skis to banana boats, Red Sail Sports also operates the *Spirit of Ppalu*. This 65-foot catamaran was originally built as a racer; it now cuts a sleek path through the waters of the North Sound, sailing to Stingray City and also offering sunset cruises and dinner sails. The catamaran has a glass bottom for a sneak peak at what lies below. They also have four dive boats. We journeyed aboard the *Spirit of Ppalu* and enjoyed a quiet sail through the channels that lead out into the North Sound. In spite of choppy conditions that day, we had a smooth sail and would recommend the catamarans for anyone who is prone to seasickness; the twin hulls make for a smoother ride. Rates on the *Spirit of Ppalu* are US $60.50 for a sail to Stingray City, including lunch.

Windsurfing

Windsurfing is enjoyed along Seven Mile Beach, although real aficionados venture to more challenging waters elsewhere on the island. If you do windsurf at Seven Mile Beach, be on the constant lookout for swimmers and snorkelers (while snorkeling, we once had a near miss as one windsurfer skimmed by way too close). Prices average about $20 per hour for windsurfing and equipment.

Sailboards Caribbean, ☎ 345-916-2820. With locations at West Bay Road at the Public Beach and the Grand Caymanian, this operator is a Mistral certified school.

Yachting

Located on Governors Creek just off the North Sound, the **Cayman Islands Yacht Club** (PO Box 30985, SMB, Grand Cayman, BWI, ☎ 345-945-4322, fax 345-4432, e-mail ciyc@candw.ky, has full facilities for travelers arriving by yacht. The 152-slip operation offers berths, fuel, electricity, and water hook-ups for craft up to 70 feet.

Sea Kayaking

Sea kayaks are a fun and fairly easy way to enjoy the water. Rent a kayak for an hour or two and paddle your way along the coastline, enjoying the casuarina-dotted strip of sand and a view of the accommodations that cling to this precious real estate. One- and two-person sea kayaks are available for rent from vendors for US $15-20 per hour.

■ In the Air

Parasailing

 The only parasailing in the Cayman Islands is offered along Seven Mile Beach. Soaring up high above the waves can be a thrilling adventure. Prices for parasailing average about $45.

PARASAILING OPERATORS

Abank's Watersports & Tours, Ltd. . . . . ☎ 345-945-1444

Aqua Delights . . . . ☎ 345-945-4786

Bob Soto's Diving Ltd. . . . . ☎ 800-262-7686

Cayman Skyriders . . . . ☎ 345-949-8745

Kirk Sea Tours and Watersports . . . . ☎ 345-949-6986

Grand Cayman

Parasailing Professionals	☎ 345-916-2953
Red Sail Sports	☎ 345-949-8745

■ On Horseback

 Honey Suckle Trail Rides (☎ 345-947-7976 or 916-3363), offers rides for both experienced and new riders with special attention given to children. Both western and English saddles are available, as are a variety of horses from thoroughbred to quarter horse. Guided trail rides and sunset rides are popular; fees start at US $65.

Experienced and new riders can enjoy beach rides with **Pampered Ponies** (☎ 345-945-2262 or 916-2540, fax 345-945-2262, www.ponies.ky). The operator offers early morning as well as romantic sunset beach rides. Moonlight excursions are especially popular, and private trips are also available. Fees start at US $75 for a one-hour beach ride; private rides are US $85 per person. Moonlight rides are US $100 per person for one hour.

Nicki's Private Beach Rides (☎ 345-916-3530 or 945-5839) offers guided 90-minute trips along quiet trails, in groups of no more than four. No children under 12 are accepted; transportation to the departure site is

Caymanian gingerbread house.

included. In summer, fees begin at CI $50 or US $63; winter rates are CI $56 or US $70.

Cultural Excursions

Visitors staying at the **Hyatt Regency Grand Cayman Resort and Villas** (☎ 800-233-1234, 345-949-1234, fax 345-949-5526) can get a glimpse into Caymanian history and customs in a unique cultural program. Local experts introduce guests to traditional Caymanian activities – such as coconut husking, rope making, and weaving silver thatch palms into baskets and hats – while local historians recall the island's past.

"We are working closely with island historians and community artists to bring the real flavor and charm of the Cayman Islands to our activities," says general manager Doug Sears. "Culture is an important part of the island experience and, with these activities, guests will have a better understanding of island life." The resort also offers horticultural tours (see pages 165-167).

Sightseeing

Governor's House, West Bay Road; not open to the public. This beachfront house was built in 1972 as the home for the Governor, appointed by the Queen.

Shopping

From books to jewelry to crafts, there is plenty to entice even the most seasoned shopper along West Bay Road.

■ Malls

Seven Mile Beach is home to several large, open-air malls that offer a selection of souvenirs ranging from T-shirts to tanzanite necklaces. The following malls are popular shopping stops, starting at the south end of Seven Mile Beach:

- **Seven Mile Shops**, just north of Sleep Inn Hotel
- **West Shore Center**, north of Grand Cayman Marriott Beach Resort

- **Galleria Plaza**, at the Galleria Loop just north of West Shore Center
- **The Strand**, just north of The Caribbean Club
- **The Falls**, across from the Westin Casuarina

■ Specialty Shops

Some of the top shopping stops include:

- **The Book Nook II**, Galleria Plaza, West Bay Road, ☎ 345-945-4686. This bookstore is one of our favorite stops on Seven Mile Beach. We always find a good selection of Caribbean guidebooks and cookbooks here. It also has a large children's section, including toys for those restless young travelers.
- **Chests of Gold**, Hyatt Regency, ☎ 345-949-8846, and Westin Casuarina, ☎ 345-949-5330. Numismatic jewelry, diamond creations, and champlevé enamel designs are set in primarily 18-karat gold at these popular shops.
- **LaHavana Restaurant and Cigar Emporium**, Queen's Court Plaza, Seven Mile Beach, ☎ 345-949-2345. This Cuban restaurant also has a showroom of Cuban cigars, including Monte Cristo, Cohiba, Romeo y Julieta and more.
- **La Perla**, The Strand, Seven Mile Beach, ☎ 345-945-4979. This exclusive boutique features La Perla Italian swimwear, lingerie and resort wear.
- **Mitzi's**, Bay Harbor Center, West Bay Road, ☎ 345-945-5014. Mitzi's specializes in fine jewelry, including beautiful gold work by Carrera y Carrera, all in 18-karat gold.
- **Pure Art Gallery and Gifts**, Hyatt Regency, West Bay Road, ☎ 345-945-5633. All types of Caymanian and Caribbean art are showcased in this gallery, along with a variety of crafts. We purchased an inexpensive woven rug with the emblem of the Cayman Islands here; you'll also find a good selection of rum cakes.
- **Venture Gallery**, West Shore Center, West Bay Road, ☎ 345-949-8657. This show has an enormous selection of rare coins, including shipwreck coins, and coin jewelry.
- **24-K Mon Jewelers**, Treasure Island Resort, ☎ 345-949-9729; Buckingham Square (in front of Hyatt Regency), ☎ 345-949-1499; and Cayman Falls (across from Westin), ☎ 345-945-7000. Coins, diamonds, gemstones, and gold jewelry are the specialty of these shops. Black coral, pearls, hand enameled cloisonné, and custom creations are other specialties.

Where to Stay

Seven Mile Beach boasts the lion's share of accommodations in the Cayman Islands. You'll find both luxury resorts and budget accommodations, lavish condominiums and economical motels. Not all accommodations are on the beach itself, but, with public beaches throughout, none are more than a few minutes' walk to the water.

ACCOMMODATIONS PRICE SCALE
Prices listed are for a standard room for one night during high season (expect prices to be as much as 40% lower during the low season). The price scale refers to US $.
$ . . . . Under $100
$$ . . . . $100-$200
$$$. . . . . Over $200

■ Hotels & Resorts

Comfort Suites and Resort, West Bay Road, ☎ 345-945-7300, fax 345-945-7400, e-mail comfort@candw.ky, www.caymancomfort.com, $$. This all-suites hotel is a good choice for those with an eye on the budget. A favorite with families, it features one- and two-bedroom units, each with two phone lines, a full kitchen, and a family atmosphere. Rooms are carpeted and cozy, each decorated in cool colors and opening onto enclosed hallways. Guests enjoy a free continental breakfast each morning as well as use of a fitness center, pool, pool bar, restaurant, dive shop, and guest laundry.

Hyatt Regency Grand Cayman, West Bay Road, ☎ 800-233-1234, 345-949-1234, fax 345-949-5526, www.hyatt.com, $$. One of Grand Cayman's most beautiful resorts, the Hyatt is located on both sides of the road. It has a private beach club with full watersports facilities. You may recognize parts of this resort from the movie *The Firm* (it's where Gene Hackman and Tom Cruise stayed).

"THE FIRM"

The first look that many visitors had of Grand Cayman was in the 1993 movie *The Firm*, starring Gene Hackman, Tom Cruise, Holly Hunter, and Jeanne Tripplehorn. The film included 350 local Caymanians as extras and prominently featured sites around the island.

Many of the scenes were shot at the Hyatt Regency. The pool bar, the garden, Loggia Lounge, the front drive, and other spots around the property were included in the film. Except for Tom Cruise, who rented a private home, the stars stayed at the Hyatt Regency and Britannia Villas. The crew members were stationed down at the Sleep Inn and George Town Villas, and the Paramount offices were set up in what's now the Clarion Grand Pavilion. Other locations that appear in the movie include:

Cheeseburger Reef: Check out the characters of Avery and Mitch scuba diving this shallow west coast site during their first stay on the island (Hackman and Cruise actually did the dive shot themselves. Bob Soto's Diving Ltd. provided the watersports services for the film and their *Holiday Diver* custom dive boat was repainted as *Abanks Dive Lodge*).

George Town: The intersection of Harbour Drive and Cardinal Avenue was the location of a phone booth that the Gene Hackman character uses as Mitch (Cruise) first sees the Abanks Dive Lodge advertisement.

Abanks Dive Lodge: This set was constructed on North Sound in Newlands. The site is still standing.

Hyatt Regency Aquas Pool Bar: The Jeanne Tripplehorn character surprises Avery (Hackman) at this bar.

Movie buffs, enjoy!

In the original section of the hotel, guests can select from 236 rooms, many overlooking the Britannia golf course or the private marina. Standard rooms, each carpeted and featuring a soft Caribbean color scheme, include a mini-bar, satellite color television, coffee makers, electronic key card system, direct dial telephones with voice mail, in-room safe, ironing board, and hairdryer. Along with standard rooms, the property has 50 one- to four-bedroom villas and 10 bi-level suites. The Britannia Villas are especially popular with families and offer all the hotel amenities except turndown service. A separate Regency Club offers 44 rooms that come with complimentary continental breakfast, evening cocktails and hors d'oeuvres, concierge service, upgraded amenities and linens, and use of the Regency Club lounge.

More rooms are available in a $15 million addition on Seven Mile Beach. This section offers 53 luxury beachfront suites, including 44 one-bedroom and nine two-bedroom units. These suites feature a separate living room with a dining area, wet bar, work station with two phone lines and upgraded amenities. All suites have sea views, and are served by a dedicated concierge.

The complex highlights a new landscaped pool area with bronze sea turtle sculptures, waterfalls, and three freshwater pools with mosaic tile designs of stingrays and other marine life.

The Hyatt also offers one of the island's most extensive children's programs. "With our Camp Hyatt program, children enjoy more than just fun activities," noted Doug Sears, general manager. "They also learn about a new place, its local flowers, animals, art and history." Activities range from nature walks to spot the island's blue iguanas and parrots to visits to the Turtle Farm to shell painting. The 1,800-square-foot Caymanian-style Camp Hyatt House includes a playground, interactive computer games, and a big-screen television for movie viewing. The program is offered daily from November 1 through August 31, and weekends from September 1 through October 31. Children age three to 12 years can enroll for the price of $62.50 for a complete day and night session. Some activities incur an additional charge. The resort also offers cribs and babysitting services.

The Hyatt Regency Grand Cayman offers a unique cultural program to introduce guests to the island's history, culture, flora and fauna. Horticultural tours, led by the resort's landscaping experts, point out sea grape, travelers' palm, silver thatch palm, and more. For a peek at the island's past, visitors can talk with a local historian. For more hands-on experiences, a coconut husker teaches the secrets of obtaining the edible portions of this thick fruit, while local artists show the skills needed to make rope, baskets and hats from silver thatch palms.

Holiday Inn, West Bay Road across from the Public Beach, ☎ 800-HOLI-DAY, 345-946-4433, fax 345-946-4434, www.holidayinn.com, $$. We've got fond memories of the old Holiday Inn. The huge tree and the funky beach bar. The Barefoot Man. The fun, family-oriented atmosphere. Alas, that hotel is no more, torn down to make way for the Ritz-Carlton Grand Cayman. Fortunately, however, the Holiday Inn has been rebuilt and is now one of the newest hotels on Seven Mile Beach. Not as atmospheric as its old self, this hotel is located across the street from the beach but still offers good bargains for families. Rooms are standard Holiday Inn fare, with mini-bar, iron and ironing board, satellite TV, coffee maker, and hair dryer.

Marriott Grand Cayman, ☎ 800-223-6388, 345-949-0088, fax 345-949-0288, www.marriotthotels.com, $$. Located two miles from George Town and about four miles from the airport, this convenient property (formerly the Radisson) sits on a beautiful stretch of Seven Mile Beach. Swimmers and snorkelers can enjoy calm waters and a small coral reef just offshore, learn scuba diving, or book dive trips through the on-site shop. Oceanfront rooms have private balconies with good beach views and are worth a somewhat long walk to the elevators in this 309-room hotel. Facilities include casual and fine dining, pool and hot tub, dive shop, WaveRunners, windsurfing boards, shopping arcade, and a full-service spa.

Ritz-Carlton Grand Cayman, West Bay Road, ☎ 800-241-3333, www.ritzcarlton.com, $$$. There's great excitement over the construction of this new property, under construction on the site of the former Holiday Inn. Scheduled to open mid-2002, the 366-room resort and 71-room condominium facility will feature three pools, a nine-hole Greg Norman-designed private golf course, a full-service 17,000-square-foot spa and fitness center, watersports, retail promenade, and a beauty salon.

Sleep Inn, West Bay Road, ☎ 800-SLEEP INN, 345-949-9111, fax 345-949-6699, $$. If you're just looking for a centrally located place to lay your head after a day of fun in the sun, the Sleep Inn is a good choice. This chain motel is just outside of George Town along the Seven Mile Beach stretch (the hotel itself is not on the beach). Rooms have air conditioning and telephones. The property has a pool and whirlpool, poolside bar and grill, dive shop, and watersports center.

Sunshine Suites Hotel, off West Bay Road at SafeHaven, ☎ 877-786-1110, 345-949-3000, fax 345-949-1200, www.sunshinesuites.com, $. When we first heard about this new resort, we didn't think we'd be impressed. After all, it's not located on Seven Mile Beach. Then we had a look at it and changed our minds: this is a great spot for travelers with an eye on their pocketbook who still want to be right in the heart of the action. These Caribbean lemon-tinted buildings offer studio rooms, deluxe rooms, and one-bedroom suites (our favorite), each with fully equipped kitchens, cable TV and movie channels. Behind the central area stands a small pool with lockers for dive gear; you're also in walking distance of the Links at Safe-Haven. Guests also have use of World Gym's facilities, a short drive away. The resort is located behind The Falls shopping center, home of Legendz and Eats, and across West Bay Road from the Westin Casuarina.

Treasure Island Resort, West Bay Road, ☎ 800-203-0775, 345-949-7777, fax 345-949-8489, www.treasureislandresort.net, $$. This 280-room resort includes an offshore snorkel trail. Now starting to look a little tired around the edges, the hotel nonetheless has a pretty pool area with waterfall cascading down from the third-floor restaurant. Facilities include two freshwater pools, two whirlpools, tennis, dive operation, shopping, informal dining, bar and lounge.

Westin Casuarina Resort, West Bay Road, ☎ 800-228-3000, 345-945-3800, fax 345-945-3804, www.westin.com or www.westincasuarina.com, $$$. This luxurious hotel is built on a strip of beach bordered by willowy casuarina trees. The hotel has 340 guest rooms, most with breathtaking views of the sea from their balconies. It has the feel of a conference property, with a slightly dress-up atmosphere in the main lobby. Facilities include beachfront, casual and fine dining restaurants, pools, whirlpools, tennis, fitness facilities, beauty salons, masseuse and masseur. Rates are high, as would be expected in a resort of this caliber.

The Westin Casuarina Resort is also home to the Westin Kids Club. Upon check-in, families receive a Westin Kids Club sports bottle (or, for families with young children, a tippy cup), which can be filled with complimentary beverages at mealtimes. Young visitors also receive coloring books and bath toys; special amenities are also available for infants. Parents receive safety kits with adhesive bandages, electrical outlet covers, identification bracelets, and a list of local emergency phone numbers. Jogging strollers are available upon request at no additional cost. Whenever possible, guest rooms are set up in advance with high chairs, cribs and other items as appropriate.

DID YOU KNOW?

The casuarina trees found along the Westin's beach have long been used by fishermen offshore to get their bearings.

■ Condos & Villas

Anchorage, 1989 West Bay Road, ☎ 345-945-4088, fax 345-945-5001, www.imexpages.com/anchorage, $$-$$$. These 15 villa units are located on the northern end of Seven Mile Beach, almost to West Bay. Each of the two-bedroom units is decorated in cool Caribbean colors; all include air-conditioning, ceiling fans, kitchens, laundry, maid service, television, and VCR. Guest facilities include a pool, snorkeling and tennis.

Avalon, West Bay Road, ☎ 345-945-4171, fax 345-945-4189, www.cayman.org/avalon, $$$. Located just south of the public beach, these elegant condominiums are some of the island's most exclusive. Each of the 14 units has three bedrooms, air-conditioning, ceiling fans, full kitchen, maid service, TV, and VCR; guest facilities include pool, snorkeling and tennis.

Aqua Bay Club, West Bay Road, ☎ 345-945-4728, fax 345-945-5681, www.aquabayclub.com, $$$. This 21-unit condominium resort (formerly Grand Bay Club) on Seven Mile Beach, recently underwent an extensive renovation. "A total remodeling within the past year, including new landscaping as well as a new roof, brought our property well above the standard," said Walter Puk, director of marketing. Honeymooners, divers, golfers, families and couples are target markets for this property with one- and two-bedroom oceanfront units. Each unit has a view of the sea and is fully equipped. Guests facilities include a freshwater pool, tennis, and Jacuzzi.

Britannia Villas, West Bay Road, ☎ 800-223-1234, 345-949-1234, fax 345-949-8032, www.britanniavillas.com, $$$. Britannia Villas lie beyond the Hyatt Regency guest rooms, adjacent to the Britannia golf course (across the road from the beach but connected with a covered walkway above the traffic). The Britannia Villas are longtime villa favorites, especially popular with families; they include all the hotel amenities, with six pools, restaurants, beach bar, spa, fitness center, tennis, and a children's club. Along with standard rooms, there are 50 one- to four-bedroom villas and 10 bi-level suites.

Caribbean Club, West Bay Road, ☎ 345-945-4099, fax 345-945-4443, www.caribclub.com, $$. Eighteen one- and two-bedroom pastel pink villas offer seaside relaxation. Six of the villas are beachfront; others have a garden view. All rooms have a full kitchen, air conditioning, ceiling fan, TV, phone, dining room, and furnished patio. Facilities here include tennis. When you get hungry, head to Lantana's, one of the island's top restaurants.

Cayman Villas, Airport Road, ☎ 800-235-5888, 345-945-4144, fax 345-949-7471, www.caymanvillas.com, $-$$$$. Some of Seven Mile Beach's most exclusive properties are handled by Cayman Villas. "More and more private houses and exclusive condos are being built," notes Penny Cumber, managing director for Cayman Villas. "Both houses and condos are becoming more deluxe; many have a private pool, a Jacuzzi, or a gym."

Cayman Villas' offerings include the **Great House** on Seven Mile Beach. This property, used by *The Firm* filmmakers, features beachfront balconies, three bedrooms, and a den that can become a private fourth bedroom; there is one king, one queen, two twin beds, and two day-beds. Three-and-a-half baths, satellite TV and VCR, kitchen with microwave, dishwasher, ice maker, wine cellar, and washer/dryer are found in the apartment as well. Guests have use of a freshwater pool, tennis courts, and gym on premises. There is a minimum one-month stay.

Cayman Villas also offers another luxury property away from the hustle and bustle of Seven Mile Beach; the **Green House**, on tranquil Spotts Beach, is a new private home on the beachfront about five minutes from the airport in George Town. The house includes four oceanview bedrooms (two masters each with king bed), four full ensuite bathrooms and a half-bath, living and dining rooms with high ceilings and French doors to let in ocean breezes, kitchen with microwave, waste disposal, ice maker, and dishwasher, utility room, satellite TV and VCR, freshwater pool, and housekeeping services.

■ Rentals

In addition to its most luxurious properties, Cayman Villas also has options for the average traveler. Over 100 properties, some starting at $99 a night, are represented. "Cayman Villas specializes in beachfront condos and private houses ranging from economy to deluxe, from studios to seven bedrooms. Most condos are on Seven Mile Beach."

Properties are closely inspected and monitored to maintain high standards. The Department of Tourism and the departments of fire and environment also inspect furnishings, linens, flooring, woodwork, metal fixtures, landscaping, beach, quality of drinkable water, and check fire extinguishers and smoke detectors.

Crescent Point, West Bay Road, ☎ 800-486-9428, 345-945-2243, fax 345-945-2263, www.crescentpoint.com, $$$. Located on the south end of Seven Mile Beach, the resort offers 27 oceanfront three-bedroom villas. Along with the beach, there's a sculptured free-form Oceanic pool, Jacuzzi and a fully-equipped fitness center. We especially liked the fact that each villa offers a private, screened patio with room for outdoor dining; villas are equipped with full kitchens, washer/dryer, central air conditioning, a VCR, two color televisions and telephones.

Discovery Point Club, West Bay Road, ☎ 345-945-4724, fax 345-945-5051, $$. This beachside condominium complex offers 45 suites. The one- and two-bedroom apartments have air conditioning, screened porches or balconies, telephone, and TV. Most units have kitchens, but some of the garden-view hotel-type units are available without kitchens. Facilities include Jacuzzi, pool, and tennis. Children under six stay free.

Grand Caymanian Beach Club and Resort, Crystal Harbour Drive at SafeHaven, ☎ 345-949-3100, fax 345-949-3161, www.grandcaymanian.ky, $$$. This timeshare is a joint venture between Royal Resorts and the local Thompson Group. The resort offers 44 "flexivillas" in a variety of sizes, as well as four grand villas and six townhouses. Each includes a full kitchen, living room, and dining room; full maid service and room service are available. The resort includes a swimming pool, children's pool, waterfront restaurant, on-site scuba diving, snorkeling, deep-sea fishing, WaveRunners, windsurfing, a private dock for boating and fishing, a kids' club and concierge services. The resort is on the North Sound, not on Seven Mile Beach, although it offers shuttle service to the beach. Its convenient location to SafeHaven makes the Grand Caymanian a favorite with golfers.

Georgetown Villas, West Bay Road, one mile from George Town, ☎ 345-949-5172, fax 345-949-0256, www.georgetownvillas.com, $$$. Located on the southern end of Seven Mile Beach, this 54-unit condo offers two-bedroom, two-bath units. The red-roofed buildings, each three stories tall, overlook the water and manicured grounds. The guest units each include air conditioning, cable TV, stereos, dishwasher, microwave, ceiling fans, a balcony or patio, and a cool Caribbean décor. Guests have use of a freshwater swimming pool and barbecue grill.

Grandview Condominiums, West Bay Road, ☎ 800-327-8777, 345-945-4511, fax 345-949-7515, www.grandviewcondos.com, $$$. This 69-unit complex is one of Cayman's newest. Located right on the beach, the complex has 63 two-bedroom units and six three-bedroom units, all with air-conditioning, cable TV, full kitchen, and screened patio. Guests find plenty of activity here: two tennis courts (including one lit for night owls), fitness room, and a large pool with Jacuzzi. You can even get married here.

Harbour Heights, West Bay Road, ☎ 345-945-4295, fax 345-945-4522, $$-$$$. These 20 beachfront apartments are surrounded by tall palms and tropical blooms. All units include two bedrooms, two baths, air conditioning, cable TV, ceiling fans, living/dining area, full kitchen, and a private balcony or patio overlooking the sea. A large kidney-shaped pool is just steps away from the units and includes a poolhouse.

Indies Suites, West Bay Road, ☎ 800-654-3130, 345-945-5025, fax 345-945-5024, $$$. Although it doesn't have a beachfront location, this property is a good choice if you're looking for suite accommodations. All rooms include either a king-size or two double beds and a full-size kitchen equipped for four. They also have satellite TV, telephone, storage locker for dive gear, and a convertible sofa bed.

The family-operated all-suites hotel has a dive shop and an introductory scuba diving course is free. There's a pool, hot tub, cabana bar, boutique, mini-mart, and complimentary continental breakfast daily.

Lacovia, West Bay Road, ☎ 345-949-7599, fax 345-949-0172, $$-$$$. This condominium complex offers one-, two-, and three-bedroom suites. You'll have a choice of oceanfront or courtyard (the most economical) and all guests have access to a freshwater swimming pool and tennis. Daily maid service is offered. You won't find any dining on the property but this complex is within walking distance of the Westin and several shopping malls.

Plantana Condominiums, West Bay Road, ☎ 345-945-4430, fax 345-945-5076, $$. This 49-unit complex offers elegant condominium accommodations just steps from the beach. Two- and four-guest units are available, all with air conditioning, ceiling fans, telephones, television, kitchens, maid service and laundry facilities.

Ritz-Carlton Condominiums, West Bay Road, ☎ 800-241-3333, www.ritzcarlton.com. Located adjacent to the 366-room resort, the condominium property will include an integrated 71-room condominium facility. Guests will have use of a nine-hole Greg Norman-designed private golf course, a full-service 17,000-square-foot Spa and Fitness Center, watersports, retail promenade, and a beauty salon. At press time, completion was planned for mid-2002.

Seven Mile Beach Resort and Club, West Bay Road, ☎ 345-949-0332, fax 345-949-0331, www.7mile.ky, $$$. Located inland but with private beach facilities, this condominium property has two-bedroom, two-bath units. Each has private balcony, air conditioning, telephone, cable TV, VCR, and a fully equipped kitchen. The complex includes a freshwater pool, Jacuzzi, lighted tennis court, outdoor grills, and children's play area. Seven Mile Watersports arranges trips to Stingray City and has complete dive facilities, including resort and certification courses. Rates are for one to four people (children under 12 free).

Silver Sands Condominiums, 2131 West Bay Road, ☎ 800-327-8777, 345-949-3343, fax 345-949-1223, www.silversandscondos.com, $$$. This complex consists of two- and three-bedroom units, each with full kitchens, telephones, air conditioning, ceiling fans, cable TV, and private patios or balconies. The complex has a beautiful stretch of beach with snorkeling right offshore; other activities on property include tennis, and beach volleyball. A freshwater pool has a nice beach view. All rooms have daily maid service except on Sundays; laundry facilities are available.

Tamarind Bay Condominiums, West Bay Road, ☎ 800-698-6593, 345-949-4593, fax 345-945-2761, $$$. This 28-condo complex is located on the beach. The tile floor units, decorated in Caribbean colors, have two bedrooms, two full bathrooms, a den, living room, full kitchen, and a screened patio. Guest facilities include tennis and a freshwater pool.

Tarquynn Manor Condominiums, 1883 West Bay Road, ☎ 800-247-9900, 800-327-8777, 345-945-4038, fax 345-945-5060, www.armadainteractive.com/tarquynn/index.html, $$$. This 20-unit complex is located on the north end of Seven Mile Beach. Targeting families as well as couples and singles, the condominium complex is right on the beach. All units include a full kitchen, air conditioning, cable TV, ceiling fan, and safe. Two-bedroom units have one bath, while three-bedroom units have two. Guests have use of a game room, beach, and freshwater pool.

Villas of the Galleon, West Bay Road, ☎ 800-328-0025 or 800-327-7777, 345-945-4433, fax 345-945-4705, www.villasofthegalleon.com, $$ (two to six guests). Within walking distance of Seven Mile Beach hotspots, this 74-unit complex is popular for its well-furnished units. Rooms include air conditioning, telephone, TV, kitchen, laundry facilities, and maid services.

Where to Eat

The Cayman Islands offer a wide variety of dining options, especially on Grand Cayman, where visitors can opt for anything from a three-course gourmet meal to fast food. Typically, vacationers at Seven Mile Beach should expect to pay about US $45-$90 per person for a three-course meal with wine in one of the island's finest restaurants; about US $10-$20 for a casual lunch or dinner. Fast food lunches or snacks can be obtained for about US $5-$10 per person.

DINING PRICE SCALE
The scale below indicates the approximate cost of a meal for one person, including drink and gratuity. The price scale refers to US $.
$ . . . . Under $15 per person
$$. . . . . $15-$30 per person
$$$ . . . . $31-$40 per person

■ American

Lone Star Bar, West Bay Road near Hyatt Regency, ☎ 345-945-5175, $-$$. This bar, next to the Hyatt Regency entrance, was named one of the "World's Top 100 Bars" by *Newsweek* magazine. The atmosphere is rollicking and fun, a mix of both locals and vacationers who come to enjoy a drink and some conversation in this T-shirt decorated bar. Every inch of available space seems to be occupied by the donated T-shirts as well as autographed memorabilia. The Lone Star is often patronized by visiting celebrities. The adjoining restaurant, decorated as a 50s diner, features an All-You-Can-Eat Fajita Rita night on Monday and Thursday, a Cayman bargain. Take-out food is available, and there's also a kids' menu.

Eats, Falls Shopping Center, across from the Westin Casuarina, ☎ 345-945-5288, $$. The first time we dined at Eats, we were staying at the Westin Casuarina and were on the lookout for a place within walking distance (it was our first night on the island and we weren't looking forward to tackling left lane driving in the darkness). We scooted across West Bay Road to Eats and quickly discovered one of our favorite casual restaurants in the region. This eatery, decorated with movie memorabilia in a diner atmosphere, is a favorite with locals and residents. We enjoyed quesadillas and old fashioned burgers that first trip, but other dishes are equally tempting: chicken fajitas, catch of the day, shepherd's pie, stir fry, hot sandwiches, and more.

Legendz, Falls Shopping Center, across from the Westin Casuarina, ☎ 345-949-6887, $$. Legendz adjoins Eats (above) and the atmosphere is a little more adult, with quieter booths where you can enjoy a brew and a conversation while dining on the same menu as found next door.

■ Asian

Canton Chinese Restaurant, The Strand on West Bay Road, ☎ 345-945-3536, $. This five-star restaurant serves Cantonese and Szechwan dishes (with a menu that includes over 100 choices; save some time for this!). The restaurant is elegant, although take-out service is also available. Open for lunch and dinner daily, the restaurant closes between 3 and 5 pm. Reservations suggested.

Thai Orchid, Queens Court Plaza, West Bay Road, ☎ 345-949-7955, $$. Chefs from Thailand cook authentic dishes at this popular restaurant, which serves lunch and dinner. Traditional dishes such as pad Thai, khaw phad (fried rice with meat), pla tod lad pnk (deep-fried fish topped with chili sauce), and ped phad khing (duck stir-fried with ginger and vegetables) are also accompanied by many vegetarian dishes.

Golden Pagoda, West Bay Road across from the Marriott, ☎ 345-949-5475, $-$$. This casual restaurant serves Hakka-style cuisine with no MSG. Lunch is served weekdays and the daily luncheon buffet is a favorite with many locals. Dinner is served daily, and take-out is available.

■ Bars & Pubs

Big Daddy's, Queen's Court Plaza, ☎ 345-949-8511, $-$$. This microbrewery has both a restaurant (indoor) and a bar, and is open for breakfast, lunch and dinner. Entrées are a far cry from pub grub; look for seafood linguine, New York sirloin, fajitas, burgers, pizza, and more. This is the island's only real microbrewery, so save room to sample the pub's product.

Fidel Murphy's Irish Pub, Queens Court Plaza, West Bay Road, ☎ 345-949-5189, $$. You'll think you're in jolly old Ireland with a look at this pub menu: Irish stew, smoked salmon salad, mussels, fish and chips, chicken and mushroom pie, steak and Guinness pie, shepherds pie, and more. The pub has a happy hour on Wednesday and Friday nights with a free buffet and drink specials. Open from 10:30 am daily until midnight on Saturday and Sundays and until 1 am other nights.

Lone Star Bar and Grill, West Bay Road near Hyatt Regency, ☎ 345-945-5175, $-$$. This bar has a happy hour every weekday from 5-6:30; the atmosphere here is casual and fun. If there's a sporting event occurring somewhere in the world, it is probably televised here.

P.D.'s Pub, Galleria Plaza, West Bay Road, ☎ 345-949-7144, $. This fun bar, much like an English pub with its dark paneling and cozy atmosphere, serves up burgers, chicken wings, quesadillas, nachos and even seafood. It's an excellent place to check your e-mail; several computers give you access to the Internet for a low charge. Open for breakfast, lunch and dinner.

■ Breakfast

Big Daddy's, Queen's Court Plaza, ☎ 345-949-8511, $. Yes, it's a pub but if you overindulge the night before, Big Daddy's also makes a great breakfast that's guaranteed to wake you up and put some spring in your step. This restaurant serves breakfast from 8-11 am and has a large selection of omelets as well as eggs benedict, steak and eggs, pancakes, and other traditional offerings.

Eats, Falls Shopping Center, across from the Westin Casuarina, ☎ 345-945-5288, $. Drive by the Falls Shopping Center during breakfast hours and you'll see people waiting in front of Eats; they're in line for the breakfast that's made this place so popular. Along with omelets (everything from cheese to vegetarian to Spanish), breakfast offerings include pancake platters, pork chop combos, steak and eggs, and more. Breakfast is served starting at 6:30 am.

Ferdinand's, Westin Casuarina, West Bay Road, ☎ 345-945-3800, $$. This restaurant is pricey as breakfast goes, but popular especially for Sunday brunch. You can eat indoors or outside, although the dining area is enshrouded with netting to keep hungry birds out of your breakfast plate. Breakfast starts at 7 am daily and Sunday brunch is served 11:30 am-2 pm.

Hook's Seafood Grotto, Treasure Island Hotel, West Bay Road, ☎ 345-945-8731, $$. Known for its seafood dinners (see page 179), Hook's also serves an extensive breakfast buffet. For $8.95 (a bargain as far as hotel breakfast buffets go on this island), you can select from all the usual breakfast fare: eggs, French toast, ham, sausage, muffins, and more.

■ Caribbean

The Peninsula, West Bay Road in the Marriott Grand Cayman, ☎ 345-949-0088, $$. Bring a big appetite for this restaurant's Friday night Pirate's Night Buffet. The food is just part of the fun, you'll be entertained by a limbo dancer as well as a fire eater. Reservations are required. The restaurant is open for lunch and dinner daily.

Ferdinand's, Westin Casuarina, West Bay Road, ☎ 345-945-3800, $$-$$$. The breakfast and lunch eatery for the Westin Casuarina, Ferdinand's has indoor and outdoor dining (the outdoor dining area, which we recommend, is covered with netting to keep the birds out of the breakfast plates); reservations are suggested. The menu is varied and rich with seafood items. Start with conch fritters or jerk pork quesadillas, then move on to Caribbean lobster tail, Malaysian satay, salmon tournedos, Mediterranean chicken kabob, or grilled tuna. Take-out is also available.

Cimboco, The Marquee off West Bay Road, ☎ 345-94-PASTA, $$. This popular restaurant, open for lunch and dinner, serves pasta and fish dishes with a Caribbean flair. Choices include fire-roasted Caribbean rotis, jerk chicken sandwiches, "Hell Hot" pasta, shrimp pesto, and daily fish specials. Cimboco is the creation of the same folks who brought Chicken! Chicken! (below) to Grand Cayman. Diners can eat in or take out.

Chicken! Chicken!, West Bay Road at West Shore Centre, ☎ 345-945-2290, $-$$. This small restaurant serves, well, chicken. Caribbean wood-roasted chicken is sold by the quarter or by the half; family-sized meals are also available. Side dishes include wild rice pilaf, tarragon carrots, buttermilk mashed potatoes, jicama coleslaw, and more. You can dine in or take out.

■ Coffee Shops & Bakeries

The Coffee Grinder, Seven Mile Shops on West Bay Road, ☎ 345-949-4833, $. Start your day indoors or outside at this bakery and deli. Morning favorites include bagels, croissants, honey pecan rolls and scones, all accompanied by a selection of over 30 coffees as well as espresso and cappuccino. Lunch specialties include soups, salads and sandwiches ranging from muffalettas to tuna salad to Reuben sandwiches.

Dickens Internet Café, Galleria Square, ☎ 345-945-9195, $. This café is popular for both its bakery and its 12-cents-a-minute Internet connections (you'll see four terminals at the front of the bakery; just sign up and keep track of your time). Order up some espresso then enjoy poppy seed bagels, quiche or deli sandwiches. The atmosphere is reserved, with hardwood floors and displays of English teapots.

PD's Pub, Galleria Plaza, West Bay Road, ☎ 345-949-7144, $. Yes, this is a pub, but during breakfast hours you'll find a full menu of eye-opening dishes: huevos rancheros, breakfast quesadillas, corned beef hash, eggs benedict, and more. A Sunday brunch is offered 11 am-3 pm; if you need to check your e-mail, do so at one of several computers with Internet service.

■ Continental

The Links Restaurant, The Links at SafeHaven Golf Course, ☎ 345-949-5988, $$$. Located upstairs in the golf club, this air-conditioned restaurant is a favorite with duffers for both lunch and dinner. The lunch menu offers fried scampi, fish and chips, burgers, and steaks. Dinner includes a wide variety of dishes, from salmon steak to Jamaican jumbo shrimp to veal schnitzel and Brazilian pork. Open for lunch from 11:30 to 2:30; dinner from 6 to 9:30.

Reef Grill, Royal Palms at West Bay Road, ☎ 345-945-6358, $$-$$$. This popular restaurant is a great place to start the evening, to be continued later at the adjacent Royal Palms for live music. You'll dine by candlelight either indoors or outside (our recommendation is outside, but call ahead to reserve a table). Start with a Caesar salad, smoked salmon with roasted corn cake or tuna sashimi. Entrées range from pepper-crusted yellowfin tuna with Oriental noodles to braised lamb shank to roasted chicken breast.

■ Delivery Services

With the high number of condominiums and villas on Grand Cayman, several delivery services offer to bring meals right to the door of your home away from home.

Fine Dine-In, ☎ 345-949-DINE. For a CI $5 (per restaurant) charge, this service will deliver meals from Bed, Casanova, Big Daddy's, Ching Chinese, Edoardo's, Chicken! Chicken!, Cimbaco, Deckers, DJ's Cantina, Pizza and Ribs, PD's Pub, Ragazzi, Thai Orchid, and others.

Pizza Hut, West Bay Road, ☎ 345-949-0404. Call this special delivery number for pizza delivery to your condo or hotel room.

■ Fast Food

It may not seem right to come to the islands and dine on fast food, but budget-conscious travelers find this is a valuable option. Fast food chains, while offering American food, also offer a slice of local life – most fellow diners are local residents. We also found the service to be friendly and prompt; Pizza Hut provided excellent table service and a kind staff member transformed a penny-pinching night out into a nice dinner for the two of us.

KFC, The Strand, West Bay Road, ☎ 345-945-8485

Burger King, West Bay Road, ☎ 345-949-7784

Grand Cayman

Pizza Hut, West Bay Road, ☎ 345-949-8687 (345-949-0404 for delivery)

■ Fine Dining

Casa Havana Restaurant, Westin Casuarina, West Bay Road, ☎ 345-945-3800, $$$. This is the Westin Casuarina's signature restaurant, complete with white glove service and a romantic atmosphere. Reservations are suggested for this elegant eatery, which is the most lauded restaurant in the Cayman Islands. Menu selections include glazed swordfish, roast pork tenderloin, and filet mignon. We recently ate a wonderfully romantic dinner here, enjoyed to the sounds of harp music. Call for reservations and ask for an outdoor table if the weather's pretty.

Lantana's Restaurant and Bar, Caribbean Club, West Bay Road, ☎ 345-945-5595, $$$. This elegant restaurant has an excellent menu featuring spicy Cuban black bean soup, jerk pork tenderloin, grilled yellowfin tuna with cilantro linguine, and more. Top it off with tropical coconut cream pie with white chocolate and mango sauce or frozen Cayman lime pie with raspberry sauce and whipped cream. Inventive presentations make this a good choice for a special night out. Dining is indoors. Reservations are recommended for this popular eatery.

Ottmar's, West Bay Road at Grand Pavilion, Commercial Centre, ☎ 345-945-5879, $$$. This fine dining restaurant handles much of the catering for special corporate events and has won numerous awards. It is open only for dinner. Start with chilled mango and orange soup, Caribbean conch chowder, conch fritters, or escargot. The menu includes many seafood specials: orange roughy "Monte Carlo," broiled lobster tail à la française, poached coquille St. Jacques. House specialties include chicken Trinidad and smoked pork tenderloin Casablanca. Ottmar's has children's and take-out menus as well.

■ Infusion

Bed, Harquail Bypass by World Gym, ☎ 345-949-7199, $$-$$$. This restaurant blends the flavors of Asia with the Caribbean and Europe. Start with surf-and-turf carpaccio or chicken and beef satay, then move on to entrées like Moroccan chicken, Uraguayan rack of lamb, black Angus beef or Thai-style curry. Late night tapas are served weekdays until 12:30 am and Saturdays until 11:30. The restaurant also has a busy night scene (see page 181). Reservations are recommended.

■ Italian

Ragazzi, Buckingham Square, West Bay Road, ☎ 345-945-3484, www.eragazzi.com, $$. This casual lunch and dinner restaurant (next door to the Hyatt Regency on the south side) has a varied menu. There's a long list of brick oven pizzas ranging from smoked salmon to Texana (with sausage, black beans, corn and jalapeños). Other options include grilled chicken, and pastas include gnocchi, shellfish linguine, saffron linguine, and tortellini. Meat lovers can opt for grilled pork or beef tenderloin, while fish fans select grilled salmon, Caribbean bouillabaisse or walnut-crusted sea bass. Reservations are suggested.

Ristorante Bella Capri, West Bay Road, ☎ 345-945-4755, $$. Enjoy seafood or Italian specialties at this casual eatery. Veal and steak round out the menu. Open for lunch 11:45 am to 2 pm on weekdays; for dinner, 5:30 to 10:30. Reservations are suggested.

■ Mexican

DJ's Cantina, West Bay Road at Coconut Place, ☎ 345-945-4234, $$. Look for all the usual Tex-Mex offerings in this fun, casual eatery. You'll find tacos, tamales, fajitas, chili and even jalapeño lime tuna. Reservations are recommended.

■ Pizza

Pizza and Ribs to Go, Falls Shopping Center, ☎ 345-945-8836, $. This take-out restaurant has several specialty pizzas: Greek, Hawaiian, veggie, Texas barbecue, and Mexican; you'll also find all the usual favorites. If you're not in the mood for pizza, you can take out barbecue baby back ribs instead. Open daily 11:30 am-11 pm.

Pizza Hut, West Bay Road, ☎ 345-949-8687, $. This restaurant has dine in, take-out and delivery service.

■ Seafood

Benjamin's Roof Seafood Restaurant, West Bay Road at Coconut Place, ☎ 345-947-4080, $$$. When you're ready to go all out, head to this elegant restaurant, which serves clams casino, marinated conch, turtle steak, lobster, shrimp, crab, scallops, and a full line of meat and pasta dishes (and don't miss the alligator tail!). Open for dinner from 3:00 until 10:30; an early bird menu is offered until 5:30 pm.

Hemingway's, Hyatt Regency Grand Cayman, ☎ 345-945-5700, $$. Located beachside at the Hyatt, this delightfully fun eatery sits right on the beach with indoor and outdoor seating. Entrées include spiny Caribbean lobster tail, roasted rack of lamb with herbed couscous and Caribbean ratatouille, and pan-fried snapper with a sweet pepper essence on a zesty couscous.

Hook's Seafood Grotto, Treasure Island Hotel, West Bay Road, ☎ 345-945-8731, $$. This restaurant looks like a set from "Pirates of the Caribbean" (you can't miss old "Hook" himself as you drive by). A favorite with families, Hook's has a full menu of seafood dishes including crab cakes, coconut shrimp, Cajun jambalaya, Cayman-style mahi mahi, rum-soaked garlic jumbo shrimp, clam chowder, and more. Surf-and-turf dishes include prime rib and lobster tail as well as New York steak with king crab legs. Kid-sized portions are available and you can dine inside or outdoors.

Deckers, West Bay Road in front of the Hyatt Regency, ☎ 345-945-6600, $$-$$$. You can't miss this restaurant: just look for the double decker bus out front. A casual eatery, located right on West Bay Road, Deckers combines a pub atmosphere with the fun of a beach bar. Options include appetizers like conch chowder, conch fritters, coconut shrimp; save room for main courses such as Caribbean lobster, mahi mahi in an island sweet potato crust, mesquite grilled shrimp, or beef tenderloin. Reservations are recommended.

The Peninsula, Marriott Beach Resort, West Bay Road, ☎ 345-949-0088, $$-$$$. Just steps off the beach, this outdoor restaurant specializes in seafood dishes: crab stuffed shrimp, Caribbean grouper filet, lobster, chili-citrus glazed tuna, ahi tuna salad, hazelnut-encrusted mahi mahi, and more. For meat lovers, options include roasted rack of New Zealand lamb, cumin spiced pork tenderloin, and New York strip steak. Every Friday, this restaurant hosts a large buffet with a Caribbean theme show (see *Nightlife*, below).

■ Steakhouses

Outback Steakhouse, West Bay Road in The Strand, ☎ 345-945-3108, $$-$$$. Part of the popular chain of steakhouses with an Australian theme, this eatery serves up a variety of steaks cooked to order. Open for dinner only, it also offers veggie dishes, from Walkabout soup to seafood and pastas. Reservations are recommended. Outback offers take-out service and a children's menu.

Nightlife

■ Caribbean Nights

 Caribbean Dinner Party, Hyatt Regency Grand Cayman, West Bay Road, ☎ 345-949-1234, ext. 5208. Held on Tuesday and Friday nights from 6:30-9:30 pm, this show features limbo dancers, fire eaters, and a steel pan musician. The evening includes dinner of pepperpot soup, spicy conch stew, salads, Jamaican barbecued fish, jerk mahi mahi, and more. The dinner and show are priced at CI $42 (plus a 15% gratuity), which includes the dinner buffet and mixed drinks. Children under 12 are admitted for half-price.

Marriott Caribbean Party, The Peninsula, West Bay Road in the Marriott Grand Cayman, ☎ 345-949-0088, $$. Bring a big appetite for this restaurant's Friday night Pirate's Night Buffet. The food is just part of the fun, you'll be entertained by a limbo dancer as well as a fire eater. Reservations are required.

■ Sports Bars

Lone Star Bar and Grill, West Bay Road near Hyatt Regency, ☎ 345-945-5175. This fun-filled bar televises all major games. Happy hour is offered weekdays from 5-6:30; you'll also find a full menu with everything from lobster to steak to barbecue.

West Bay Polo Club Sushi Bar and Grill, Seven Mile Shops, West Bay Road, ☎ 345-949-9892. This bar has over 15 television screens broadcasting just about every sporting event available. Pizza is served nightly until midnight. Kids are welcomed and children under 12 eat lunch or dinner free when dining from the children's menu and accompanied by an adult.

■ Clubs

Sharkey's Niteclub, Cayman Falls Shopping Centre, ☎ 345-945-5366. This club is known for its dancing with live rock and roll Tuesdays, comedy on Wednesday, Thursdays, Saturdays and Sundays, and big screen music theme nights.

Two comedy clubs pack in crowds looking for laughs. **Coconuts Comedy Club** (☎ 345-949-NUTS) at Legendz in The Falls Shopping Centre features traveling comics on Wednesday, Thursday, Saturday and Sunday nights at 9 pm. **Chuckles Comedy Club** (☎ 345-945-5077) moves between the West Bay Polo Club and Sharkey's, depending on the night of the week.

■ Live Music

Royal Palms Beach Club, West Bay Road, ☎ 345-945-6358. The music starts up about 9 here and expect a full house. A favorite nightspot for both locals and visitors, this open-air bar has live music, dancing, and TV sports at the bar. Here, you can dance under the stars just steps from the sea. One of our favorites.

Bed, Harquail Bypass next to World Gym, ☎ 345-949-7199. Live music fans will want to make their way to this restaurant on Wednesday and Saturday nights when a local band headlines the evening, starting at 9:30 pm.

Cruise to Rum Point: Another popular evening outing is a cruise over to Rum Point (for more on Rum Point, see the *East End* section of this chapter). Cruises on the *Rum Pointer Ferry* depart from the Hyatt Regency

Grand Cayman; the ride takes about 40 minutes. For reservations, ☎ 345-949-9098; tickets are about US $15 round-trip. Rum Point showcases the Barefoot Man, the musician whose name is synonymous with Cayman music (you may have seen him in *The Firm*). He plays at Rum Point on Monday and Friday nights from 5-10 pm at the Rum Point Restaurant (and from 2-6 pm on Saturdays on the beach).

■ Movies

If you're ready to enjoy a quiet, cool evening, catch a film at **Cinema I & II** on West Bay Road (across from the Marriott), ☎ 345-949-4011 for listings and times.

■ Quiet Evenings

Looking for a quiet evening where you have the opportunity to unwind or to converse about your day? You'll find several quiet lobby shows and restaurant musicians favored by lovers and travelers looking for a quiet end to their day.

The Wharf, West Bay Road, ☎ 345-949-2231. A harpist provides the perfect accompaniment to the waves just steps from the restaurant.

Westin Casuarina, West Bay Road, ☎ 345-945-3800. A harpist also entertains diners at the restaurants at the Westin (both Casa Havana and Ferdinand's); the harpist plays Monday through Saturday nights. The lobby of the Westin also features an excellent pianist at the lobby bar.

Loggia Lounge, Hyatt Regency Grand Cayman, West Bay Road, ☎ 345-949-1234. The lounge has a piano player tinkling out quiet favorites as well as a humidor filled with Cuba's finest.

■ Sunset Cruises

Red Sail Sports, Multiple locations, Seven Mile Beach, ☎ 345-945-5965, US $30 per person and up. We recently took a sunset dinner cruise with Red Sail Sports – it was one of the highlights of our trip. Red Sail Sports offers this sunset cruise from Rum Point on Sundays and other days from Seven Mile Beach. The two-hour sunset cruise departs at 5 pm during the winter months and 5:30 during the summer. Complimentary appetizers are served, and there's a full cash bar.

West Bay

Vacationers along fun-loving Seven Mile Beach miss the "real" Grand Cayman, a place where homes, not condos, line quiet streets; where children grow up in cozy neighborhoods; where friends take time from their day to stop and say hello or to sit out in the yard and just enjoy a Caribbean afternoon.

That feeling of real life is found in West Bay, directly north of Seven Mile Beach, but a great distance away in terms of atmosphere. Don't look for slick swimwear shops or shipwreck jewelry here. Hotels are few. But West Bay, like the East End, is the heart of Grand Cayman.

The shape of West Bay somewhat resembles a hammerhead perched atop the hammer handle of Seven Mile Beach. The head of the hammer is the most developed area of West Bay. Here you'll find the **Cayman Turtle Farm** and numerous dive sites. Traveling north from Seven Mile Beach along West Bay Road, the name of the road changes to North West Point Road and follows the coastline, becoming more and more residential. At the Cayman Turtle Farm, a less-traveled road traces the far northern edge of this region, continually switching names along the route: Boatswains Bay Road, King Road, Birch Tree Hill Road, Conch Point Road, Palmetto Point Road. Traveling east, houses become fewer and fewer and the area gives way to a swampy habitat that attracts birds.

If you turn away from the coast and head to the inland area of West Bay you will find a community called **Hell**, a popular stop on island tours. Located, appropriately enough, on Hell Road, this small town cashes in on its unusual moniker with the expected T-shirt shops and a post office that sends off postcards franked with the obligatory Hell postmark. Nevertheless, it's a small, homey community that's worth a visit.

Follow Hell Road east, first onto Reverend Blackman Road and then Batabano Road, to travel to the North Sound and the fishing community of Batabano. This is home of **Morgan's Harbour**, starting point for many deep-sea fishing cruises and some trips to Stingray City. It's not as glitzy as Seven Mile Beach, but offers an interesting look at the working side of Grand Cayman.

Back to the hammerhead image: The claw of the hammer is the **Barkers** area of West Bay. Located north of Batabano on the North Sound, Barkers is also popular with birders, who find good sites off Palmetto Point Road on its northern reaches and along its many ponds.

Grand Cayman

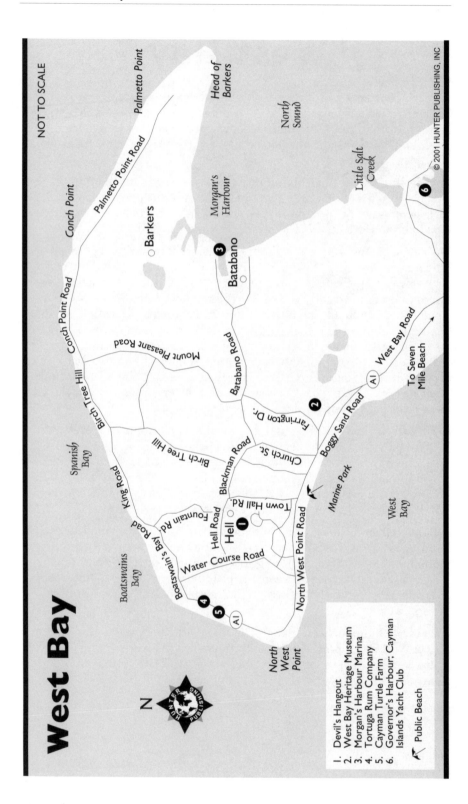

West Bay

NOT TO SCALE

N

1. Devil's Hangout
2. West Bay Heritage Museum
3. Morgan's Harbour Marina
4. Tortuga Rum Company
5. Cayman Turtle Farm
6. Governor's Harbour; Cayman Islands Yacht Club

↗ Public Beach

© 2001 HUNTER PUBLISHING, INC

Adventures

■ On Foot

Walking Tour

A brochure describing a self-guided walking tour of central West Bay is available from the National Trust (see page 92). The 37-stop tour begins at the West Bay United Church and continues on to many historic sites. Some of the most interesting of the locally used architectural styles are pointed out on buildings along the way, including the wattle-and-daub houses typical of those built on the island from the 17th through the early 19th centuries.

WATTLE & DAUB

Handmade using few tools, the homes were built of mahogany, ironwood, wattles, daub, and thatch and had outdoor bathrooms and kitchens as a safety feature. Wattles are woven wood panels covered by a coral lime plaster substance called daub. Making the daub was often a neighborhood-wide activity, since it was so labor-intensive. Coral rocks were broken up and baked in a large kiln to create lime ash. This was mixed with sand and water then daubed onto the wattles, usually about six inches thick. Although a fairly simple construction method that used locally available materials, this style was sturdy and could withstand the hurricanes and tropical storms as well as rain and sun.

Wattle and daub houses built from the mid-19th century to the present are called **manor houses**. Showing American influences, the modern homes have indoor baths and kitchens as well as verandahs. You'll see several examples on your walking tour.

Timber houses, constructed of imported lumber using ship-building tools, were built starting in the mid-19th century. The most striking feature of these homes was their intricate fretwork, or gingerbread trim. Towards the end of the century, the bungalow style became a favorite, using pre-cut lumber and, later, cement and blocks.

Traditional Caymanian **sand gardens** are unique. Raked clean, the sand gardens are often trimmed with conch shells and have paths paved with coral. Again, you'll have a chance to view these traditional gardens as you walk. An excellent spot to see sand gardens is on Boggy Sand Road in West Bay.

Grand Cayman

■ In the Water

Scuba

 The West Bay area has some of the best diving sites on Grand Cayman. For a list of dive operators, see pages 71-73.

Bonnie's Arch: Just off North West Point, this 50- to 70-foot dive is a favorite with underwater photographers because of its arch formation, which is covered with corals and sponges. Good for beginners, the dive offers a good opportunity to view many types of marine life, from tarpon to tangs.

Hepp's Pipeline: This 30- to 60-foot dive for beginners and intermediate divers is not far from the Cayman Turtle Farm. It has two mini-walls and can be a shore dive.

Big Tunnel: Swim-throughs, canyons and a depth of 60-100 feet make this a favorite with intermediate and advanced divers. It is located off the North West Point (close to Bonnie's Arch and the Orange Canyon).

Ghost Mountain: This deep dive, ranging from 80-120 feet, features a pinnacle covered with corals, some black. Located off the north end of the island.

Hepps Wall: This 60-foot wall drops steeply, and is lined with soft corals.

Orange Canyon: A 60- to 100-foot dive, the canyon is favored by intermediate and advanced divers. This wall dive is filled with color and is named for its orange elephant ear sponges. Near Bonnie's Arch.

Trinity Caves: Located in West Bay, the caves sit at 40-100 feet. Beginners can enjoy a look at spectacular corals and fans, while intermediate and advanced divers can enter the three channels that wind their way to a wall where large species might be spotted. Look for turtles on this dive.

Ghost Mountain: At North Point, West Bay, you will see a large coral pinnacle, the base of which lies on a sand slope at a depth of 140 feet. Large schools of jack swim in and out of the cave at the base. This 70- to 100-foot wall dive is for intermediate to advanced divers.

Spanish Bay Reef: Walk right out to this shallow reef dive (30-60 feet) near Spanish Bay Reef Resort. This site is also good for snorkeling, although the waters can be rough.

Tarpon Alley: This site, divided into east and west sections, is home to a large school of tarpon. The dive is off the north end of the island.

Turtle Farm Reef: Just east of the turtle farm, a short swim from the shore, this site offers a steep mini-wall rising from a 60-foot deep sand bottom. You can do this as a shore dive or enjoy the site as a snorkeler.

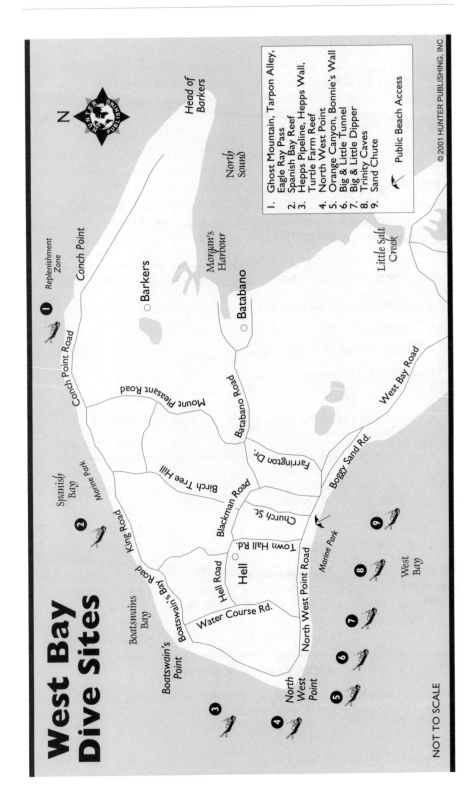

West Bay Dive Sites

N

Replenishment Zone

Conch Point

Conch Point Road

Spanish Bay
Marine Park

Boatswains Bay

Boatswain's Point

Boatswain's Bay Road

King Road

Mount Pleasant Road

Birch Tree Hill

Blackman Road

Hell Road

Water Course Rd.

Hell

North West Point Road

North West Point

Batabano Road

Farrington Dr.

Church St.

Town Hall Rd.

Marine Park

Boggy Sand Rd.

West Bay Road

West Bay

Barkers

Morgan's Harbour

Batabano

North Sound

Head of Barkers

Little Salt Creek

1. Ghost Mountain, Tarpon Alley, Eagle Ray Pass
2. Spanish Bay Reef
3. Hepps Pipeline, Hepps Wall, Turtle Farm Reef
4. North West Point
5. Orange Canyon, Bonnie's Wall
6. Big & Little Tunnel
7. Big & Little Dipper
8. Trinity Caves
9. Sand Chute

↙ Public Beach Access

© 2001 HUNTER PUBLISHING, INC

Grand Cayman

NOT TO SCALE

Snorkeling

One of the top snorkel spots on the island is located near the cemetery. Follow West Bay Road north from Seven Mile Beach. As the road begins turning west into West Bay, you'll see a small cemetery between the road and the sea. Nearby, there's public access to the beach and it's a short swim from here to **Cemetery Reef**.

Another popular snorkel spot is the **Turtle Farm Reef**. It's just a short swim from the shoreline and offers snorkelers a look at a mini-wall and abundant marine life.

These West Bay operators offer guided snorkel trips of either a full or half-day. They provide a good opportunity to travel to the reefs beyond the reach of shore swimming. Great for beginners to get an introduction.

WEST BAY SNORKELING OPERATORS

Captain Marvin's Aquatics . . . . ☎ 345-945-6975

Cayman Delight Cruises. . . . . ☎ 345-949-8111

Jackie's Watersports. ☎ 345-945-5791

Kelly's Watersports . . . . ☎ 345-949-1193

Oh Boy Charters. . . . . ☎ 345-949-6341

Resort Sports Limited. . . . . ☎ 345-949-8100

Seasports . . . . ☎ 345-949-3965

Many of the West Bay snorkel operators offer trips to Stingray City (see the *East End* section of this chapter).

■ On Horseback

Most horseback riding on the island is along the powdery beaches, an excellent place for practiced riders to romp and gallop and for beginners to enjoy a slow walk on cushioned sand (a comfort to those who feel they may fall off). Both experienced horsemen and those new to the sport can enjoy beach and trail rides. Fees start at $65.

HORSEBACK RIDING

Honey Suckle Trail Rides. . . . . . . ☎ 345-947-7976 or 916-3363

Pampered Ponies. . . . . ☎ 345-945-2262 or 916-2540
fax 345-945-2262, www.ponies.ky

Nicki's Private Beach Rides . . . . ☎ 345-916-3530 or 945-5839

Sightseeing

 Cayman Turtle Farm, 825 Northwest Point Road, West Bay, ☎ 345-949-3893/3894, www.turtle.ky. The chief sightseeing stop on the West Bay is also one of the island's most popular. The world's only turtle farm, it had over 260,000 visitors last year. Since 1968 this unique farm has offered visitors the chance to get up close and personal with green sea turtles.

Green turtles, named for the color of their fat, can weigh 700 pounds and you can watch them slowly swimming in open-air tanks in the center of the farm. You'll even have the opportunity to pick up one of the small reptiles. The turtle farm has been both praised and criticized for its operation. Many turtles are released into the sea every year from this farm, although others find their way onto Cayman dinner tables. Turtle meat served at local restaurants comes from the Cayman Turtle Farm, which defends its efforts and points out that by providing turtle meat – a longtime Caymanian favorite – to the local market, it diminishes the need for turtle hunting. Also, the sur-

A hatchling at the Cayman Turtle Farm

vival rate of turtles bred at the farm is much higher than in the wild. Here, nine out of every 10 turtles survive, as compared to one out of 10 hatchlings in the wild.

TURTLE TRIVIA

- The sex of green sea turtles is dependent on the temperature during incubation. At 82°, an equal number of males and females are born. If the temperatures are cooler, all males are produced. At warmer temperatures, the hatchlings will all be female.

- Only one mature turtle is expected to survive from an average 10,000 eggs in the wild.

- Mating season for green sea turtles lasts from April through July; the pair may mate for as long as six days.

- Nesting season occurs from May through October.
- At the turtle farm, single individual turtles have laid as many as 690 eggs in a single clutch. A female may nest one to 10 times a season, producing up to 1,700 eggs in a year. She may nest every year or skip several years.
- Mature green sea turtles have been observed to stay underwater for several days without surfacing for air.

The turtle farm displays the life cycle of the green sea turtle from birth through breeding stage. A nursery shows where the eggs, which are laid by the big breeder turtles on a sand beach, are incubated. The hatchlings live in tanks and are fed high-protein pellets similar in appearance to dog food. This diet accounts for the rapid growth of the farm's turtles compared to their relatives in the wild.

The self-guided tour of the turtle farm takes you past many tanks filled with turtles in various life stages. A special tank contains turtles that you may pick up and hold, an excellent photo opportunity. Reach down and clutch the turtle's body just behind his front flippers. He'll flip and flap around, trying to swim away in mid-air, unless you hold him vertically. The farm is also home to several other turtle displays.

- **Hawksbill turtle** (*Eretmochelys imbricata*). With a narrow, sharply serrated carapace and a bird-like bill, the hawksbill turtle is easy to identify. Specimens range from 90 to 180 pounds.
- **Kemp's Ridley sea turtle** (*Lepidochelys kempii*). The most endangered of the sea turtles, these are being raised at the farm for future release into the wild.
- **Loggerhead turtle** (*Caretta caretta*). Found off the Florida, Georgia, and Carolina coasts, these weighty (200 to 350 pounds) turtles have large heads that give them their name.

The turtle farm also recognizes the land residents of the Cayman Islands in several exhibit areas. Look for the agouti (*Dasyprocta*) or the Cayman "rabbit" in one area. These rodents, found in the eastern districts of Grand Cayman, have long, thin legs, hoof-like claws, with three toes on their hind feet and five toes on the forefeet. Once a food source, today the rodents are rarely spotted. Nearby, another display area houses the American crocodile. Early verbal records speak of sightings of this reptile (*Cocodylus acutus*), which reaches 20 feet in length, in Grand Cayman and Little Cayman; recent archaeological finds have proven this claim.

Admission is US $6 for adults, US $3 for children six to 12 (under six free). The farm is open daily 8:30 am to 5 pm. Allow about 45 minutes at the farm, which makes an excellent rainy day distraction.

The devil at Hell.

Hell: East of the turtle farm lies an attraction that is pure Hell. This oddly named place is actually a community named Hell, a moniker derived from the time an English commissioner went hunting in the area, shot at a bird, missed, and said, "Oh, hell." The name must have seemed appropriate for the devilishly pointed rocks near town, a bed of limestone and dolomite that, through millions of years, have eroded into a crusty, pocked formation locally called ironshore.

To reach this small community, follow West Bay Road north from Seven Mile Beach. At the intersection of Town Hall Road, turn right; continue to Hell Road and turn left.

Hell trades upon its unusual name as a way to draw tourists to the far end of West Bay. Visitors stop at the **post office** (and the three shops directly adjacent) to buy postcards and have them postmarked from Hell. Nearby, **The Devil's Hangout**, the original post office, ships out its share of postcards. The store is manned by Ivan Farrington, who dresses as the devil himself to greet tourists who come to buy the obligatory postcard and other Hell-related gifts, from hot sauces to T-shirts.

Step behind the store or the nearby post office for a close-up look at the ironshore that gave this region its unusual name. Even with all the Hades-related attention this small community draws, a stroll along its streets will show that this is a quiet, heavenly town. And, yes, there are churches in Hell.

Conch Shell House: Interesting as a drive-by attraction, the conch shell house on North Sound Way is included on most island tours. It's privately owned, so you can't enter the premises, but the house is often photographed. Handmade from conch shells, it's charming and certainly one of the most picturesque homes in the Caribbean. Ask locally for directions.

Heritage Museum, West Bay. This small museum was once a schoolhouse; today it is filled with Caymanian artifacts that recall the island's early residents. At the four-way stop in West Bay, turn toward the sea (left if heading north); the museum is on the left before you reach Boggy Sand Road. Admission to the museum is free; it is open Monday through Friday, 9-12 and 1-4; and Saturday, 9-12.

Shopping

 West Bay isn't know for its shopping; you'll have to head back down West Bay Road to Seven Mile Beach's malls for a big selection. In this area, you will find a few good souvenir shops.

Cayman Turtle Farm, 825 Northwest Point Road, West Bay, ☎ 345-949-3893/3894, www.turtle.ky. You can't miss the turtle farm's gift shop; you'll walk right through it on your way in. It has everything turtle-related: turtle socks, turtle jewelry, toy turtles, the list goes on and one. Steer clear of the turtle oil and turtle shell items, however; they'll be confiscated by US Customs.

Tortuga Rum Company, Northwest Point Road on north side of the turtle farm, ☎ 345-949-9247. This expansive gift shop sells Tortuga Rum Cakes; on weekdays you can even watch through a window at the bakery for a look at the cakes in progress. The shop displays the many rums manufactured by Tortuga Rum, but they are not for sale.

Devil's Hangout, Hell. This shop is worth a stop if only to see the owner, Ivan Farrington, in full devil costume. Many people stop here and write a postcard to be postmarked from Hell.

Where to Stay

ACCOMMODATIONS PRICE SCALE
Prices listed are for a standard room for one night during high season (expect prices to be as much as 40% lower during the low season). The price scale refers to US $.

$.	Under $100
$$.	$100-$200
$$$.	Over $200

■ Hotels & Resorts

Spanish Bay Reef, Barkers, ☎ 800-482-DIVE, 345-949-3765, fax 345-949-1842, www.caymanresorthotels.com, $$. This resort on the north end of West Bay, tucked away on a sandy stretch of beach shaded by tall palms and willowy casuarina trees, is casual and fun. The sea here is somewhat choppy, although a barrier creates a swimming area, and it is a favorite spot with divers. Dive sites include No Name Wall, Chinese Wall, Lemon Drop-Off, Grand Canyon, The Pinnacles, and more, each offering a peek at an undersea world filled with marine life, fascinating formations, and beautiful corals.

All rooms have air conditioning, private balcony or patio and satellite TV. The resort features the Spanish Main Restaurant and Calico Jack's Poolside Bar as well as a private beach, freshwater pool, Jacuzzi, and dock. An all-inclusive package covers all meals and beverages (other than wine or champagne), use of sightseeing cars on a shared basis, bicycles, introductory scuba and snorkeling lessons, unlimited scuba diving from shore for certified divers (including tanks and weight belt), boat dives (usually a two-tank dive), airport transfers, and all taxes and gratuities. The three-night dive package starts at $756 per person ($568 for non-divers; standard room) and includes one two-tank dive per day. Low-season rates, from the end of June through August, drop to $692 for divers and $505 for non-divers.

■ Guest Houses

White Haven Inn Guest House, Batabano Road, ☎ 345-949-1064, fax 345-945-4890, $. Located in a quiet residential neighborhood, this modest guest house offers a slice of real Caymanian life at a reasonable price. Three units feature air conditioning, ceiling fans, telephone, televisions, and VCRs. A full American breakfast is included, along with free airport pick-up. After a day spent scuba diving and exploring the island, guests can enjoy quiet walks in this neighborhood, where cattle peacefully reside in large fields.

Where to Eat

■ Caribbean

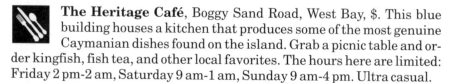 **The Heritage Café**, Boggy Sand Road, West Bay, $. This blue building houses a kitchen that produces some of the most genuine Caymanian dishes found on the island. Grab a picnic table and order kingfish, fish tea, and other local favorites. The hours here are limited: Friday 2 pm-2 am, Saturday 9 am-1 am, Sunday 9 am-4 pm. Ultra casual.

Calypso Grill, Morgan's Harbour, Batabano Road, ☎ 345-949-3948, $$-$$$. This new, colorful restaurant is right on the water and packed with flavor. Start with marinated conch, peppered tuna carpaccio or pesto bruschetta. Leave plenty of time for preparation of the special entrées, dishes like seafood paella, grilled prime rib chop, Cajun chicken linguine, and shrimp linguine; enjoy the view across the water as you wait. Reservations are suggested.

Liberty's, West Bay, ☎ 345-949-3226, $$. This Caribbean restaurant is a favorite with local residents. The all-you-can-eat seafood buffet is especially popular and is served Sunday, Wednesday, and Friday nights from 6:30-10 pm, as well as for Sunday brunch.

■ Italian

Ristorante Pappagallo, Conch Point Road, ☎ 345-949-1119 or 949-3479, $$-$$$. The beauty of this restaurant hints at the specialness of a meal here. Its thatched roof, made from over 100,000 thatch palm leaves, shields a building designed from bamboo, local stone, and marble. Parrots, cockatoos, and macaws lend their voices to create an exotic atmosphere that's echoed in the setting. The restaurant is perched on the shores of a small natural lake in a bird sanctuary.

Meals here are special, featuring Northern Italian cuisine. Homemade pastas, seafood, and fine wines make this restaurant well worth the drive for those staying in the Seven Mile Beach area. Dinner is served from 6 to 10:30 pm daily.

Cayman Brac

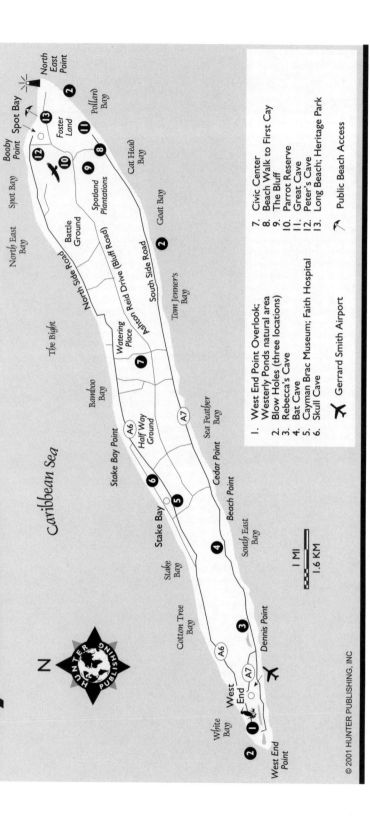

Caribbean Sea

White Bay
West End
West End Point

Cotton Tree Bay
Dennis Point

Stake Bay
Stake Bay

Bamboo Bay
The Bight

Stake Bay Point
Half Way Ground

South East Bay
Beach Point
Cedar Point
Sea Feather Bay

North East Bay

Watering Place

Battle Ground

North Side Road
Ashton Reid Drive (Bluff Road)
South Side Road

Tom Jenner's Bay

Goat Bay

Spotland Plantations

Cat Head Bay

Spot Bay
Booby Point
Foster Land
Pollard Bay

North East Point

A6
A7
A6
A7

1 MI
1.6 KM

N

1. West End Point Overlook;
2. Westerly Ponds natural area
   Blow Holes (three locations)
3. Rebecca's Cave
4. Bat Cave
5. Cayman Brac Museum; Faith Hospital
6. Skull Cave

7. Civic Center
8. Beach Walk to First Cay
9. The Bluff
10. Parrot Reserve
11. Great Cave
12. Peter's Cave
13. Long Beach; Heritage Park

✈ Gerrard Smith Airport

⚓ Public Beach Access

© 2001 HUNTER PUBLISHING, INC

Cayman Brac

Cayman Brac is the larger of the sister islands. If Grand Cayman is the flashy big brother, swelling with pride about its lavish condominiums, full-service resorts, international dining, and top-notch diving; and Little Cayman is the family's youngest sibling, favored for its petite size and almost shy demeanor; then Cayman Brac (rhymes with Jack) is the middle child. Have no fear, though; this sibling is not at all overlooked.

A favorite of scuba divers, this island boasts world-class diving along undersea walls, a neighborly feeling, a sense of peace, and a striking landscape. This most "mountainous" of the Cayman Islands offers good hiking as well as numerous caves, which invite exploration. Birders also find plenty of challenge here.

Its people are another of this island's true treasures. "Brackers are all nice and enjoy talking," explains Terri Scott, the Cayman Islands Department of Tourism representative on the island. "People come back often to the island because they feel welcome; they feel like they know people here. There's very little crime here because everyone knows everyone."

The island is named for the "brac," Gaelic for bluff, which soars up from the sea to a height of 140 feet on the island's east end. It's the most distinct feature of this 12-mile-long, one-mile-wide island, which sits 89 miles east-northeast of Grand Cayman and just seven miles from Little Cayman.

With a population of under 1,300 residents, Cayman Brac is closer in pace to Little Cayman than to Grand Cayman. Residents, or "Brackers," are known for their personable nature and welcome vacationers to their sunny isle.

Cayman Brac has all basic services, including a bank (the **Cayman National Bank** at Tibbetts Square, Cross Road at West End, ☎ 345-948-1551; also has an ATM), **dental clinic** (☎ 345-948-2618), medical clinic (**Brac Clinic**, ☎ 345-948-1777), and hospital (the 16-bed **Faith Hospital** at Stake Bay, ☎ 345-948-2356). Several **grocery stores** provide all the necessities, although at a slightly higher price than on Grand Cayman.

A Brief Island Tour

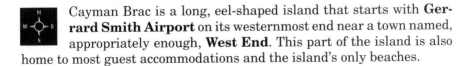

Cayman Brac is a long, eel-shaped island that starts with **Gerrard Smith Airport** on its westernmost end near a town named, appropriately enough, **West End**. This part of the island is also home to most guest accommodations and the island's only beaches.

Two roads etch the perimeter of the island. **A6** (locals refer to it as the **North Side Road**) traces the northern coast, starting at West End and working east past Knob Hill, Banksville, Half Way Ground, Molusca Heights, Tibbetts Turn, and Spot Bay, the most populated area of the island. Along the way, the road looks out on a sea that hides several good dive sites beneath its placid waters.

On this eastern end of the island, you'll see traditional Cayman building styles; these were the first houses built on the island. Spot Bay is now constructing **Heritage Park**, an area that will recall the heritage of the island and offer nature tourism sites and trails.

On the southern shore, **A7** (usually just called the **South Side Road**) traces its way from West End Point all the way northeast, journeying past the island's resorts (Brac Reef Beach Resort and Divi Tiara Beach Resort), past several good caves that are favorites with outdoor adventurers, and up to Pollard Bay.

A small center road (labeled **Ashton Reid Drive** on the maps but known as **Bluff Road** by residents) works through the center of the island, and this is the route to Cayman Brac's best known attraction: the **bluff** or the Brac. From this road, turn east on the gravel **Major Donald Drive** (a.k.a. Lighthouse Road) and continue to the Parrot Reserve and the Lighthouse.

Getting Here

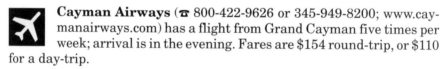

Cayman Airways (☎ 800-422-9626 or 345-949-8200; www.caymanairways.com) has a flight from Grand Cayman five times per week; arrival is in the evening. Fares are $154 round-trip, or $110 for a day-trip.

Island Air (☎ 345-949-5252, www.islandaircayman.com) provides daily service from Grand Cayman to Cayman Brac. Some flights are direct; others make a quick stop in Little Cayman. Fares from Grand Cayman to Cayman Brac are US $154 round-trip.

PRIVATE PILOTS

Gerrard Smith Airport is an official port of entry for private planes. For information on bringing your plane to the Cayman Islands (including how to get an overflight permit from the Cuban government), contact the Airport Officer, PO Box 58, West End, Cayman Brac, British West Indies, ☎ 345-948-1222, fax 345-948-1583.

Getting Around

 Upon arrival at Gerrard Smith Airport, continue through the airport past the baggage claim and outside to the pick-up area. Several rental-car offices are located just across the parking lot; you'll also find taxi service here most of the time.

■ By Car

Rental companies include: **T & D Avis**, ☎ 800-228-0668 or 345-948-2847; **Brac-Hertz Rent-a-Car**, ☎ 345-948-1515, www.bracrentals.com; **B&S Motor Ventures**, ☎ 345-948-1646, www.bandsmv.ky; and **Four D's Car Rental**, ☎ 345-948-1599. Rental prices range from US $40-$45 for a Jeep and about US $30 for a compact car.

■ On Foot

With the low crime rate on Cayman Brac, sightseeing on foot is fun and safe. You will find, however, that the distance between communities is too far for casual walkers. Remember to look right when crossing the street.

■ By Scooter & Bicycle

Cayman Brac makes a great destination for cycles and scooters because of its light traffic and primarily flat road grade. Check with **B&S Motor Ventures**, ☎ 345-948-1646, www.bandsmv.ky, for rentals of scooters and bicycles. The company will provide free pickup islandwide.

■ Guided Tours

Free guided nature tours are available with local resident **T.J. Sevik**. T.J., a young man with an extensive knowledge of the island's flora and fauna as well as its history, can tailor a tour to your specifications. For arrangements contact Kenny Ryan or Mrs. Wanda Tatum, ☎ 345-948-2651, fax 345-948-2506.

You may also arrange a private, half-day tour for about US $30 from one of these taxi services.

D&M Taxi-N-Tours, Spot Bay, ☎ 345-948-2307. Customized tours around the island, including trips to the bluff and the lighthouse, are available through this company.

Elo's Tours and Taxi Service, The Bight, ☎ 345-948-0220. This company offers guided tours around the island including the caves. Trips to the lighthouse cost extra.

Hill's Taxi, Spot Bay, ☎ 345-948-0540. These tours cover the caves, light-house, museum, and more.

Maple Edwards Taxi, Spot Bay, ☎ 345-948-0395. These tours include the museum, bluff, caves, and more.

Adventures

■ On Foot

Hiking

NATURE TRAILS: One of the best nature trails in Cayman Brac is at the **Parrot Reserve**. Located in the center of the is-land, this trail is great for self-guided tours. The trail is a mile long and takes hikers through the reserve, which is home to the endangered Cayman Brac parrot. There is no charge to enter the reserve and trails are always open. Bring your own water; there are no facilities on the trail. You'll also want to wear long pants and good shoes for the trek, which traverses ironshore.

To reach the reserve, travel from either the North Side Road or the South Side Road to the center road called Ashton Reid Drive (but known as Bluff Road). Take this road to the intersection of the gravel Major Donald Drive (a.k.a. Lighthouse Road) and continue to the Parrot Reserve and the lighthouse. For more information, contact Wallace Platts, chairman of the trust's district committee, at ☎ 345-948-2390.

The gravel road is well graded and can be maneuvered by bicycles (just watch out for the stray cow or two!). This road has long been used by Brackers who once planted "grounds" or small gardens in the pockets of dirt found here (remember, much of the island is ironshore and just about impossible for gardening).

From the Parrot Reserve, continue traveling on Major Donald Drive east to the **lighthouse**, located at the end of the road (and high atop the bluff; don't get too close to the edge!). There are actually two beacons at this point; an historic lighthouse and a newer model. Both are just lights atop tall towers, but the view from this area is dramatic; the 140-foot-high **bluff** is the highest point in the Cayman Islands. A trail weaves its way to the edge and provides excellent photo opportunities. Rocky paths snake their way along the bluff; wear hiking boots for this challenge.

The Cayman Bluff.

DID YOU KNOW?

As you drive along Major Donald Drive, keep an eye out for the fences built of cut birch. A branch from these trees, reddish in color, can take root so you'll see many fences that look like they're made from growing trees. The trick: the birch was cut into fence posts, used to string the fence and, over the years, the birch took root and formed a row of new trees, complete with barbed wire running through them.

On the lower bluff area, you'll also find some challenging hikes that cut through rugged brush on trails once used by farmers. Just look for road signs that appear without roads. Bring along water for these excursions. Most of the trails average about a mile, but can take considerably longer than you might expect due to the dense foliage.

HERITAGE SITES & TRAILS: Don't miss this extensive island-wide network of 35 marked trails, which was recently instituted by the Department of Tourism. Some are easy to reach while others require more hiking. You can obtain a free map and brochure of the trails from the Department of Tourism office (located adjacent to the Cayman Brac Community Park; call ☎ 345-948-1849). Some sites include:

Cayman Brac

West End Point Overlook, South Side Road west of Brac Reef Beach Resort. Located on the far west end of the island, this lookout is an easily accessible point, good for a little birdwatching as well as the island's best sunset view.

Westerly Ponds, South Side Road across from Brac Reef Beach Resort. These two ponds are good spots for watching wetland birds. You'll find boardwalks across the marsh here and a small viewing area. Sit quietly, get out your binoculars and your copy of *Birds of the Cayman Islands*, and try your luck. Parking is on the side of the road (you don't have to worry about creating a traffic jam here).

Beach Walk to First Cay, southeast shore at southeast end of South Side Road. This hike takes about two hours and follows the shoreline below the bluff. Watch for brown boobies, magnificent frigate birds, and tropicbirds along this stretch. The hike goes to the large rock known as the First Cay; beyond that point the sea can get hazardous.

Long Beach, far east end of Spot Bay Road. Travel as far as you can on Spot Bay Road then park and walk through the sea grape-lined path. The trail widens into a rock- and coral-filled area with ironshore to the water; you're rewarded for the somewhat difficult walk with a beautiful view of the bluff. Hiking too far east can be dangerous because of hazardous seas.

Tennis

If tennis is your game, you'll find courts at **Brac Reef Beach Resort** on the South Side (see page 211).

Caving

The bluff is pocked with caves, which frame beautiful seaside views. No one really knows the history of these caves. Some guess that pre-Columbian Indian settlements used them; others say they were the lair of plundering pirates who used their dark recesses to hide their loot. None of these legends has been proven, but one use of the caverns is known for certain. During the Great Hurricane of 1932, the caves offered shelter for many Brackers. During Hurricane Gilbert, some longtime residents also turned to the caves for safety.

Several of the 18 caves on Cayman Brac have been explored. Five are frequently visited by vacationers.

- **Rebecca's Cave**, east of Divi Tiara Hotel (see page 211), this cave is marked with signs. The best known of the island's caves, it is named for a young child who died here of exposure during the Great Hurricane of 1932. The child's grave is seen in the center of the largest cave room. Rebecca's Cave is located at ground level and is the easiest to reach.

- **Skull Cave**. This interesting cavern is on the north coast near the high school and east of Faith Hospital.

- **Peter's Cave.** This cave requires either a climb down a steep path or a hike downhill, so bring along good shoes for this task. From the cave, you can view the community of Spot Bay below.

- **Bat Cave.** On the south side of the island, this two-level cave is marked with signs. A short ladder leads up to the cave, but access is easy. You'll want to bring a flashlight to view the resident Jamaican fruit bats, seen on the ceiling of the leftmost room.

- **Great Cave.** Also on the south side, Great Cave also requires a steep climb. A nearly vertical ladder makes this cave more challenging than most but a sea view on the climb makes this worthwhile for many.

AUTHOR TIP *Visitors to Cayman Brac should bring along a pair of old jeans for exploring caves and a pair of old sneakers with good soles for walking on the ironshore beaches. And don't forget a flashlight for the caves!*

Some of the caves on Cayman Brac.

Cayman Brac

■ In the Water

Scuba

Without a doubt, the diving off Cayman Brac is one of the island's prime attractions. Over 50 prime sites tempt all levels of divers.

The newest attraction is a Russian frigate deliberately sunk in September 1996. Renamed the **MV *Captain Keith Tibbets***, this 330-foot freighter was built for use by the Cuban navy. It lies about 200 yards off-

Divers explore the
MV Captain Keith Tibbetts.

shore northwest of Cayman Brac. The bow rests in 90 feet of water; the stern is just 40 feet below the surface. This is the first Cayman wreck site to allow multi-level computer diving experience. The site is marked with three permanent dive moorings.

The sinking of the vessel was recorded by Jean-Michel Cousteau Productions in a documentary film, *Destroyer at Peace*. Before the ship was sunk, it was modified to make it safe for divers, who can now swim through the three upper decks, although the hull and lower decks cannot be entered. Divers can see into most of the ship and should be able to spot the missile launcher, fore and aft deck cannons, and living quarters. Often seen here are eagle rays, stingrays, Queen angelfish, filefish, four-eyed butterfly fish, puffer fish, batfish, snapper, red soldier fish, sergeant major, French grunt, barracuda, jack, and more.

COST OF SCUBA DIVING ON CAYMAN BRAC

(Prices quoted are in US $)

1-tank dive	$40-$45
2-tank dive	$70-$75
3-tank dive	$95-$110
Certification course	$350-$400
Night dive	$50
Resort course	$90-$100

Dive Sites

Anchor Wall: Located on the south side of the island off Dennis Point, this wall dive is considered intermediate level. Don't miss the anchor of an old Spanish galleon; it marks the entrance to a tunnel leading to a vertical wall that drops into the deep blue abyss.

Charlie's Reef: On the north side of the island near Cotton Tree Bay, this 20- to 60-foot dive is a favorite with beginners and is named for a green moray eel.

Inside Out: This wall dive off South East Bay is a favorite with beginners because of its shallow (15 to 50 feet) depth. With coral heads, a tunnel, and plenty of marine life, it's a good choice for anyone.

Radar Reef: Off Half Way Ground on the island's north side, this shallow dive can be reached from shore and is a favorite for night diving. Look for octopus!

East Chute: This all-level dive, on the north side of the island in White Bay, has something for everyone. Wreck divers will find the remains of a 65-foot vessel in its waters; those looking for spectacular formations will find canyons and tunnels.

Rock Monster Chimney: Located off the island's south side, this 66- to 100-foot dive has a sharp drop-off dotted with sea caves.

Scuba Operators

Brac Aquatics Ltd., ☎ 800-544-BRAC, 345-948-1429. For over 20 years this operator has offered dives for all levels. Three dives are run daily with a 14-diver maximum. PADI and NAUI affiliated. There's also a photo center with camera rentals, film processing, and video post-production services.

Dive Tiara, ☎ 800-661-DIVE. This PADI 5-star dive and photo center leads visits to over 50 sites on Cayman Brac and neighboring Little Cayman. Located at the Divi Tiara Beach Resort, it also offers photo and video camera rentals. PADI, NAUI, SSI, and NASDS affiliated.

Reef Divers, ☎ 800-327-3835, 345-948-1642, www.bracreef.com. At Brac Reef Beach Resort, this dive service includes a full photo and video center. Three dives daily; 20-person maximum. PADI, NAUI, SSI, and NASDS affiliated.

Village Scuba School, ☎ 345-948-1497, e-mail weedee@candw.ky. This PADI affiliate offers advanced certification courses as well as resort courses.

Snorkeling

The wreck of the **MV *Captain Keith Tibbets*** can be enjoyed by snorkelers, as it is located just a short swim off shore. The wreck sits in 50-100

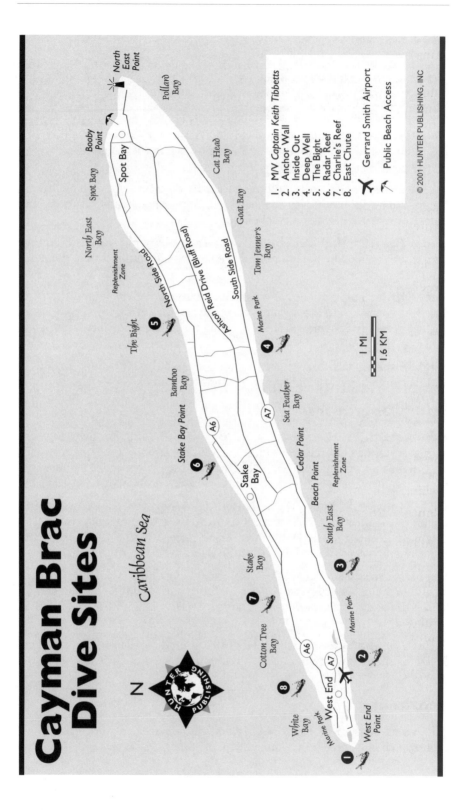

Cayman Brac Dive Sites

Caribbean Sea

1. M/V Captain Keith Tibbetts
2. Anchor Wall
3. Inside Out
4. Deep Well
5. The Bight
6. Radar Reef
7. Charlie's Reef
8. East Chute

✈ Gerrard Smith Airport
🚶 Public Beach Access

© 2001 HUNTER PUBLISHING, INC

feet of water and is already home to a good selection of marine life. Snorkel trips run about US $15-$30 per person.

Scuba operators generally do two dives per day, and some will make their afternoon dive a shallow one that can accommodate snorkelers; check with the scuba operators listed above for details. Other snorkel operators include **Shelby Charters**, ☎ 345-948-0535; **Barefoot Watersports**, ☎ 345-948-1299; and **Condor Watersports**, ☎ 345-948-1226.

Underwater Photography

Rent professional-grade equipment (both photo and video), buy film, process your shots, and more at one of these dive shops' underwater photo centers:

Brac Aquatics Ltd., ☎ 800-544-BRAC, 345-948-1429, e-mail bracdive@candw.ky

Reef Divers, ☎ 800-327-3835 or 345-948-1642, www.bracreef.com

■ On the Water

Fishing

 Barefoot Watersports, ☎ 345-948-1299, fax 345-948-1350, e-mail barefeet@candw.ky. This operator has a 28-foot boat and offers full- and half-day deep-sea cruises for a maximum of six persons.

Brac Caribbean Beach Village, ☎ 800-791-7911; www.brac-caribbean.com. Groups of up to four people can book a full- or half-day of deep-sea fishing or bone, tarpon, and reef fishing.

Captain Edmund "Munny" Bodden, ☎ 345-948-1228. In operation 38 years, this guide specializes in bonefishing. Up to four fishermen can book a full- or half-day of either deep-sea or bone, tarpon, and reef fishing.

Condor Watersports, ☎ 345-948-1226, fax 345-948-2570, e-mail kirkconn@candw.ky. This operator offers deep-sea, bottom and bonefishing cruises with a 21- , 27- , and 30-foot boats.

Gemini Sportfishing, South Side, ☎ 345-948-2517, www.bandsmv.com. This 30-foot boat takes up to four anglers for a half- or a full-day of deep-sea fishing.

Shelby Charters, ☎ 345-948-0535. Captain Shelby Scott offers full- and half-day excursions – either deep-sea or reef fishing – for up to eight participants.

COST OF FISHING ON CAYMAN BRAC

(Prices quoted are in US $)

Half-day deep-sea fishing $350

Full day deep-sea fishing . . . . $500-$600

■ In the Air

Day-Trip to Little Cayman

Hop aboard with **Island Air** for a 15-minute jaunt over to Little Cayman, a popular day-trip from Cayman Brac. With twice-daily service, they offer round-trip fares for just US $40. For schedules or reservations, call Monday through Friday, 9 am to 5 pm, ☎ 345-949-5252, fax 345-949-7044, www.islandaircayman.com. Special fares are available for children under age 12. The day-trip is a favorite with bonefishermen and beach lovers.

■ On Wheels

Bicycling

B&S Motor Venture's Car Rentals (422 Channel Road, South Side, ☎ 345-948-1646, www.bandsmv.ky) offers bicycle rentals with free pickup around the island. Cayman Brac is a good environment for cycling because of light traffic, flat terrain, and plenty of beautiful scenery.

Eco-Travel

■ Birding

Birdwatching is a favorite activity on Cayman Brac. Some of the most popular spots for sightings of the island's most sought-after species are **Saltwater Pond** on the southwest coast (best known as the home of the West Indian whistling duck), and the **Parrot Reserve** (page 200), located on the bluff. This 180-acre preserve is home to many of the endangered **Cayman Brac parrot**. Only 400 of the birds remain in the wild on this island. The best time to catch a glimpse of the emerald green parrot is from July through September (they breed from March through July and can be tough to see during those months). They're often spotted on top of the bluff, as well as around Stake Bay. Just keep an ear out for their unmistakable cry.

During the winter months, birders can look for **peregrine falcons**. Other top birding times are during the spring and winter migrations, in February and March, and November and December. Birders may spot any of 120 species, including the **brown booby**, **Vitelline warbler**, and the **white-tailed tropicbird**.

The reserve is also a good destination for those interested in the flora and fauna of the island. Thirty-eight plant species can be seen here; a two-mile trail is open for self-guided hikes. Look for candlewood, mastic, wild banana orchid plants, and other exotic species along the trail.

Exhibits at the Cayman Brac Museum.

■ Guided Tours

Ecotourists don't want to miss the opportunity to take a guided tour with local resident **T.J. Sevik**. These tours are free and can be customized to your own interests, whether that includes bird watching, caving, or identifying the island's flora. For arrangements contact Kenny Ryan or Mrs. Wanda Tatum, ☎ 345-948-2651, fax 345-948-2506.

Sightseeing

 The Cayman Brac Museum, Stake Bay, ☎ 345-948-2622. This charming museum recalls the early history of this seafaring island. Located in a building constructed in 1933 as a bank, and later used as a customs office, treasury and, finally, post office, the museum houses ship building tools, photos, and even a replica of a turtle schooner. An exhibit explains more about thatch-rope making, once a popular craft using the island's silver thatch palm fronds. The museum is open Monday through Friday from 9-12 and 1-4 pm and on Saturday from 9-12. Free.

The Brac, East Point. This sheer bluff is Cayman Brac's most notable feature and worth a visit by hikers and non-hikers alike. To reach the bluff, follow the gravel road north off Ashton Reid Road, the island crossroad. The gravel road runs six miles to a lighthouse. Free.

*To learn more about Cayman Brac's ecology and to assist in preservation efforts, consider becoming a member of the National Trust's **Cayman Brac District Committee**. For information, contact Wallace Platts at ☎ 345-948-2390.*

Spot Bay Community Cove, Spot Bay. This public park has a beach with tables and a nice atmosphere for a picnic.

Cayman Brac Community Park, West End. This park, dedicated by Governor Michael Gore in 1995, includes a short nature trail, where about 10 types of indigenous trees are identified. The park is popular with families. The Department of Tourism office is adjacent to the park. Open daily. Free.

Shopping

Kirk Freeport (☎ 345-948-2612) has a shop at Stake Bay with a selection of duty-free goods. The popular Grand Cayman company also has a duty-free shop at the airport where you can pick up some last-minute jewelry, perfumes, or gifts.

In Tibbetts Square, you'll find the **Treasure Chest**, with T-shirts, windsocks, postcards, and books.

For locally made goods, don't miss **NIM Things** (NIM stands for "Native Island Made") in Spot Bay, ☎ 345-948-0461. This shop sells Caymanite jewelry as well as crocheted items and straw bags.

Where to Stay

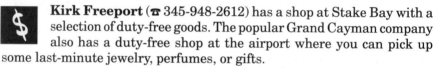

ACCOMMODATIONS PRICE SCALE
Prices listed are for a standard room for one night during high season (expect prices to be as much as 40% lower during the low season). The price scale refers to US $.

$	Under $100
$$	$100-$200
$$$	Over $200

■ Hotels & Resorts

 Brac Caribbean Beach Resort, South Side, ☎ 800-791-7911, 345-948-2265, fax 345-948-1111, www.brac-caribbean.com, $-$$. Located at Stake Bay, this 16-room resort has a restaurant, bar, scuba, snorkeling and a dive shop. Rooms here are sunny and decorated in Caribbean style furnishings, with white rattan furniture and island-inspired prints. All rooms have air conditioning, ceiling fans, telephones, and televisions. This family-friendly resort is quiet and in easy walking distance of the new Carib Sands Beach Resort.

Brac Reef Beach Resort, South Side, ☎ 800-327-3835, 345-948-1323, fax 345-948-1207, www.bracreef.com, $-$$. This 40-room resort sits on the prettiest beach on Cayman Brac, overlooking Channel Bay on the island's southeast shore. The atmosphere here is fun and friendly (just have a look at the signs guests have painted on driftwood for proof!). Guest rooms have air conditioning, ceiling fans, telephones, televisions, and porches or patios. The resort also offers a pool, Jacuzzi, restaurant, bar, scuba, dive shop, snorkeling, fishing, tennis, underwater photo center and gift shop.

Carib Sands Beach Resort, South Side, ☎ 345-948-1121, www.carib-sands.com, $$. This condominium resort has one- , two- , and three-bedroom units, all housed in coral pink buildings. Each unit has tile floors, full kitchens, a pull-down Murphy bed, and all the comforts of home. Cribs and playpens are available for families. We especially liked the long dock, which provides not only access to fishing vessels, but also shady places for quiet hammock time with a view of the shallow sea. The atmosphere here is extremely quiet and peaceful. The resort is, at press time, still under expansion. The first phase of the project opened 18 units, while the new phase will add 17 additional units as well as a weight room.

Divi Tiara Beach Resort, South Side, ☎ 800-367-3484, 345-948-1553, fax 345-948-1316, www.diviresorts.com, $-$$. Cayman Brac's largest resort offers 59 guest rooms, both standard and deluxe. Guest rooms feature air conditioning, ceiling fans, telephones, televisions, and porches or patios. The resort also has a pool, Jacuzzi, restaurant, bar, scuba, dive shop, snorkeling, fishing, tennis, underwater photo center and gift shop.

■ Condos & Apartments

La Esperanza, Stake Bay, ☎ 345-948-0531, fax 345-948-0525, $-$$. Visitors can choose from one of four two-bedroom apartments or a three-bedroom house. Located on the island's north side near The Bight, this property has a restaurant and bar. Rooms have air conditioning, ceiling fans, and telephones plus kitchens and laundry facilities. Guests also have use of gas grills, hammocks, and clothes lines (important for drying out those scuba skins).

Visitors leave homemade driftwood signs on the island.

■ Small Inns

Walton's Mango Manor, Stake Bay, ☎/fax 345-948-0518, $. Cayman Brac's first bed-and-breakfast is within walking distance of the Cayman Brac Museum. The community of Stake Bay and both snorkeling and shore diving are accessible. Walton's Mango is housed in an historic Caymanian house that formerly operated as a retirement home for Bracker seamen. Today, it's a five-room guest house. Rooms include air conditioning, ceiling fans, telephones, and television; each has a private bath. A full breakfast is served daily. Guests have use of a barbecue, patio and microwave; rental bicycles are also available.

This B&B is a favorite with nature lovers. Named for a large mango tree in the front yard, the garden features guinep, breadfruit, buttonwood and poinciana trees as well. Cayman Brac parrots are sometimes spotted here.

Where to Eat

■ Eclectic

 La Esperanza Restaurant and Bar, Stake Bay, ☎ 345-948-0531, $-$$. Located on the island's north side near The Bight, this casual eatery specializes in local seafood and is also known for its jerk chicken, served on Wednesday, Friday, and Saturday nights.

Aunt Sha's Kitchen, West End, ☎ 345-948-1581, $-$$. Order up a plate of fresh seafood cooked with island spices at this charming eatery. You can't miss it: just look for the bright pink restaurant. That's Aunt Sha's (pronounced Shaws).

Captain's Table, Brac Caribbean Reef Resort, ☎ 345-948-1418, $$. This casual restaurant serves lunch and dinner; you can opt for the relaxed dining room or dine at poolside. The menu always includes a fresh fish and seafood dish, along with popular favorites such as conch fritters. Sundays bring a popular buffet.

Coral Gardens Dining Room, Brac Reef Resort, ☎ 345-948-1323, $$-$$$. Coral Gardens is known for its breakfast buffet (US $17.25), lunch buffet (US $21.56) and dinner (US $35.94). Entrées change daily but expect to see seafood and fish most days.

G&M Diner, West End, ☎ 345-948-1272, $. Local fish tops the menu at this diner.

■ Pizza

Domino's Pizza, West End, ☎ 345-948-1266, $. This take-out place is the only "fast food" on the island.

Nightlife

Nightlife is limited on Cayman Brac; most travelers hit the sack early to prepare for the next day of scuba diving. If you are in search of evening fun, you will find that on most nights there is one hot spot on the island, either featuring a live band or a DJ. Check with your hotel concierge for the night's best entertainment.

Aunt Sha's has a disco several nights per week; ☎ 345-948-1581 for specifics. If that doesn't suit your tastes, another option is a romantic sunset cruise offered by **Condor Watersports** (☎ 345-948-1226).

Little Cayman

ittle Cayman is the Cayman Islands' tiniest treasure. Vacationers looking for secluded scuba diving, fly- or light tackle fishing, and nature appreciation find that Little Cayman fits the bill.

Appropriately named, Little Cayman is only 10 miles long and two miles across at its widest point. Boasting none of the glitz of Grand Cayman, 80 miles to the southwest, Little Cayman does greet guests with all the basic comforts, including several small lodges and condominiums with air conditioning, satellite television, and telephone service. A favorite with birders and anglers, this 10-square-mile island is a giant in the scuba diving world and home of **Bloody Bay Wall**, named by Philippe Cousteau as one of the best dive sites in the world. Although a veritable metropolis exists below the surface, with high-rise coral heads and a marine population explosion, on land all's quiet and secluded. Only a handful of permanent residents are lucky enough to make their home on this limestone isle.

This island, which offers accommodations in quiet inns and a few condominiums, is truly for those looking to get away from it all. Don't come here expecting even a fraction of the action found on Grand Cayman. Shopping is nil, nightlife hasn't even been considered. But for those seeking solitude, this is the place to be.

Little Cayman was once the home of a few die-hard anglers and scuba divers who were willing to live without any creature comforts. One of the earliest residents was actor Burgess Meredith, who had a vacation home on the northwest side of the island in the 1970s, back in the days when electricity was produced only by home generators (the first electrical service came to the island in 1991).

With a permanent population of fewer than 170 people, the island's primary residents are birds and iguanas. Over 2,000 Little Cayman rock iguanas inhabit the island, so many that "Iguana Crossing" and "Iguana Right of Way" signs are posted throughout the island to protect the five-foot-long lizards. Local artists Janet Walker and John Mulak painted the popular signs.

A Brief Island Tour

 Most of Little Cayman's residents live in a community called **Blossom Village**, on the southernmost tip of the island. Here you'll find most services, including the airport, car rental, grocery store, gas station, real estate office, restaurant, and several accommodations. The island's main road curves through town, but there's certainly no

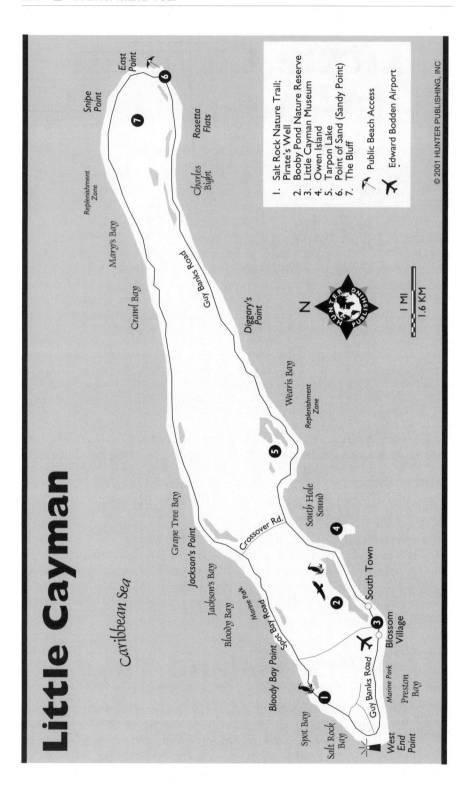

Little Cayman

Caribbean Sea

West End Point

Spot Bay
Salt Rock Bay

Preston Bay
Marine Park

Guy Banks Road

Blossom Village

South Town

Bloody Bay Point
Spot Bay Road

Bloody Bay
Jackson's Bay
Jackson's Point
Marine Park

Grape Tree Bay

Crossover Rd.

South Hole Sound

Wearis Bay

Replenishment Zone

Diggary's Point

Guy Banks Road

Crawl Bay

Mary's Bay

Replenishment Zone

Charles Bight

Rosetta Flats

Snipe Point

East Point

N

1 MI
1.6 KM

HUNTER PUBLISHING

1. Salt Rock Nature Trail;
   Pirate's Well
2. Booby Pond Nature Reserve
3. Little Cayman Museum
4. Owen Island
5. Tarpon Lake
6. Point of Sand (Sandy Point)
7. The Bluff

Public Beach Access

Edward Bodden Airport

© 2001 HUNTER PUBLISHING, INC

need to worry about traffic. So little happens here, in fact, that there's only one policeman (locals warn that he enjoys using his new radar speed gun) and one taxi (but the driver has another job, so don't expect to be picked up at a moment's notice).

Past the main road, side streets wind through Blossom Village, curving past cheery neighborhoods where everyone knows one another and visitors are greeted with waves and smiles. A small cemetery, many of its graves marked with conch shells and white crosses bleached even whiter by the Caribbean sun, marks the final resting place of former Little Cayman residents.

A Little Cayman tour bus.

Just offshore from Blossom Village stretches a protected **marine park**, with some of the top snorkeling and dive spots on the island. Here, divers find Grundy Gardens, Windsock, Harlod's Holes, Jay's Reef, Charlie's Chimney's, Patty's Point, Pirates Reef and Preston Reef, each the location of myriad varieties of marine life and underwater formations. Several dive operators offer trips to these popular sites.

Beyond Blossom Village, the main road, known formally as Guy Banks Road on the southern stretch of the island, winds north past scrubby brush land. Soon the road passes the **Booby Pond Nature Reserve**, a brackish mangrove pond. Trees are dotted with white birds, the red-footed boobies, and overhead the distinct shape of the magnificent frigate bird can been seen soaring on the trade winds.

Continuing north, **Owen Island** is seen just offshore to the right. This uninhabited island spans just 11 acres and is a popular day-trip destination for picnickers, who can reach the island's sandy beaches by row boat.

Owen Island is in a bay called **South Hole Sound**, and this inlet marks one of Little Cayman's few intersections. Here, the Crossover Road, more formally called Spot Bay Road, crosses to the other side of the island.

The main road soon loses its pavement and gives way to packed dirt and sand, safe for all vehicles. Stay on the road, however, because deep sand is found at some turnoffs. Along this stretch you'll pass many shallow ponds on the left side of the road, each lined with low-growing vegetation that forms a home for the island's bountiful bird population. Birders enjoy a drive by **Tarpon Lake**, a brackish 15-acre lake that is a favorite spot with anglers. The tarpon caught here range from three to 15 pounds. Birders will find plenty to interest them along the lake's shoreline.

Scrubby undergrowth becomes thick as you work your way to the north side of the island, climbing a slight rise. This is the island's driest end, a place where the terrain becomes marked with tall cacti and century plants (agave).

Swimmers and picnickers often head to the excellent beach at **Point of Sand**, a.k.a. Sandy Point. Turn right off the main road where you see a stop sign at the approaching road. The sand is packed for the first half of the drive, but be sure to stop at the wide section. The route soon turns to deep sand, so do not attempt to take vehicles down it. It's a long walk back to town and there are no facilities or telephones in this park.

Beyond Sandy Point lies the **East Point**, the easternmost point of the island. From here you can see nearby Cayman Brac seven miles across the channel. This stretch of Little Cayman is nearly deserted, with just a few cacti overlooking acres of undeveloped land.

The road then turns back south and traces the northern coast of Little Cayman, a stretch that's a favorite with divers. By far the most popular area is Bloody Bay Wall, found near where the Crossover Road comes out on the north coast road. This stretch of coastline is a marine park, safeguarding what has often been called one of the best dive locations on the globe.

TIP: *To sound like a local when saying Little Cayman, pronounce Cayman with an equal emphasis on each syllable (k-man).*

Getting Here

Arrival on Little Cayman is half the fun – you land in a cloud of dust. The dirt airstrip is next to a tiny one-room building that shades a desk and a phone; this is the **Edward Bodden Airport**. Service is available four times per day from Grand Cayman on **Island Air**. Departures from Grand Cayman on the 45-minute flight are at 8 am and 3:50 pm; return flights depart Little Cayman at 9:55 am and 5:45 pm. Round-trip tickets are US $154; a day-trip package is also available for US $110. Passengers may check up to 55 pounds of baggage free of charge; excess baggage is charged at US 50¢ per pound.

Flights are also available on Island Air from Cayman Brac to Little Cayman and cost US $40, round-trip. Special fares are available for children under age 12. Call Island Air at ☎ 345-949-5252, Monday through Friday, 9 am to 5 pm, fax 345-949-7044, or see www.islandaircayman.com.

Getting Around

∎ By Car

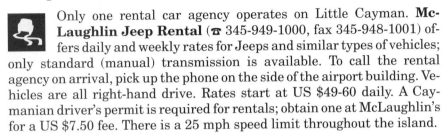

Only one rental car agency operates on Little Cayman. **Mc-Laughlin Jeep Rental** (☎ 345-949-1000, fax 345-948-1001) offers daily and weekly rates for Jeeps and similar types of vehicles; only standard (manual) transmission is available. To call the rental agency on arrival, pick up the phone on the side of the airport building. Vehicles are all right-hand drive. Rates start at US $49-60 daily. A Caymanian driver's permit is required for rentals; obtain one at McLaughlin's for a US $7.50 fee. There is a 25 mph speed limit throughout the island.

∎ By Bicycle

Another popular mode of transportation is the bicycle. Most resorts provide complimentary use of bicycles and, with practically no traffic on the roads, they offer a peaceful way to see the island, journey to a secluded beach, or pop into Blossom Village. The old cycles may not be the fastest vehicles, but this is Little Cayman. What's the hurry?

∎ Guided Tours

If you are looking for a specialized tour, these organizations have a variety of options.

- ∎ **LCB Tours**, Blossom Village, ☎ 800-327-3835 or 345-948-1033, fax 345-948-1040, e-mail lcbr@candw.ky. This tour company visits the Bird Sanctuary, museum, and more; snorkel trips are also available. Tours start at US $20 per person.

- ∎ Guided tours of the island are led by Gladys Howard, **National Trust** Chapter Chairman and owner of the Pirates Point Resort. Tours are conducted every Sunday morning; for more information contact the Cayman Islands National Trust, ☎ 345-949-0121, or Gladys Howard, ☎ 345-948-1010. A CI $1 donation to the Little Cayman National Trust is requested.

Little Cayman

Adventures

■ On Foot

Hiking

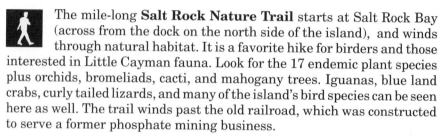

The mile-long **Salt Rock Nature Trail** starts at Salt Rock Bay (across from the dock on the north side of the island), and winds through natural habitat. It is a favorite hike for birders and those interested in Little Cayman fauna. Look for the 17 endemic plant species plus orchids, bromeliads, cacti, and mahogany trees. Iguanas, blue land crabs, curly tailed lizards, and many of the island's bird species can be seen here as well. The trail winds past the old railroad, which was constructed to serve a former phosphate mining business.

Another highlight is **Pirates Well**, a cave fed by a freshwater well. Discovered in 1994, the cave has not yet been fully explored.

Aside from guided hikes, Little Cayman presents travelers with plenty of walking and hiking opportunities. Almost non-existent traffic, a flat grade on all but the island's easternmost end, and wide roads make Little Cayman perfect for a stroll or hike. Stroll the quiet streets of Blossom Village, the main road out to Tarpon Lake, or the island's beautiful beaches.

Tennis

Tennis courts are available at **Little Cayman Beach Resort** and **Southern Cross Club** (see *Where to Stay*, pages 228-231).

■ In the Water

Scuba

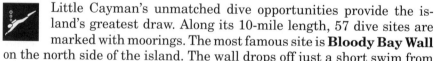

Little Cayman's unmatched dive opportunities provide the island's greatest draw. Along its 10-mile length, 57 dive sites are marked with moorings. The most famous site is **Bloody Bay Wall** on the north side of the island. The wall drops off just a short swim from the shore at a depth of only 20 feet, making it a favorite with snorkelers as well.

Dive Sites

Bloody Bay Wall: Starting at a depth of just 25 feet, this site is nonetheless a favorite with divers of all skill levels and is considered one of the best dive sites in the Caribbean. Named one of the top dive sites by the late Philipe Cousteau, the wall is thick with sponges and corals and is home to many formations – chimneys, canyons, coral arches. The wall is a spectac-

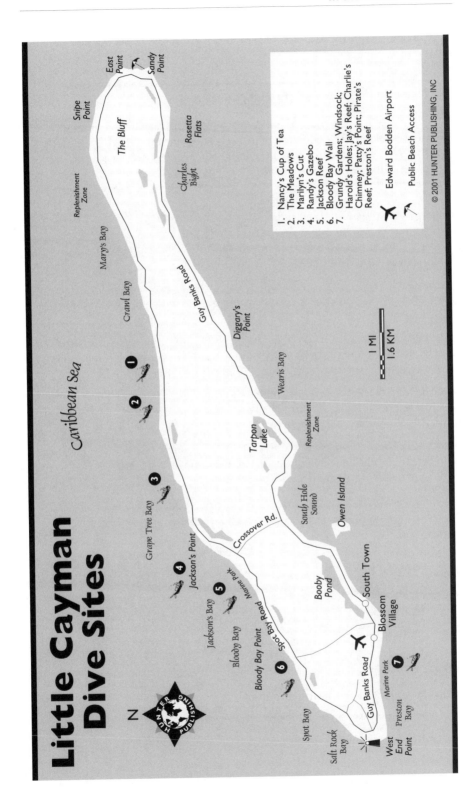

Little Cayman
Dive Sites

Caribbean Sea

East Point
Sandy Point
Snipe Point
The Bluff
Rosetta Flats
Charles Bight
Replenishment Zone
Mary's Bay
Crawl Bay
Guy Banks Road
Diggary's Point
Wearis Bay
Tarpon Lake
Replenishment Zone
South Hole Sound
Owen Island
Crossover Rd.
Grape Tree Bay
Jackson's Point
Marine Park
Jackson's Bay
Bloody Bay
Bloody Bay Point
Bloody Bay Road
Booby Pond
South Town
Blossom Village
Spot Bay
Salt Rock Bay
West End Point
Preston Bay
Marine Park
Guy Banks Road

N

HUNTER PUBLISHING

1. Nancy's Cup of Tea
2. The Meadows
3. Marilyn's Cut
4. Randy's Gazebo
5. Jackson Reef
6. Bloody Bay Wall
7. Grundy Gardens; Windsock;
   Harold's Holes; Jay's Reef; Charlie's
   Chimney; Patty's Point; Pirate's
   Reef; Preston's Reef

✈ Edward Bodden Airport

⚓ Public Beach Access

1 MI
1.6 KM

© 2001 HUNTER PUBLISHING, INC

Little Cayman

ular sight, dropping into sheer blackness from the clear turquoise shallows just inches away.

BLOODY BAY

Why was Bloody Bay given its name? According to a local legend, in the early 18th century, the Royal Navy ambushed pirates at this site when they tried to escape the island. As the name suggests, the pirates didn't make it.

Nancy's Cup of Tea: Located on the north side of the island off Big Channel, this dive site begins a depth of just 35 feet before plunging into deep waters. Decorated with multicolored sponges as well as gorgonians. Look for lots of marine life here.

Meadows: West of Nancy's Cup of Tea, this shallow site is home to eagle rays, groupers, and more. Small caverns and overhangs make this spot special.

Marilyn's Cut: Off Grape Tree Bay on the north side of the island, this crevice leads to a wall filled with sponges and gorgonians. This site is also home to a favorite resident: Ben, a Nassau grouper.

Randy's Gazebo: Out from Jackson's Point, Randy's Gazebo is noted for its tunnels and swim-throughs. This wall dive includes a natural arch, which is a favorite with underwater photographers.

Jackson Reef: This site, located on the island's north side, is shallow enough to be enjoyed by scuba divers and snorkelers, starting at just 18 feet below the sea's surface.

COST OF DIVING ON LITTLE CAYMAN

(Prices quoted are in US $)

1-tank dive	$35-45
2-tank dive	$65-$75
3-tank dive	$65-$100
Certification course	$290-$500
Advanced course	$200-$345
Nitrox course	$200-$225
Resort course	$75-$200

Scuba Operators

Conch Club Divers, ☎ 800-327-3835 or 948-1026, www.conchclub.com. This NAUI- and PADI-affiliated operator offers dives for up to 15 people. Three daily dives are provided.

Little Cayman Divers, ☎ 800-458-2722, 345-948-1429, www.littlecaymandiver.com. Their 90-foot yacht takes divers to Cayman Brac as well as Little Cayman. Only 10 divers are taken by this PADI-affiliated operation.

Sam McCoy's Diving & Fishing Lodge, ☎ 800-626-0496 or 345-948-0026, www.mccoyslodge.com.ky. Located at the lodge on Little Cayman's north shore, this operator runs excursions to the Bloody Bay Wall as well as shore diving along Jackson's Point. PADI, NASDS, SSI, and NAUI affiliated.

Paradise Divers, ☎ 877-3-CAYMAN, 345-948-0001, www.paradise-divers.com. Groups of up to 16 can be accommodated by this PADI-affiliated facility, which offers two or three dives daily, as well as advanced and certification courses.

Pirates Point Resort, ☎ 345-948-1010. Located at the resort, this dive shop offers two dives daily for groups of up to 20 divers. PADI, NAUI, and SSI affiliated.

Reef Divers Little Cayman, ☎ 800-327-3835, 345-948-1642, www.littlecayman.com. Little Cayman Beach Resort is home to this facility, which includes a full-service photo and video center. Three dives offered daily for groups of up to 20 divers. PADI, NAUI, SSI, and NASDS affiliated.

Southern Cross Club, ☎ 800-899-2582, 345-948-1099, www.southerncrossclub.com. This fishing and diving resort leads four dives daily for small groups (no more than 12 divers). PADI affiliated.

Snorkeling

Snorkeling can be done just about anywhere along the island's rim, but the top spot is **Bloody Bay Wall**. Snorkel trips range from US $10-$25.

Many of the island's shallower dive sites are also favored by snorkelers. **Nancy's Cup of Tea**, **The Meadows**, and **Jackson Reef** are among the most popular.

Owen Island, on the south side of the island, is also home to good snorkeling, especially on the south side. The island is accessible by boat.

Point of Sand, on the eastern end, is not only one of the island's best beaches, but it is also a good snorkel site.

Check with scuba operators to arrange a snorkeling trip.

MOLLY THE MANTA

A favorite resident of Little Cayman was Molly the Manta, a giant manta ray often seen on night dives in this region. The manta, which measured 12 feet across, was spotted along the north coast and on the south coast flats from 1991 through 1995. She was seen off Bloody Bay swooping through the water, scooping up plankton that were attracted by divers' lights. Today Molly is no longer spotted on night dives; she is believed to have reached maturity and gone off in search of a mate.

Underwater Photography

Underwater photography rentals are available from **Little Cayman Divers**, ☎ 800-458-2722 or 345-948-1429, www.littlecaymandiver.com, and **Reef Divers Little Cayman**, ☎ 800-327-3835 or 345-948-1642, www.littlecayman.com, or **Reef Photo & Video Centre**, Little Cayman Beach Resort, ☎ 345-948-1033, fax 345-948-1040.

■ On the Water

Fishing

 Fly- and light tackle fishing attract anglers to the waters of Little Cayman, which offer excellent **bonefishing** in the shallow flats. Other anglers come to catch **tarpon** or **permit**. Little Cayman is the top destination of the three Cayman Islands for those looking for light tackle and fly-fishing.

 AUTHORS' NOTE: *Bonefishing is a favorite activity here, and a challenge to anglers (although the sport here is not on par with other islands in the Caribbean or the Florida Keys). These fish are seen in the shallow areas called* **muds**, *places where the sea is churned up by the bottom-feeding fish.*

Guides recommend baiting with fry (very young fish). Bonefish can be caught all day, although, as with other types of fishing, the success rate depends on factors such as weather and tides. The best bonefishing around Little Cayman is usually found at the South Hole Sound.

Tarpon fishing is also popular on Little Cayman. Tarpon Lake, a brackish body of water north of Blossom Village, is home to many 20-lb tarpon. Fly-fishermen will have best luck at this site in early morning and late afternoon.

Permit are also a favorite catch, ranging from 15 to 35 pounds. They're found in schools on the southeast end of Little Cayman and on the northwest coast flats.

Whether you're staying on the island or coming over on a day trip, you can enjoy some fishing with a local guide if you make advance arrangements.

COST OF FISHING ON LITTLE CAYMAN

(Prices quoted are in US $)

Bone fishing, full day $220

Bone fishing, half-day $110

Deep-sea fishing, full day . . . . $550-$1100

Deep-sea fishing, half-day . . . . $300-$600

Fishing Charter Operators

McCoy's Diving and Fishing Lodge, ☎ 800-626-0496 or 345-948-0026, www.mccoyslodge.com.ky. McCoy's Lodge has guides on staff year-round and offers light tackle fishing and fly-fishing. Fishermen should bring their own fly-fishing equipment, but light tackle equipment is available. McCoy's is also fully equipped for deep-sea fishing; ice, bait, and tackle are provided.

Southern Cross Club, ☎ 800-899-2582 or 345-948-1099, www.southerncrossclub.com. Three vessels, 16 to 24 feet in length, take groups of two, three or four deep-sea fishing. Full- and half-day reef fishing also available.

Beaches

Point of Sand: This beach, luminescent with beautiful pink sand, is one of the island's prettiest and most secluded. You may spend the entire day here and never see another person. On weekends, visitors from Cayman Brac often come over to enjoy the solitude. A covered picnic table invites you to enjoy a quiet lunch with the sound of the sea as background music. Turn right off the main road where you see a stop sign at the approaching road. The sand is packed for the first half of the drive, but do not attempt to take vehicles down to the beach; park at the wide section to avoid getting your vehicle stuck in the deep sand.

■ On Wheels

Biking

 The island has over eight miles of paved roads, and even the unpaved sections are passable on mountain bikes. Many of the accommodations include free use of bicycles. Rentals are available at

McLaughlin's Enterprises, Little Cayman Beach Resort, Pirates Point, and Paradise Villas; see *Where to Stay*, beginning on page 228, for contact information.

Eco-Travel & Sightseeing

■ Birding

Booby Pond Visitors Centre, ☎ 345-948-1010, fax 345-948-1011. Operated by the National Trust, Booby Pond, the 1.2-mile-long brackish mangrove pond is home to a breeding colony of magnificent frigate birds and the Caribbean's largest breeding colony of red-footed boobies (*Sula sula*). Approximately 30% of the Caribbean population of red-footed boobies resides at this pond. Even without the help of telescopes or binoculars, you can view the large white birds (or their large, gray offspring) in the trees surrounding the pond. Over 7,000 of the birds make their home here. The area is home to egrets, herons, West Indian whistling ducks, black-necked stilts, and more.

Visitors Centre at the Booby Pond Nature Reserve.

The visitors center is set in the 206-acre Booby Pond Nature Reserve. It includes exhibits on the island's indigenous species, from the common crab (*Eurytium limosum*) to the seed shrimp (*Ostracoda*) to the pond's many resident birds. Friendly volunteers staff the center and welcome questions about the wildlife and island life. Admission is free, although donations are welcomed.

The reserve, which has been designated an international RAMSAR site. For this recognition, which falls under the United Nations convention to protect wetlands for waterfowl habitats, a site must meet strict environmental criteria.

Occasionally, Booby Pond will smell like rotten eggs or sulfur. The odor is the result of hydrogen sulfide gas created from decomposing organic material in the pond. Under normal conditions, the gas is dissolved in the pond water, but when the water level drops occasionally the harmless gas is released into the air.

Even non-birders enjoy this facility. Ride a bicycle up to the center in early morning to relax on the covered porch watching the show of birds. For a close-up look you can use one of two telescopes available at all times on the visitors center porch. One telescope is positioned low, to accommodate those in wheelchairs. The boobies fly about 40 mph and nest in crude constructions made of rough sticks. After a look at the birds, step inside the visitors center to see exhibits on the birds of Little Cayman. A small gift shop sells locally made crafts and artwork.

THE NATIONAL TRUST

The National Trust welcomes members and donations. Annual dues are US $30; membership includes updates on projects such as Booby Pond. For information on the Little Cayman District Committee for the National Trust, contact Gladys Howard, Pirates Point Resort, ☎ 345-948-1010.

Little Cayman Museum, Blossom Village, ☎ 345-948-1033. Learn more about the history of this small island in this museum. You'll discover that Blackbeard stopped here with his pirates for fresh water (and, some say, to bury his treasure in a brick-lined cave). Other exhibits recall the battle of Bloody Bay.

Shopping

This is not a shopper's paradise, but you will find assorted small gift stores around the island, primarily at the resorts. At Little Cayman Beach Resort, **Mermaids** sells jewelry, Spanish coins, clothes, and gift items; the shop is open afternoons only, Monday through Saturday. T-shirts and some souvenir items can be found at the grocery store and the small shop adjoining **McLaughlin's** rental agency in Blossom Village. A small gift shop at **Pirates Point** sells a variety of items, including a Little Cayman cookbook prepared by Gladys Howard for the National Trust.

Where to Stay

Small resorts, condominiums, and an efficiency apartment complex make up the accommodations offerings.

ACCOMMODATIONS PRICE SCALE
Prices listed are for a standard room for one night during high season (expect prices to be as much as 40% lower during the low season). The price scale refers to US $.

$	Under $100
$$	$100-$200
$$$.	Over $200

■ Rentals

Cottages

Cayman Villas, ☎ 800-235-5888, www.caymanvillas.com, $-$$$. Cayman Villas represents several properties on Little Cayman in a variety of price ranges. Properties include **Sunset Cottage** (☎ 345-945-4144, fax 345-949-7471), a two-bedroom, two-bath home for up to six guests, located seaside, with a screened porch off the master bedroom and another off the living/guest bedroom; **Suzy's Cottage**, a one-bedroom property on a white sand beach, which can host up to six guests and has air conditioning, ceiling fans, telephones, television, and more; and **Little Cayman Cottage**, a two-bedroom cottage set on the beach, which can accommodate up to six guests.

Villas

Paradise Villas, ☎ 877-3-CAYMAN, 345-948-0001, fax 345-948-0002, www.paradisevillas.com, $$. Next door to the Hungry Iguana restaurant (and just steps from Blossom Village), these cozy villas are perfect for those who'd like housekeeping facilities but the option of both a nearby eatery and a grocery store. These villas, two units to a cottage, lie right on the beach. Each includes two twin beds or one king, a futon that can sleep one adult or two kids, a back patio overlooking the sea, full kitchen with microwave, toaster and coffeemaker, and air conditioning. There's also a swimming pool.

Condos

Conch Club Condominiums, Blossom Village, ☎ 800-327-3835, 345-948-1033, fax 345-948-1040, www.conchclub.com, $$$. Located just north of Blossom Village, this condominium and townhouse project is the island's newest development. The lemon-yellow units are excellent for several couples traveling together or for families. The Conch Club is within walking distance of one of the island's best dive shops, and the two-story condominiums are just steps from a powdery beach.

The complex offers two- and three-bedroom units. Two-bedroom units, spanning 1,700 square feet, include one queen, two twins, and one double convertible bed, as well as two baths. At 2,000 square feet, the three-bedroom units offer one queen, one double, and two twin beds, with three baths. All units have a fully equipped kitchen, living and dining room, laundry facilities, ceiling fans, daily housekeeping, and use of the pool, Jacuzzi, and dock on the property.

Several meal plans are available for guests. Meals are taken at the Bird of Paradise Restaurant at Little Cayman Beach Resort, next door.

Guests at the Conch Club can also enjoy scuba diving at Little Cayman Beach Resort. Full equipment rental, diving courses, and underwater photography equipment are available.

AUTHORS' NOTE: *Most Little Cayman condominium units offer cribs. However, parents with infants should bring baby needs, including disposable diapers, formula, and baby food. Such items are difficult, if not impossible, to find on-island.*

■ Hotels & Resorts

Little Cayman Beach Resort, Blossom Village, ☎ 800-327-3835 or 323-8727, fax 813-323-8827, www.littlecayman.com, $$$. Little Cayman's largest property is specially tailored for those who want luxury with their adventures. This two-story conch-shell pink resort overlooks a shallow area inside the reef on the south side of the island. Just outside the reef lie top scuba spots, accessible through **Reef Divers**, the on-site operator. Packages including dives, room and meals run $622-$671 for three nights. Beginners can learn with a resort course or obtain open-water certification. Underwater photographers can see their shots the same day; an underwater photo and video center has E-6 processing and rentals.

Non-divers also enjoy this resort for its laid-back atmosphere. Hammocks sway just yards from the shore; chaise lounges line the freshwater pool just steps from the bar. Rooms have air conditioning, balcony or patio, color TV, ceiling fan, private beach. New oceanfront rooms feature wet-bars, microwaves, and coffee-maker. Other facilities include a restaurant, bar, gift shop, fitness center and hot tub. The resort is also home to the Nature Spa, which offers a range of massages as well as a hair and beauty salon. Spa packages are available.

■ Small Inns

Little Cayman Diver II, ☎ 800-458-BRAC, $$ (all-inclusive). Well, it's not exactly a small inn, but this live-aboard operates much like one. Based off Little Cayman, the boat accommodates 10 passengers in five cabins, each with a private bath. PADI, NAUI, SSI, NASDS, and YMCA affiliated, this operator has been in business for 10 years. It has video camera rentals.

Pirates Point Resort, Preston Bay, ☎ 345-948-1010, fax 345-948-1011, $$. This 10-room resort is a favorite with divers and it's easy to see why. Four dive instructors reveal the secrets of Bloody Bay Wall, from sheer cliffs to delicate sponges and coral formations.

Non-divers find plenty of activity (or non-activity, if they so choose) at Pirates Point as well. Owner Gladys Howard is the chairperson of Little Cayman's National Trust committee and active in eco-tourism. The lobby of Pirates Point is filled with nature guidebooks, and Gladys also has a nature trail guide and fishing guide to take visitors out for a day or half-day of fishing or birding.

The resort offers plenty of temptation to just laze away the day on the powdery white beach as well. Guest cottages are simple and light, decorated in Caribbean colors. Rooms include ceiling fans, tile floors, and private baths. Drinking water is produced by the resort's own reverse-osmosis plant.

After a day in the sun, guests can relax in the island's most unusual bar, which features artwork created by previous guests. (The grounds of Pirates Point also feature guest-donated artwork, charmingly produced out of everything from coconut shells to driftwood.)

But there's no doubt that dining ranks as one of the top attractions of Pirates Point. Along with her expertise in natural history, Gladys Howard is also a Cordon Bleu-trained chef. While guests may rough it during the day, at night they enjoy gourmet meals as elegant as those found at any of the Caribbean's finest resorts. Gladys boasts, "My kitchen never closes."

An all-inclusive dive package is available, including a deluxe room with private bath, three gourmet meals daily (with wine), open bar with unlimited drinks, two boat dives daily, use of all dive equipment, airport transfers, use of bicycles, and hammocks, lounges, and beach towels. For non-divers, an all-inclusive package has all of the above except diving. Hotel tax and gratuity are not included.

Southern Cross Club, south side of island, ☎ 800-899-2582, 345-948-1099, fax 345-948-1098, www.southerncrossclub.com, $$. The Southern Cross holds the distinction of being the island's first resort. Located along South Hole Sound with 800 feet of beachfront, this resort was renovated in 1998. Today, five beachfront duplex cottages offer 11 guest rooms decorated in island colors; each room has air conditioning, ceiling fans, (no phones or TV) and plenty of water from the inn's own desalinization plant. In 2000, the resort added a honeymoon suite. Facilities include a freshwater swimming pool and two outdoor bars, one of which is on the dock.

Southern Cross has long been a favorite destination with Caribbean anglers. Both deep-sea and tackle fishing for bonefish, tarpon, and permit are offered here. The Southern Cross Club has a 24-foot deep-sea fishing boat available for charter. A resident fishing guide will make sure you return home with plenty of fish tales.

Two dive boats offer daily dives at this PADI certified shop. This is now an IANTD Nitrox facility. Dive boats take a maximum of 12 guests per dive.

The Southern Cross Club specializes in service, with one of the highest staff-to-guest ratios on the island. And they go the extra mile to make vacations here memorable, organizing day-trips to offshore islands, romantic dinners for two at the end of the dock and more. Call to discuss your request. This all-inclusive property allows children over age five.

McCoy's Diving and Fishing Lodge, Bloody Bay, ☎ 800-626-0496, 345-948-0026, fax 345-948-0057, www.cayman.com/ky/com/sam, $$. One of the island's earliest accommodations remains one of its favorites, especially with divers and fishermen. Two dive boats, the 30-foot *Caymaniac* and the 28-foot *Caymanak*, transport divers to sites around the island. Anglers can head out aboard the 32-foot *Reel McCoy* deep-sea fishing boat.

Eight guest rooms greet visitors with rustic charm. Tucked beneath shady trees and always in sight of the deserted beach, the rooms feature private baths and air conditioning. Guests can dine right on premises. Other facilities include a small freshwater pool with Jacuzzi jets.

Where to Eat

To cut food costs, many guests on Little Cayman opt for buying a few groceries. The lone grocery store is the **Village Square**, next to the car rental agency. Open 9-1 and 4-6, Monday through Saturday, the store stocks a little of everything: housewares, bait and tackle, VCR rentals, medicines, and groceries. A surprising number of resorts feature top-notch dining; advance reservations are required for non-guests. Check with resorts to make dining arrangements.

DINING PRICE SCALE		
The scale below indicates the approximate cost of a meal for one person, including drink and gratuity. The price scale refers to US $.		
$		Under $15 per person
$$		$15-$30 per persons
$$$		$31-$40 per person

■ Eclectic

Hungry Iguana, ☎ 345-948-0007, $-$$. The Hungry Iguana, the island's only stand-alone restaurant, is near the airport. The namesake of the seaside eatery is an iguana often seen at the airport. To honor the hungry herbivore, the restaurant sports a 40-foot mural of the local lizard. Continental buffet breakfasts start the day; lunch and dinner feature jerk chicken, grouper sandwiches, prime rib, and burgers.

Appendix

Living in the Cayman Islands

With its beautiful setting, low crime rate, and high standard of living, it's no surprise that many visitors to the Cayman Islands wonder what it would be like to live on one of these sunny isles. Although it's a pricey proposition, visitors can relocate to the Cayman Islands.

When moving to the Caymans, you'll basically fall into one of two categories: a worker, with or without dependents, or a person coming to reside and not work, either permanently or temporarily, on the islands.

■ Work Permits

To work in the Cayman Islands, you must obtain a work permit from the Department of Immigration (see below). This permit allows you and a limited number of dependents to live on the island during the term of your employment (any dependents will need to obtain their own work permits, though). If you are self-employed, you'll need to obtain the work permit; otherwise it is obtained by your employer.

■ Initial Residency Permits

If you are considering a move, you'll need to apply for residency before moving. Make your application to the Chief Immigration Officer, Department of Immigration, PO Box 1098, Grand Cayman, Cayman Islands, British West Indies, ☎ 345-949-8344, fax 345-949-8486; www.gov.ky/immigration. The initial residence permit is granted for a six-month period.

When you apply to live in the Cayman Islands, you'll need to write a letter requesting short-term residence. With that letter, you'll need to supply a police clearance certificate covering the past 10 years. You will obtain this from your last place of residence (every member of the family age 16 or over will need this). If you are from the UK, you can provide an affidavit that you do not have criminal convictions. You'll also need to supply a medical report of health for each family member, with results of an HIV test and VDRL test. Three references from persons not related to you are required as well as evidence of your financial status, such as a letter from your banker. You'll also need photographs.

The initial residency permit, if approved, costs CI $250 for US residents, CI $500 for Canadian residents, CI $1,000 for citizens of Great Britain and Ireland, and CI $1,500 for citizens from other European and Mediterranean countries.

■ Permanent Resident Status

If you would like to obtain permanent resident status, you may do so after a six-month stay. With that status, however, you'll be expected to invest in property to the tune of US $180,000 or more – and one look through the real estate listings will tell you that you will be lucky to find anything for $180,000! You will also need approval to obtain employment. If you are of independent means and don't require employment, you'll pay a one-time fee of CI $15,000 to be granted permanent residency. The best source of information on obtaining permanent residency is a booklet published by the Cayman Islands Government Information Services, titled *Acquisition of Permanent Residential Status in the Cayman Islands*. You can obtain a copy by calling the Government Information Services office at ☎ 345-949-8092 or fax 345-949-5936.

■ Real Estate

When it comes time to shop for Cayman real estate, take a deep breath (or maybe take a good drink of Caymanian rum; you'll need it). Prices are incredibly steep by any standards. Million-dollar condominiums are routine; empty lots can easily run half a million dollars.

You will find numerous real estate agents on the islands (especially Grand Cayman) and many properties for sale.

REAL ESTATE BROKERS

Crighton Properties . . . . ☎ 345-949-5250
www.crightonproperties.com

Coldwell Banker . . . . ☎ 345-945-4411
www.caymanislandsrealty.com

ERA . . . . ☎ 345-945-7955
www.eracayman.com

RE/MAX . . . . ☎ 345-949-9742
www.remax-cayman.com

Tranquil Realty Sister Islands
www.tranquilrealty.com
Cayman Brac. . . . . ☎ 345-948-1577
Little Cayman . . . . ☎ 345-948-1077

■ Pets

If you are bringing pets with you to the Cayman Islands, you'll need an import permit or a valid animal passport issued by the Department of Agriculture. To obtain a form for the import permit, contact the Department of Agriculture, Plant Quarantine/Veterinary Service Units, Box 459GT, Grand Cayman or call ☎ 345-945-2267 or 949-4932, fax 345-947-1476. You'll need to submit the forms with a fee of US $61. You'll also need an official health certificate issued by an accredited veterinary inspector in your country. Start the paperwork well before your travel dates.

■ Customs

When you move to the Cayman Islands, you are allowed to bring personal and household goods duty free. Don't rush out and buy all new appliances to ship to the islands, however; the goods must have been in use for six months. Special rules apply to the importation of a car.

To simplify the customs process, many new residents hire a customs broker to get through the paperwork. A few brokers are listed below.

CUSTOMS BROKERS

Brac Business Brokers and Agents . . . . ☎ 345-948-1438

Cayman Islands Customs Agency. . . . . ☎ 345-949-2350

Economy Custom Brokers . . . . ☎ 345-945-3443

Emery Worldwide . . . . ☎ 345-949-5989

IMP Agency . . . . ☎ 345-949-0066

Miracle Brokers . . . . ☎ 345-949-5989

Sta-Mar Enterprises . . . . ☎ 345-949-2399

■ Taxation

Ahh, now we come down to one of the real beauties of the Cayman Islands: taxation, or, rather, lack thereof. There are no direct taxes in the Cayman Islands, period. That means no income tax, no gift tax, no corporate tax, no inheritance tax, no capital gains tax.

That makes these islands extremely attractive. While there are no taxes, however, you will find a few miscellaneous charges including a stamp duty on real estate. You'll pay a stamp duty of 7.5% (higher in some areas) on the value of the real estate at the time of the sale and a fee of 1% on mortgages under CI $300,000 and 1.5% on mortgages greater than CI $300,000.

You'll also pay an annual fee for garbage collection (CI $50 per year for houses, CI $150 for condos).

The government does collect much of its money on duties. Some food items, such as cheese, fish, rice, water, and others, are not dutiable but most goods do carry both the cost of duty and of importation. Look for higher grocery prices on just about all items.

■ Education

If you are bringing young family members to live in the Cayman Islands, you'll soon learn that the mandatory education system is much like the British. Children of non-Caymanians are charged a fee, ranging from CI $150 per term for primary schools to CI $210 per term for high school. Several private schools are also located on Grand Cayman.

PRIVATE SCHOOLS

Cayman Preparatory School . . . . ☎ 345-949-9115

Faulkner Academy . . . . ☎ 345-945-4664

Grace Christian Academy . . . . ☎ 345-945-0899

St. Ignatius Preparatory School . . . . ☎ 345-949-9250

Triple C School . . . . ☎ 345-949-6022

Truth for Youth School . . . . ☎ 345-949-2620

Grand Cayman also offers limited higher education opportunities. The International College of the Cayman Islands (☎ 345-947-1100) offers degrees in accounting, business administration, banking, and other topics. The Community College of the Cayman Islands (☎ 345-949-9580) offers classes on a variety of topics.

Conference & Meeting Facilities

Are you combining your visit to the Cayman Islands with a business trip? If so, you'll have plenty of company. With its position as the world's fifth-largest financial center, the Cayman Islands is as well prepared to meet the needs of business travelers organizing a conference as those of individuals or groups organizing a family reunion or a wedding.

■ Grand Cayman

Resorts

Several resorts along Seven Mile Beach – Hyatt Regency Grand Cayman, Westin Casuarina Resort Grand Cayman, Grand Cayman Marriott Beach Resort, and Treasure Beach Resort – offer facilities and staff for large- and medium-sized groups.

Recently the **Hyatt Regency Grand Cayman** (☎ 800-55-HYATT, www.hyatt.com) added an additional 5,000 square feet of beachfront meeting and event space as part of its $15 million beach suite addition. The new areas include a 4,800-square-foot pavilion adjacent to its existing ballroom. This flexible space is designed to accommodate all types of events from meetings to elegant evening functions. The property also added the 925-square-foot Royal Crown meeting space, which can be used as either one or two rooms, and a 4,000-square-foot rooftop deck overlooking the beach.

The 309-room **Grand Cayman Marriott Beach Resort** (☎ 800-228-9290, www.marriott.com) is home to a 3,657-square-foot ballroom with a capacity of 500 when used theater-style, or 300 for a banquet. The resort also offers a 1,113-square-foot meeting room.

Westin Casuarina Resort Grand Cayman (☎ 888-625-5144, www.westincasuarina.com) offers a 2,560-square-foot ballroom, which is divisible into two rooms, as well as two executive board rooms, each capable of hosting 15 attendees in a conference setting.

Treasure Island Resort (☎ 800-203-0775 or 800-448-8355) offers three meeting rooms with over 1,500 square feet. The Spinnaker Room has a capacity of 70 persons theater-style, while the Leeward and Windward Rooms each can seat 80 attendees theater-style.

In mid-2002, these resorts will be joined by the **Ritz-Carlton Grand Cayman** (☎ 800-241-3333, www.ritzcarlton.com). This 366-room and 71-condominium resort will offer 17,450 square feet of meeting facilities, including a 12,000-square-foot ballroom and six meeting rooms totaling 5,450 square feet.

Smaller groups will find conference space as well. **Seaview Dive Centre** (☎ 345-945-0558, fax 345-945-0559) offers a small meeting facility for up to 60 participants; groups also have use of a slide projector and TV/VCR as well as catering. Casual meeting space is available at the new **Royal Reef** (☎ 888-373-5959, www.royalresorts.com), a complex of 30 two-bedroom villas with an additional 50 villas planned for construction within the next year. Small groups can book the villas as meeting and function space.

Alternative Venues

Smaller groups may prefer an alternative to the resort-based conference facilities. Meeting planners will find a range of activities and off-site venues, whether your group's interests lie in history or horticulture.

The **Queen Elizabeth II Botanic Park** (☎ 345-947-9462, fax 345-947-7873, www.botanic-park.ky) is home to a self-guided trail of native plants as well as a newer garden featuring imported tropical plants and blooms. The park offers a small conference room with space for up to 50 attendees classroom style or up to 20 for a board meeting; the gardens are also available for both after-hours events and functions during normal working hours.

The **Cayman Islands National Museum** (☎ 345-949-8368, fax 345-949-0309, mussdl@candw.ky) offers a small meeting space for up to 10 guests; food and beverage as well as special tours of the museum can also be arranged. The museum regularly hosts special events, from balcony lunches overlooking the George Town harbor to after-hours cocktail parties. The courtyard is also available for dinner under the stars with catering by one of many local restaurants as well as full or partial bar service and local entertainment.

The **Hyatt Regency Grand Cayman** (☎ 800-55-HYATT, www.hyatt.com) offers programs highlighting local culture and customs. Horticultural tours, storytelling, rope making, and coconut husking can be arranged with local experts. "We are working closely with island historians and community artists to bring the real flavor and charm of the Cayman Islands to our activities," says Doug Sears, General Manager. "Culture is an important part of the island experience and, with these activities, guests will have a better understanding of island life."

One of the island's most historic sites is also one of its newest group venues. Following a $7.5 million renovation, **Pedro St. James Historic Site** (☎ 345-947-3329) now transports groups back to the days of 1780. The island's oldest known existing stone structure is considered the birthplace of democracy in the Cayman Islands. Today the three-story greathouse is home to a 49-seat multimedia theater as well as a café. The grounds are available for group functions of up to 800 participants.

Theater space is also available at the **Harquail Theatre** (☎ 345-949-4519 or 345-949-5477). The site has auditorium seating for 350 attendees, a stage, and state-of-the-art facilities. Catering and bar service can be arranged.

Group Activities

GOLF: For free-time fun or competitive tournaments, two golf courses offer challenges. The **Links at SafeHaven** (☎ 345-949-5988, fax 345-949-5457) is the only championship 18-hole golf course in the Cayman Islands. At the **Hyatt Regency Grand Cayman**, the Jack Nicklaus-designed Britannia course (☎ 345-949-8020) can be played as a nine-hole championship course, an 18-hole executive course, or an 18-hole Cayman ball course.

When completed, the **Ritz-Carlton Grand Cayman** resort (see above and page 158) will include a nine-hole Greg Norman-designed private golf course.

WATERSPORTS: For all its land-based venues, Grand Cayman is especially well-known for its water-based group activities. One of the island's largest watersports operators is **Red Sail Sports** (☎ 877-RED-SAIL, www.redsail.com). Along with scuba diving, excursions to Stingray City, and watersports, the operator offers catamaran trips aboard its luxury catamarans, the 65-foot *Spirit of Ppalu* and the 62-foot *Spirit of Cayman*. Both are available for private charters, including four-hour day sails for 50 to 70 participants; three-hour dinner sails for 35 to 40 attendees; and two-hour sunset sails for groups of 50 to 70 people. The charter price for the *Spirit of Ppalu* is $550 per hour; the rate is $650 per hour for the *Spirit of Cayman*. There is a minimum rental of two hours. Red Sail Sports also offers dive boat charters for 20 to 24 divers (or 30 snorkelers) at $330 per hour. Sportfishing is another popular option for small groups or incentives; deep-sea charters for four persons are $650 for a full day or $450 for a half-day. Other watersports options include sailing for $25 per hour, water-skiing for $75 per half-hour, and personal watercraft rentals for $50 per half-hour for single riders.

TEAMBUILDING: Teambuilding exercises are another corporate group option, and **Red Sail Sports** offers several, including beach games such as coconut bowling and kayak races. The **Jeep Rally Treasure Hunt** makes a good option for groups who want to see more of the island. For $22 per person, groups spend a day searching for clues around the island, ending the day at Rum Point for beach relaxation. Cost of Jeep rental is $125 and includes insurance, Cayman Islands temporary driver's license, a full tank of gas, and transportation to and from your hotel. Other options include a raft building competition and Pirates' Capture, with a beach dinner invaded by "pirates."

On Grand Cayman, group functions don't just take place on water, they continue underwater as well, thanks to *Atlantis* **Submarines** (☎ 800-253-0493, fax 345-949-8574, www.goatlantis.com). Up to 46 attendees can take part in a charter submarine dive. Rides can be modified to feature a corporate theme. In the past, meeting planners have arranged to highlight companies by putting a CEO in scuba gear outside the submarine and submerging logos and corporate symbols so the vessel "discovers" the items on the dive. See page 110 for information about trips with *Atlantis* Submarines.

■ The Sister Islands

Opportunities can also be found for smaller conferences and group activities on the sister islands. Little Cayman and Cayman Brac are good choices for quiet incentives, pre- or post-trips, or intense strategy meetings.

The 40-room **Little Cayman Beach Resort** (☎ 800-327-3835, www.littlecayman.com) offers groups the use of the Grouper Room Conference Center. This 1,270-square-foot facility can accommodate 54 classroom style or 70 for a cocktail party. A complete list of AV equipment is available. On Cayman Brac, the 71-room **Divi Tiara Beach Resort** (☎ 800-367-3484, www.diviresorts.com) is home to the Coconut Conference Centre. Accommodating up to 80 attendees, the center has full AV facilities. **Brac Reef Beach Resort** (☎ 800-327-3835, www.bracreef.com) has added a new conference facility, the Governor's Conference Room. The 2,000-square-foot room will seat 150 for dinner or 180 theater style. A new telephone system has also been added to all guest rooms to allow for Internet access.

Useful Web Sites

The world's interest in the Cayman Islands has spawned a wealth of web sites. Throughout the book, we've included Internet addresses for businesses, accommodations, and attractions wherever possible. This chapter lists web sites that offer more than just information about a particular business but also helpful material about the islands, such as activities and accommodations.

■ Airlines

www.caymanairways.com – Cayman Airways

www.islandaircayman.com – Island Air

■ General Travel Information

www.parisandjohn.com – Check out our web site for information on our latest finds in the Cayman Islands. There's an e-mail link to tell us about your most recent discoveries and photos from our island excursions.

www.caymanislands.ky – This official site of the Cayman Islands Department of Tourism has Cayman news and current weather conditions. Tourism information includes hotels and condominiums, restaurants, transportation, attractions, fishing, scuba diving, snorkeling, group and meeting facilities, watersports, information on the sister islands, visitor services, links to other Cayman sites, an e-mail link to the DOT and a brochure request form.

www.travelfacts.com – These pages offer a wealth of information on the Cayman Islands, including a calendar of events, history, sightseeing and side trips, maps, sports, beaches, hotel guide, dining guide, shopping and travel tips.

www.cayman.org – This Web site, portions of which are still under development, offers information on transportation, accommodations, what's new, watersports, and a short picture tour of the island.

www.destination.ky – You can make accommodations reservations online here. A neat feature is a WebCam connection to the Turtle Farm so you can see what's going on right now.

www.caribbeansupersite.com – Learn about shopping, news, business, excursions and the national symbols of these islands on this site.

wwwcaymansonline.com – Resources on each of the islands as well as diving, hotels, snorkeling, fishing and more.

www.caymans.net – Information on business services, including accounting firms, banking, captive insurance, company formation, mutual funds, real estate, ship and yacht registration and trustee services.

www.caymanport.com – The Cayman Islands Port Authority operates this site, which includes cruise ship schedules, port business, and attractions; you can also send a Cayman postcard from the site.

■ Business Information

www.candw.ky – Information about communications services in the Cayman Islands, such as phone and Internet connections, with links to other Cayman Islands sites of interest.

www.segoes.com.ky – The Cayman Islands-based Segoes offers a full range of financial services for its account holders.

www.boddencorporateservices.com – Bodden Corporate Services, Ltd., provides information about doing business in the Cayman Islands.

■ Recreation

Scuba

www.divecayman.ky – Official dive site of the Cayman Islands Department of Tourism.

www.oceanfrontiers.com – This site, operated by Ocean Frontiers scuba diving, offers information on dive sites, accommodations, and information specifically for divers. You'll also find a link to weather. A newsletter has information on recent sightings.

Underwater Photography

www.cathychurch.com – Cathy Church's Underwater Photo Centre

www.donfosters.com – Don Foster's Ocean Photo

www.fisheye.com – Fisheye Photographic Services

Festivals

www.piratesweekfestival.com – Pirates Week Festival

www.caymanmadness.ky – Cayman Madness SCUBA promotion

Horseback Riding

www.ponies.ky – Pampered Ponies

Sailing

www.redsail.com – Red Sail Sports

Attractions

www.goatlantis.com/cayman – *Atlantis* Submarines

www.nautilus.ky – *Nautilus*: The Undersea Tour

■ History & Culture

www.caymannationaltrust.org – The official National Trust Web site

www.museum.ky – Cayman Islands National Museum

www.botanic-park.ky – Queen Elizabeth II Botanic Park

www.pedrostjames.ky – Pedro St. James National Historic Site

■ Cuisine

www.rumshop.net – Whether you want to learn more about Cayman's rums or the product of other Caribbean islands, this is the place.

www1.netaxs.com/8080.people/caymans/Cayman_Foods.html – Netaxs has a good overview of the dishes and ingredients of the Cayman Islands, along with some recipes.

■ Real Estate

www.cayman-realestate.com/caymanrealty.html – Learn all you need to know about buying real estate in the Cayman Islands.

www.century21cayman.com – Offers a lot of real estate information and listings for those who are considering Cayman as a first or second home.

www.gobeach.com/cayman/ – Information on villas, a map of Grand Cayman, travel tips on the Cayman Islands, and more.

www.dreamfinders.com – RE/MAX Cayman Islands

www.caymanislandsrealty.com – Cayman Islands Realty

www.cireba.com – Cayman Islands Real Estate Brokers Association

www.eracayman.com – ERA

www.crightonproperties.com – Crighton Properties Ltd.

www.remax-cayman.com – Lund Real Estate. This site has a very good map of Grand Cayman.

■ Services

Reservations Services

www.silvanaus.com/travel.htm – This site, called Caribbean Dreams, is operated by Destination Management and Reservations Services. Here you can make online accommodation reservations and get information on dive packages, weddings, and more.

Weddings

www.cayman.com.ky/com/weddings – Cayman Weddings has resources for planning your island wedding.

Booklist

Bradley, P. *Birds of the Cayman Islands*. Italy: Caerulea Press, 1995.

Brunt, M.A., Ed. *The Cayman Islands: Natural History and Biogeography*. Kluwer Academic Publishers, 1995.

Cancelmo, Jesse. *Diving Cayman Islands*. Aqua Quest Publications, Inc. 1997.

Dailey, Barbara Currie. *Tortuga Rum Fever and Caribbean Party Cookbook*. Island Fever Press, 2000.

Frink, Stephen (Photographer) and William Harrigan. *The Cayman Islands: Dive Guide*. Abbeville Press, 1999.

Lumry, Amanda, Loren Wengerd, and Laura Hurwitz. *Cayman: A Photographic Journey Through the Islands*. Vista Press, 2000.

O'Keefe, M. Timothy. *Sea Turtles: The Watchers' Guide*. Lakeland, Florida: Larson's Outdoor Publications, 1995.

Philpott, Don. *Cayman Islands Landmark Visitors Guide.* Hunter Publishing, 2000.

Pierce, Jean and Kris Newman. *Cayman Islands: Diving and Snorkeling.* Lonely Planet, 1999.

Pitcairn, Feodor U. and Paul Humann. *Cayman: Underwater Paradise.* Reef Dwellers Press, 1979.

Potter, Betty. *Grand Recipes from the Cayman Islands.* Cayman Islands: Potter Publications, 1985.

Raultbee, Paul G., comp. *Cayman Islands.* ABC-CLIO, Inc., 1996.

Roessler, Carl. *Diving and Snorkeling Guide to the Cayman Islands.* Gulf Publishing Co., 1993.

Sauer, Jonathan D. *Cayman Islands Seashore Vegetation: A Study in Comparative Biogeography.* Books on Demand (University of California Publications in Entomology), 1982.

Smith, Roger C. and James C. Bradford. *The Maritime Heritage of the Cayman Islands.* University Press of Florida, 2000.

Terry, Lindsay. *Grand Cayman: Colourful Reflections of Yesteryear.* Grand Cayman, 2000.

Trout, Richard E. *Cayman Gold: Lost Treasure of Devils Grotto* (children's book). Langmarc Publishers, 1999.

Wood, Lawson. *Dive Sites of the Cayman Islands.* NTC Publishing Group, 1997.

Index